ValueSpace™

ValueSpace™

Winning the Battle for Market Leadership

Lessons from the World's Most Admired Companies

BANWARI MITTAL, PH.D.

JAGDISH N. SHETH, PH.D.

McGraw-Hill

New York   Chicago   San Francisco   Lisbon   London
Madrid   Mexico City   Milan   New Delhi
San Juan   Seoul   Singapore
Sydney   Toronto

McGraw-Hill

A Division of The McGraw·Hill Companies

1 2 3 4 5 6 7 8 9 0 DOC/DOC 0 9 8 7 6 5 4 3 2 1

ISBN 0-07-137527-9

This book was set in Janson Text by North Market Street Graphics, Lancaster, Pennsylvania.

Printed and bound by R. R. Donnelley & Sons Company.

This publication is designed to provide accurate and authoritative information in regard to the subject matter covered. It is sold with the understanding that the publisher is not engaged in rendering legal, accounting, or other professional service. If legal advice or other expert assistance is required, the services of a competent professional person should be sought.

> —*From a declaration of principles jointly adopted by a committee of the American Bar Association and a committee of publishers.*

 This book is printed on recycled, acid-free paper containing a minimum of 50% recycled de-inked fiber.

McGraw-Hill books are available at special quantity discounts to use as premiums and sales promotions, or for use in corporate training programs. For more information, please write to the Director of Special Sales, Professional Publishing, McGraw-Hill, Two Penn Plaza, New York, NY 10121-2298. Or contact your local bookstore.

To Jag, my coauthor, whose passion for
constant cogitation inspires my own.

B.M

To Dr. John A. Howard, my mentor, who introduced me to the
fascinating world of customer understanding nearly four decades ago.

J.S.

Contents

Preface

Valuespace—we hold it in utmost admiration.

ValueSpace—it is to us the be-all and the end-all of all business activity, the only purpose of all organizations, all business enterprises. It is the only justifiable goal of all reengineering, organizational renewal, entrepreneurship, and corporate innovation. And it is the only path for sustained growth, for winning the battle for market leadership. It is the space where true market value is created—for shareholders, for employees, and most of all, for customers.

We present in this book a blueprint for how companies can build enduring ValueSpace for their customers.

This book is at the intersection of our two long-held obsessions: As university professors, we view ourselves as lifelong learners; and for decades, we have been students of customer behavior on the one hand and of business organizations on the other. We have studied theories of customer behavior—indeed, we created some of them ourselves—and for decades we have observed, analyzed, and written about business processes, precepts, and practices. In this book we bring these two streams together—our knowledge of customers and our knowledge of businesses. This is our ValueSpace for you, the reader: Uniquely in the current sea of business advice books, we combine the customer and business perspectives. No longer do we need to pay mere lip service to customer orientation; we show how you can do well by doing good for the customer.

We set out to understand what constitutes value for the customer and how companies can create it. Our research method was to study companies that were admired both on Main Street and on Wall Street—we chose a sample of 11 of *Fortune* magazine's Most Admired Companies. With financial support from the Marketing Science Institute (a Cambridge-based nonprofit research organization), we crisscrossed the country, visiting these companies, observing their operations, and interviewing senior executives. What we learned from these observations and interviews, and from our reflections, we report in this book.

Our framework, comprising the components of ValueSpace and its drivers, is quintessential—no matter what else you do or do not do, you must create these value components. Our framework is enduring—it is not the "project of the month"; long after the current fads have vanished, you must still build the value components we describe. Our framework is universal—it applies to all companies: manufacturing and service; small business or global enterprises; business-to-business or business-to-consumer; physical or digital; dot-com or not-com.

We intend this book to be a blueprint for thought as well as practice. We present conceptual framework to help you plan; we provide a self-audit form that you can use to assess your company's current standing in the ValueSpace; and we present case histories, stories of the most admired companies, and insights from interviews with executives that you will find both inspirational and implementable. It is a hands-on guide to launching your journey into the customer ValueSpace.

Our own journey has been fascinating. We have learned a lot—from the Most Admired Companies we studied; from the executive interviews we did specifically for this research; and from thousands of conversations over the years with consumers, managers, and corporate leaders just like yourselves. It is a pleasure and privilege to share with you our view of Customer ValueSpace, and our total fascination with it.

Ban Mittal
Jag Sheth

Acknowledgments

The authors deeply appreciate the help and support of the following:

- Marketing Science Institute for providing financial support for the research on which this book is based
- Senior executives we interviewed, both for sharing their insights and enabling access to other executives within their companies: Jim Despain (vice president, Caterpillar); Mike Eskew (executive vice president, UPS); Dave House (group president, American Express); Dieter Huckestein (president, Hilton Hotels); Mike Jackson (CEO, AutoNation); Kosta Kartsotis (president, Fossil); Ernie P. Maier (director, corporate development, 3M); Bill McDermott (former senior vice president, Xerox Business Services, now president, Gartner Group); Hal Rosenbluth (Chairman and CEO, Rosenbluth International, Inc.); Rick Schneiders (president, SYSCO); and Tom Von Lehman (vice president, Fine Chemicals, PPG Industires)
- Numerous senior executives in the companies we studied, who are named inside the book
- Mike Carrell, dean, and Matt Shank, department chair, College of Business, Northern Kentucky University, for understanding my absence from many a meeting over the last three years as I researched this book (BM)
- Meena, Pratik, and Mayank for managing their lives while I was preoccupied with the writing of this book (BM)

- Beth Robinson, my personal assistant, who provided excellent support throughout this project as well as Executive MBA students and faculty at the Goizueta Business School (Emory University) who reviewed and provided feedback on the book (JS)

And

- Mary Glenn (senior editor, in charge of the project team), Patricia Amoroso (senior editing supervisor), Elizabeth Strange (production supervisor), Maarten Reilingh (copyeditor), and other members of the book team at McGraw-Hill, for painstaking assistance and patience in bringing the manuscript to print

To all these fine individuals, our sincere gratitude.

ValueSpace™

ValueSpace: The Magic Land for Winning Customers

Y OU ARE THE CEO of a mining company, and you are digging through a difficult minefield with uneven topography. An operator sits atop a tractor mounted with cutting blades, maneuvering through the minefield diligently, cutting here at one angle, chiseling there at another. The task is difficult, the extreme skill of the operator notwithstanding, and the trial-and-error digging is nowhere near the pace it should be. As the CEO of the mining company trying to deliver this multimillion-dollar project on time, you wish there were some way for the tractor to find the best cutting path. If only it could sense the topography and automatically adjust its cutting angles! It could eliminate all the guesswork, reduce demands on the operator's skill, and cut the cutting time by half.

Take heart! There actually is. If your tractor is a CAT D11R, you can actually program it for autopiloted optimum cutting path. CAT's Computer Aided Earthmoving System (CAES) technology actually relays the topography of the ground under the machine to a remote CAT site on a real-time basis; there, CAT engineers calculate the optimum path and beam it right back to the computer on the machine. Now, the operator can simply sit back and watch the machine do its job.

* * *

You are a small business, selling widgets to another company. You ship your product by UPS—by Air or Ground, depending on the customer requirement. The customer wants this one particular shipment in three days. An air shipment will reach the customer a day early but will cost more; the ground shipment is cheaper but will miss the deadline. So, reluctantly, you ship by air, paying more. UPS says, "Don't!" Unless you like spending more. "Just tell us where you want it and by when," says UPS, "and we will figure out the best mode, combining ground and air for different sectors of the journey if necessary, and save you money."

This means UPS will make less money on each shipment. So, why would UPS do it?

* * *

Andrew Sterner is a district sales manager in the Jacksonville, Florida, operating division of SYSCO, the nation's premier foodservice company. He also happens to be a former chef. So one recent month, he was helping a customer—a restaurant—organize a benefit dinner for the Alzheimer's Association on the anniversary of the sinking of the *Titanic*. He had already secured 90 percent of the required food as donations, and he borrowed waitstaff from yet another customer (restaurant). As for finding some cooking help, he donned the apron himself and cooked a 13-course meal for 160 persons. And no ordinary meal it was—it was identical to the one served on the *Titanic* itself!

* * *

Caterpillar, UPS, SYSCO. Isn't it nice to be a customer of these companies?

It is. And it is because these companies are masters at creating new *ValueSpace*, the space that delivers us, their customers, great value.

What Is the #1 Goal of a Business?

We recently asked this question of one of our MBA classes. Their answers: to make money (67 percent), to sell what they make at a profit (15 percent), to satisfy their customers (10 percent), miscellaneous—for example, to create new products, to expand their market share, to beat the competitors, to give employment to people (8 percent). Indeed, most businesses measure their success by how well they serve their shareholders. This is not wrong. Money, after all, is the lifeblood of business. Without investors willing to provide money, there will not be any business to run. Investors invest money to make a profit. The more profit a business makes, the more value it delivers to its shareholders. Delivering value to shareholders can thus be a principal measure of a business's success. It is, however, a measure, not a means. A business cannot succeed, and value to shareholders cannot accrue, without value to two other constituencies—employees and customers.

The three value-constituencies reinforce each other. Although a business that ignores value to customers and employees can still deliver value to shareholders in such limited circumstances as a monopoly, a product shortage, or a speculative financial market, to do so in the long run and on a sustained basis is impossible. Without also delivering value to customers and employees, the business will slowly but certainly languish. When a business delivers the desired level of value to its employees, by compensation and job satisfaction, its happy employees help create value for the other two constituencies.

Happy employees are resources to be deployed; but managers must know how best to deploy them. They, as well as nonhuman resources, must be deployed to produce outcomes that customers value. Only when employees succeed in creating customer value, do they (the employees) become the source of shareholder value. In the same vein, nonhuman resources—equipment, technology, and business processes—must also be deployed to create value for customers. Their deployment merely to reduce costs, raise productivity, or produce new concoctions of products or services of no new value to customers will not raise the top line; nor the bottom line. As Figure 1.1 shows, creating customer value is the key to creating shareholder value. This book is therefore about customer value. It is about the ValueSpace where customers are owned for life or lost forever, where the battle for market leadership is won, where global market leaders thrive.

Customer Value

Value, not money, is the basic currency of all human interaction. When we meet someone, we try to quickly assess how long would it be worth

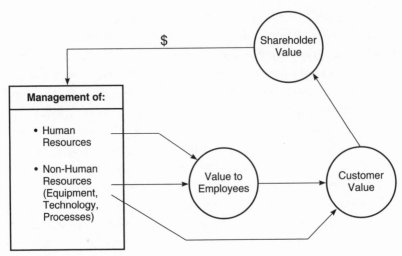

Figure 1.1   Managing resources to create value.

our while to be talking to that person. If an incoming phone call shows up on our caller ID, we promptly decide if we would gain anything by taking the call at that time. If we get 10 letters in the mail, we look through them and choose to open only those that we expect to contain some information of value to us. This is even more true for marketplace exchanges. The only reason the customers are even in the marketplace is that they are looking for something of value. The business that can deliver that value, and deliver more of it than its competitors, will gain the customer's patronage.

Customer Value: The Missing Link

More than 20 years ago, management guru Peter F. Drucker proclaimed that "The purpose of business is to create a satisfied customer." Later, Tom Peters and Robert Waterman, in their 1982 business classic, *In Search of Excellence*, extolled management to get "close to the customer." Since that time, businesses in droves have pursued customer satisfaction—albeit, some only in words, but many in deeds as well. This pursuit has led companies to acquire and practice a new marketplace discipline, focusing on customer satisfaction rather than just making a sale. But even customer satisfaction as a business goal seems to have run out of steam. Companies today are realizing that seeking cus-

Customer Value Critical for Shareholder Value

On July 26, 2000, Intel "dropped a bomb" on Rambus, a developer of chip connector technology based in Mountain View, California. Intel had earlier agreed to use Rambus technology to make its PC processors. Intel then conducted benchmark tests comparing Rambus-technology-based Intel's 820 chip set and Intel's 815 chip set that uses standard high speed memory from Rambus competitors. In 11 out of 14 such tests, Intel found that the Rambus technology had no advantage over its less expensive rivals. Consequently, it announced that it would no longer use Rambus as the exclusive supplier of chip connector technology. That day, Rambus stock plummeted 12 percent to $75, and continued its slide to $65 on July 27.

Earlier in the year, when Hitachi and Infineon had announced that they had successfully completed validation tests on Rambus RDRAM memory and would adopt it in their products, the stock had soared 25 percent to $300. Although most high-tech stocks have experienced a roller-coaster ride during much of 2000, stock-specific price swings have been fueled by their company's success in the customer marketplace, sometimes in directions opposite to the NASDAQ movement. Whenever one or more business customers have judged a company's product or service to be of value, the news of their adoption of its product or service has generally produced an upswing in that stock's price. Conversely, upon a negative evaluation by a customer, the stock has fallen. By July 31, the Rambus stock had risen again to $75. Why? Because on July 30, Rambus announced that it had developed the first DRAM (its memory technology) capable of transferring data at speeds exceeding 1 GHz (an industry first). To its customers, this would mean, potentially, an unprecedented performance value. "Samsung has been first to market with leading edge RDRAMs (licensed from Rambus). We are proud to continue this tradition with the announcement of manufacturing and marketing support for the world's highest bandwidth DRAM—the 1066MHz RDRAM," said a spokesperson from Samsung Semiconductor Inc., a Rambus customer.

Thus, customer value is a necessary and sufficient driver for shareholder value!

tomer satisfaction is a step in the right direction, but that it is by no means a surefire solution to an aggressively competitive marketplace. For one thing, today's satisfied customers will tomorrow switch to your competitors, in the blink of an eye, if someone can offer them better value. For another, customer satisfaction is an outcome, not a business action. You can do nothing with it unless you know what moves it. That prime mover of customer satisfaction is customer value. Keep your eyes on the value you offer your customers and keep ahead of your competitors on delivering those specific values, and you will have some assurance that today's customers will be with you tomorrow, and the day after. The new miracle medicine for continued customer patronage is customer value, rather than customer satisfaction.

Haven't we already heard all the management wisdom there is? We have tried, after all, one-to-one marketing, frequency marketing, loyalty programs, relationship marketing, customer partnering, among others. And we have tried other prescriptions. We have adopted TQM and we have reengineered our business processes; we have identified and honed our core competencies; we have learned to stick to our knitting; we have become a learning organization; we have deployed technology; and we have become lean, agile, and even virtual. What else remains to be learned? What is still missing?

What is missing is a clear guide to the values that customers seek in the marketplace. What do they want in products and services? How do they want businesses to act? How do they want to be treated? And how much sacrifice are they willing to make in return? What, in other words, is their ValueSpace? Make no mistake about it: There is no lack of desire anymore among most companies for satisfying the customer. And there is no lack of action, either. Whatever the customer satisfaction surveys reveal as gaps, companies rush to fix them. But these actions are often piecemeal, and there frequently is no comprehensive, compelling framework for understanding the customer ValueSpace. And certainly no guidance on how to build and deliver in that ValueSpace.

But a framework is badly needed. Profiting from such classics as *In Search of Excellence, Reengineering the Corporation, Built to Last, Direct from Dell, The Loyalty Effect,* and *Competing for the Future,* among others, progressive companies have pursued excellence with dogged diligence. These books have served their readers well, making their reengineered and renewed organizations fit and ready to launch a journey. What should be the destination of that journey? What should that organizational energy be channeled to produce? To what ends should the organization deploy its core competence? What should it offer its customers? Again, we come full circle to the need for a blueprint for understanding and creating the customer ValueSpace.

We present a comprehensive framework for building ValueSpace for the customer. And we link it to the organizational processes needed to drive it. To preview this framework briefly, there are three components in the customer ValueSpace: performance, price, and personalization, or what we call "the 3P's of ValueSpace." Like the three basic human needs for survival—food, shelter, and clothing—performance, price, and personalization are basic and universal market values all customers seek.

Performance, price, personalization—these concepts are familiar enough to most managers. Indeed, we have chosen the familiar names on purpose. After all, there is no need to reinvent the wheel. What we do need to invent, however, is *meaning*—the meaning that makes sense to customers; the meaning that captures the essence of the ValueSpace they are in fact seeking.

We do this in the next chapter, spelling out the core meaning of the 3P's, and then also identifying their fundamental building blocks. These building blocks, eight in total, and their driver processes are described

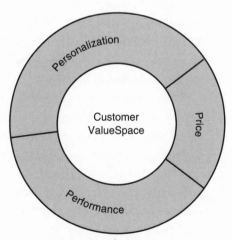

Figure 1.2 The 3P's of customer ValueSpace.

in the chapters that follow, and they are illustrated with case studies from 11 of the world's Most Admired companies. We argue that to craft the complete ValueSpace, all 3P's must be pursued, and all of the building blocks must be deployed. A trade-off is not allowed. The three vignettes at the beginning of this chapter are exemplary instances of each customer value creation. Caterpillar, UPS, SYSCO, the subjects of these stories, are leaders in delivering not just one, but each of the 3P's of the ValueSpace. They, and eight other global market leaders, are also the subjects of our research reported in this book.

Our Research Project: Lessons from the Most Admired Companies

To understand how market-leading companies create customer Value-Space, we researched 11 companies with reputations for delivering exemplary customer value. The research project was sponsored and supported by Marketing Science Institute, a nonprofit organization based in Cambridge, Massachusetts.

We call these companies "the world's Most Admired companies." Seven of them—American Express, AutoNation, Caterpillar, 3M, Xerox, UPS, and PPG—are called just that (actually, they are called *Global* Most Admired) by *Fortune* magazine. We chose two more— Hilton and SYSCO—from a similar list of America's most admired companies, because, for its global list, *Fortune* does not cover the industries to which these companies belong.

Every year, *Fortune* publishes a list called "Global Most Admired Companies," and likewise, a list called "America's Most Admired Companies" (AMACs). To prepare the list, the magazine surveys a large sample of senior business executives and financial analysts, asking them to rank all the Fortune 1000 companies on nine criteria: overall management quality, product or service quality, innovation, long-term investment value, financial soundness, getting and keeping talent, social and environmental responsibility, wise use of corporate assets, and global business acumen. The AMAC list excludes the last attribute. A company's overall ranking is derived by averaging these eight or nine (as applicable) attribute rankings. The list is organized by industry groups, and company rankings reported within each industry. We chose only one company from a given industry.

Since the exact rank within the industry changes somewhat from year to year, our goal was not necessarily to choose the #1 company but rather sample companies from among the top five (out of as many as 15). In the resulting, necessarily a convenient sample, three companies were ranked #1 (UPS, Caterpillar, and American Express), while others ranged from #2 to #5 at least on one of the two lists (Global and North American).[1]

To these nine from the *Fortune* list, we added two more, not covered by either of the two *Fortune* lists (due to their limited scope) but, in our view, world-class and possessing some unique attributes. One of these is Rosenbluth International, the world's third largest privately held business travel services company. And the other is a niche company, Fossil, the innovative maker of fashion watches and related accessories. Each of these eleven companies has created admirable ValueSpace for its customers.

Our study was *not* a typical, quantitative survey research. We wanted to understand in qualitative and process terms how customer Value-Space is created. We researched published information about the operations of each company, visited its headquarters, and interviewed its senior executives in order to understand their efforts at value creation. What we learned, from the interviews and from our reflections, we report in the subsequent chapters in this book.

A Framework for Creating ValueSpace

"I don't believe in customer satisfaction as a goal; it is simply a waste of time because satisfied customers buy your competitors' products. . . . So what I care about is 'delivering the best value' to the customer."

Ernie P. Maier,
3M's director of corporate development

THERE IS HARDLY A COMPANY these days that does not measure, in one form or the other, its customers' satisfaction. 3M measures it too. However, 3M realizes that although measuring customer satisfaction is essential to keeping score, the real game is someplace else. Measuring customer satisfaction is like counting the duration of a standing ovation a contestant receives after a difficult performance. The performer can take pleasure from the applause or feel disheartened from a lack of it, but there is no telling what would have pleased the audience more. To elicit better applause, the performer would have to know what value the audience was looking for, and what elements of his or her performance would translate into those values. The real game is in the customer's *ValueSpace*. That is why 3M and other Most Admired companies are now focusing on creating the best ValueSpace for their customers.

What is the best ValueSpace for the customer?

3P's of ValueSpace

Ask a customer what he or she wants from a business company, and his or her answer will revolve around three things: First, the product or service should do the job it is supposed to do, and do it well; second, its price should be fair and reasonable; and third, it should be easy to deal with the company. That is it. Direct and simple. There is no rocket science to it; no great mystery about what customers want.

There is a lot of cynicism about the customer, though. "Customers want everything fast, free, and now," claim some. "They want a miracle product but they don't want to pay for it," proclaim others. Market leaders know better. They don't promise miracles from products of shoddy performance. They don't scream from the top of their lungs that their prices are the lowest. And they don't mindlessly lip-sync the hype of "Great service is our motto."

Instead, market leaders respect the customer as a rational seeker of solutions—rational enough to want to identify and isolate products of superior performance; rational enough to desire and prefer hassle-free dealings; and rational enough to be willing to pay a reasonable price for those attributes. They respect and view the customer as one who is *seeking value* rather than as someone eager to get "something for nothing" or naive enough to give "more for less." When market leaders work hard to create value for their customers, they create a win-win situation for themselves and their customers. They take the time to understand what customers truly want and value—that is, what their ValueSpace consists of.

It consists of what we call the 3P's of the customer's ValueSpace: performance, price, and personalization. Of these 3P's, price is familiar to all. So is performance, although companies and customers alike often speak of it as *quality*. As we will explain below, performance is a more comprehensive term, and we believe, it is also more accurate in capturing the value customers in fact seek. Of the 3P's, personalization is new to most managers. New not to their vocabulary but new in the sense that they seldom use it to describe what they offer their customers. The prevalent term is *service* or *customer service*. The trouble with the term *service* is that it is overused; so overused in fact that it has become a catchall word, thereby becoming nearly meaningless. "Easy to do business with" is a better phrase, and some firms use it. Customers do want "ease of doing business with," but they want more; they want a personal touch in their interactions with the business company. Personalization is intended to capture that, and more. Let us look at each briefly.

Performance ValueSpace

In the performance ValueSpace, customers look for products and services that will meet their requirements and deliver the outcomes they are seeking. If a customer is seeking a bonding resin, for example, that would hold two objects together at up to, say, 120 degrees Fahrenheit, and withstand a force of 175 pounds, and if the resin manufacturer promises that it will, then that is what the resin must do. If it falls short of that performance, then the customer has been short-changed. Likewise, if as a business company, you have outsourced your payroll, then you expect all of your employees to get paid on time. Absolutely. Every time. That is performance ValueSpace.

Remember the mining-applications tractor from Caterpillar—the one that automatically maps the optimal path for removing a certain amount of earth in mining and construction applications? We described it as the first opening vignette in Chapter 1. We will revisit Caterpillar in Chapter 8. For customers needing to move some earth, Caterpillar is (and for customers in other markets, our other sample companies are) creating *performance ValueSpace*, par excellence.

Price ValueSpace

Price ValueSpace is where customers are concerned that the price they pay be fair and reasonable and that other financial costs incurred in acquiring and in using the product (for example, shipping, maintenance, etc.) also be minimal. The customers seek, in effect, lowest total lifetime costs of a product or service.

When customers consider prices and costs, of course they also consider the payoffs they will receive. Thus, judgments about the *reasonableness* of price and other costs are always made within the context of product benefits. If you are a company that has outsourced its payroll, for example, you want the payroll service to deliver good performance, but also at the lowest price. You are perfectly happy to pay a higher price rather than buy your payroll services cheaper from a company that is unreliable. However, for the level of reliability in the payroll service that you have opted for, you want the best price—better than or compatible with what other suppliers of comparable services would charge, or better than what it would cost you to do the payroll in-house.

This point about price value is important, otherwise one would mistake a lower price (in absolute terms) for a better price value. A discount merchandiser would then always be viewed as offering a better customer value than a full service retailer. This would be misleading, and, of course, it would also be entirely at odds with how customers actually view price value. Thus, price value is the lowest total cost to customers for products and services with a *given* performance value.

Remember how UPS doesn't want you to specify that the package you send be shipped by air? It wants to find you the cheapest combination of ground and air and save you money. Never mind that it will get less of your money for that package. We described this as the second opening vignette in Chapter 1. We will revisit UPS in Chapter 9. Actions like these, from UPS and our other sample companies, create *price ValueSpace*, par excellence.

Personalization ValueSpace

Finally, customers seek companies that are easy to do business with. Basically, customers want a hassle-free purchase experience. This includes convenience, prepurchase assistance, and efficient order fulfillment. If you are a company buying bonding resin, for example, then you want to deal with a company that will promptly provide you with the product sample and all the information you need to evaluate the resin for your specific application. You will want the product to be delivered on time and in a manner most suitable for your inventory management. You will like a company that you can reach easily whenever you need to talk to someone about resin needs; a company that will promptly rectify its mistakes, like a wrong shipment or a wrong invoice. Beyond these cut-and-dried functional attributes, you also want a company that deals with you as an individual. That responds to *your* queries and *your* concerns, rather than give you stock answers. That doesn't quote company policy at the slightest instance of accommodation. That doesn't treat you like a number. That is there for you in your hour of need. You want a company, in other words, that personalizes its dealings with you. You want a company that not only makes it "easy to do business with" but, in fact, makes it a pleasant experience. That is what we mean by personalization ValueSpace.

Remember how Andrew Sterner, a district sales manager at SYSCO in Jacksonville, Florida, cooked a 13-course authentic meal similar to the one served on the *Titanic?* Though he was an ex-chef, cooking a meal wasn't his current job. He was merely doing whatever it took to help one of his foodservice customers. That was our third opening vignette in Chapter 1. It is immediately obvious that such behavior goes way beyond "ease of doing business with." One really gets here a feel of personal touch, even personal warmth. Only a term like *personalization* can capture that attribute, that value. In Chapter 6, we will discuss similar personalization feats from other Most Admired companies. Acts such as these are the epitome of *personalization ValueSpace.*

Building Blocks for the 3P's of ValueSpace

Each of the three ValueSpaces is comprised of certain building blocks. Let us look at these briefly.

Performance ValueSpace Builders

What makes up the performance ValueSpace? How can companies build performance value in their products or services? We believe that there are three drivers of performance value: quality, innovation, and customization.

Quality
Most managers know what quality means. It means, simply but importantly, that the product or service works reliably and consistently. Every time, throughout its life. The bonding resin must hold up against the

specified temperature and tension; the phone service should always have a dial tone; the communications network should not crash; the overnight package should always be delivered on time. And so on.

A company's quality orientation can take many forms. At the most basic level, quality can be viewed as reduction in manufacturing defects so that the product or service conforms to design specifications. The history of the American automobile industry in the 1980s exemplifies this view. In the 1970s the industry was taking a heavy beating from the Japanese automobile makers whose cars were perceived by American consumers to be of higher quality. After losing a significant market share, the American automakers realized that they had to bridge that quality gap. They focused on improving quality by reducing defective parts and assembly mistakes. The typical tools of this quality improvement process were Statistical Quality Control (SQC) and Quality Circles (QCs).

At the next level, the view of quality is broadened to accommodate customer requirements—quality in products and services means it satisfies all of the customer requirements in the product or service. Thus, the cars would not only be efficient and reliable, but also be comfortable for drivers and passengers, for example. At the third level, the quality view broadens further to include not just the product but also other things that would affect the customer—for example, product delivery, billing, technical support, and so on.

Finally, at the highest level, quality becomes a way of life for the company. Here, the company improves on *all* of its business processes. The concept of *internal customer* is adopted so that every process, every activity is improved to meet the requirements of the person whom that activity serves. Total quality management (TQM) is the primary tool in this transformation. The result is that rather than just focusing on delivering good product and service quality, the company itself becomes a quality company. A premier measure of this fourth and highest level of quality endeavor is the Malcolm Baldrige National Quality Award for the American Industry. The award is based on documented achievements in product and service quality, but also on the quality of production and business processes, human resources management, information use, strategic planning, leadership commitment, and, most importantly, commitment to customer satisfaction.

Whether or not a company has actually won the Baldrige or even applied for it, it should endeavor to measure up to the Baldrige criteria, using them as guides to become a quality company. A cornerstone of that effort is top management commitment to quality; quality becomes an integral part of the very culture of the company. Only such a company can create and sustain the desired performance ValueSpace for its customers.

We might clarify that the pursuit of quality in products and services results in all internal processes being improved. Waste is reduced; cycle times are slashed; production costs are lowered; productivity goes up. But there is danger in confusing the process with the purpose. Total Quality Management (TQM) focuses on processes whose purpose is to produce a quality product or service for the customer. However, many companies using TQM become too fixated with *processes*, losing sight of the ultimate *purpose*. If a quality project does not produce a product that customers will value and pay a commensurate premium for, then that effort is misdirected. That is the rationale behind the Return on Quality (ROQ) initiative, in which informed companies now invest in quality effort only if that investment returns good earnings. We believe that a prerequisite for obtaining good ROQ is that the quality projects ultimately create new ValueSpace for customers.

Innovation

Quality obsession creates performance value by ensuring that the product or service lives up to the expectations of the brand. But to stretch the boundaries of that ValueSpace, companies have to innovate. The resin that withstands up to 120 degrees heat and 230 pounds of force—if it can be reformulated so that it will also withstand extreme temperature variations, for example, then that would mean more performance value for the customer. The goal of innovation is to raise the level of functionality of the product or service. American Express company recently introduced a new function for its cardholders: When you want to buy something on the Web, you can get a card identification number good for just one transaction! And you can get one every time you buy something. No longer do you have to worry that someone would steal your card number for fraudulent use. As another example, 3M has coated its roofing granules with copper so that the roofing shingles will not develop a "blackish streak." Thus, product and service innovations that invest a product with benefits greater than those currently available—these products and services create enhanced performance ValueSpace for customers. We describe 3M's and other Most Admired companies' amazing innovations in performance ValueSpace in Chapter 4.

Customization

The third building block for performance ValueSpace is customization. If a product can be formulated to specifically match your needs and desires, then that would be a greater performance value to you than an off-the-shelf product. Product or service quality delivers good, consistent performance; innovation takes that performance to a higher level; customization delivers performance value beyond quality and innovation—it delivers value by adapting or configuring the general product to fit more closely your own individual, specific requirements. Imagine if a car company could design a car just as you dream it, or an airline could fly you on demand, or a university could design an executive program to perfectly match your idiosyncratic needs. That would be the ultimate performance value for customers. Rosenbluth International, the world's third largest business travel services company, configures its travel service operations for one customer at a time. And other Most Admired companies we describe later in the book are coming close.

Builders of Price ValueSpace

Essential to understanding what constitutes price value to the customer is to learn how customers *code* a price. That is, how they decide that the price is or is not right for them to consider buying the product. Customers code prices by various labels, such as "low," "high," "reasonable," "exorbitant," "rip-off," "bargain," "a steal," and so on. These codes can be grouped broadly into two categories: fair price and value price.

Fair Price

According to numerous studies by marketing scholars, customers have a *reference price* in mind—the price that they use as a point of reference in judging whether the price offered by a vendor is high or low. Their idea of a reference price is based on a combination of factors: their awareness of the price other vendors are charging; the cost of a substitute product or service, or how much it might cost if they were to make it themselves; an analysis of what goes into the making of the product or service, or (if an OEM component) how much value it would add to the final product. Included here are considerations of fairness on the part of the vendor—that the vendor is charging a reasonable profit on his or her cost of producing it, and that the vendor is not exploiting a monopolistic or temporary supply shortage situation. A fair price is what they believe it genuinely takes someone to place a product in the marketplace. That judgment is not scientific, of course; but customers make it as best as they can, based on their personal knowledge of the marketplace. You can educate them to make a better judgment, but you can't deny the fact that they make that judgment and that is the price they are *willing* to pay. You better give them that price or else they will go somewhere else.

AutoNation, one of our Most Admired companies, will quote you a nonnegotiable price right on its Web site. It may not be the lowest price you will get if you keep looking for another ten hours or shop six more stores, but it is close. And as a customer, you would know that it is, because if you are ready to buy a car, then you have done some homework and formed a judgment as to what price would be a fair price.

Value Price

Value price goes beyond. It is *more* than worth the benefits of the product or service. As an OEM component, for example, it adds considerably more value to the final product/service than its price. The price is also better than that of alternative vendors or of substitute products/services. Value price may sometimes need some customer educating, but once that is done, the customer is in no doubt that it would be unwise not to grab that product at that offered price. Value price is a price, in other words, that the customer is *happy* to pay.

SYSCO Corporation sells its own brand of canned prunes at $48 a case, $2.50 more than its nearest competitor. But it can demonstrate that when you consider the higher quality of its product and consequent higher yield (that is, fewer prunes that must be discarded), the customer's cost would be 7 percent lower than the competing brand. That is what we mean by value price. And that is what customers are seeking in the price ValueSpace.

Companies must strive to offer customers a fair price at the minimum, and a value price, in fact, to gain their loyalty. Companies must be organized to be able to offer good price value to customers and still meet the desired profit and ROI goals. There are two drivers of price ValueSpace for the customer: target costing and lean operations. Although each driver can help enable both fair price and value price, target costing is specially suited for fair price and lean operations for value price.

Target Costing

Target costing is a program of managing the costs of product development, production, distribution, and marketing so as to contain them at a level that would allow the company to price its product attractively for the customer and at the same time yield the desired profit margin. To achieve target costs, firms may have to redesign a product, substitute less expensive materials, or save money on procurement by finding cheaper sources of raw materials. For automobile makers today, for example, target cost is an overriding goal that both drives and constrains the entire design, development, and manufacturing cycle. Through extensive customer and market research, automobile companies identify the price point at which the proposed new car model will appeal to customers; working backwards, the automakers then develop cost targets. This is in contrast to a *cost-plus* model—setting the price by adding desired margins on to whatever turns out to be the final cost. The problem with the cost-plus approach is that it does not ensure that the resulting price will be a good value to the customer.

When Hilton Hotels Corporation designed its recently launched Hilton Garden Inn, it knew it was targeting a business traveler who wanted the quality assurance of the Hilton name but was looking for a midpriced accommodation. That midprice-enabling target cost then dictated its entire design and implementation effort—from site selection to furnishings to in-room technology to the choice of amenities.

Lean Operations

The second driver of price value is lean operations. It is related to target costing but requires attention in its own right. Target costing is most pertinent at the time of first-time product design; it entails target-cost based design and manufacturing requirements. Lean operations go beyond, applicable to ongoing products and processes as well. Without altering the design and manufacturing requirements, the production processes are made more efficient. Production includes not just the factory processes but office and management processes as well. Waste must be eliminated from all processes and all operations. The factory itself must be modern and cost efficient. Employee jobs must be designed for maximum productivity, aided by necessary computers and technology. Management costs must be trimmed by, for example, removing excess layers of management. General sales and administration (GSA) expenses must be controlled.

There are at least four subprocesses to achieve lean operations—operations defined broadly as any organizational activity that produces, hopefully, an outcome. The first is process *reengineering*. Business processes are redesigned for greater efficiency, eliminating all unnecessary process steps. The movement in corporations around the world for process reengineering is a business response to the increasingly important need for lean operations. The second subprocess is *automation*. Companies automate not only their own operations but also the means by which customers interact with the company. Third, *supply chain management* entails reducing the costs of material procurement, storage, and handling throughout the system. Often inventories are a big cost to a business, and managing lean inventories through *just-in-time manufacturing, supplier partnering,* and other related moves can reduce the total operations costs significantly. The final subprocess is *modular or flexible manufacturing.* Once companies have achieved a lean and streamlined production system for a set of standardized products and services, they can turn their attention to giving their production system the requisite flexibility so that production runs can be switched from one product to another, and the production system becomes capable of responding to custom-configured product orders without a notable loss of efficiency. Management expert Joseph Pine calls this process *mass customization.* Mass customization is necessary especially if the company has moved to offering customization as a means of building enhanced performance ValueSpace.

Fossil offers its watches at value prices, enabled largely by its super-efficient inventory management. 3M is trimming production costs through what it calls "focused factories" that can be switched on and off for small runs. And American Express is automating its dealings with merchants to save costs and to improve its service to merchants. These and other lean production stories we present later in this book illustrate how market leaders build superior price ValueSpace for their customers.

Building Blocks for Personalization ValueSpace

The building blocks for the personalization ValueSpace are also three: easy access, rapid response, and relational nurture.

Easy Access

Customers demand easy means of accessing the company; demanding, in effect, the ability to do business "anytime, anywhere, anyhow." Companies enable this by establishing multiple channels of contact—stores and outlets, phone, mail, fax, even the Internet. Home shopping networks, banking by computer, shopping on the Internet, or home delivery of products such as pizza, groceries, and office supplies, are other examples of easy access. Stores and outlets should be located within easy distance and open for business during hours convenient to customers. The parts and service departments of automobile dealers, to use a familiar example, have until recently been open only on weekdays; some dealers have now begun to offer Saturday morning hours. That is an improvement, but it is still a far cry from "anytime, anywhere" availability.

Easy access is easy to grasp; but don't think it is a breeze to implement. As recently as April 2000, one of us needed a new phone connection. It was difficult to get a service rep on the phone; if you dialed them, you would be taken through a voice menu a mile long, and if and when someone answered, you would be put on hold for so long that you would begin to wonder if you really needed a phone service after all. (We are told that the situation has improved since.) As a business company, we should never underestimate the importance of easy access. Deny customers that and you won't even know they were there!

Rapid Response

Easy access by itself is of little help, however, if there is no response to the customer need of getting business done or if the response is inordinately slow or grossly inadequate. Supermarket customers want short checkout lines, bar-coding of the merchandise that can be scanned quickly, and quick credit check procedures. For services, customers seek rapid response in the provisioning of the service—for example, the installation of a phone or cable service. There was a time when your local cable company could not tell you when the repair person would show up for service installation, forcing customers to stay home and wait the whole day. Now many cable and other utility companies have improved their operations and can give you a two-hour time window during which their repair person will show up. Whether the requirement concerns an initial order fulfillment, or after-sale assistance or fixing an error, the firm has to respond rapidly to meet the customer need or resolve the problem. If you go to a store and there is nobody to help you pull down the merchandise from 10-ft high shelves, or no salesperson to answer your questions, or if the checkout lines are too long, then the store has failed on rapid response. Your business customers may want you to deliver materials and parts for the production line as close to the production schedule and as close to the production line as possible. And if a mistake has been made, or the product or service develops some deficiency, you must rush to solve the problem with a "fix it yesterday" mindset.

Such rapid response and full and satisfactory recovery requires in turn a number of infrastructural resources. Among the important ones: The customer contact personnel should be professional and competent with adequate product knowledge, and empowered to resolve the problem; and there should be an adequate frontline information system so that customer service reps can look up the relevant customer information and product information on their desktop terminals. Armed with such data, as well as the authority to act, a service rep can resolve a problem in one call and immediately.

If you are a PPG customer buying phosgene derivative chemicals, and if you need an urgent shipment and it is Saturday midnight, what do you do? Just call the PPG plant direct, and they will ship it the next flight out. They will inform their own sales account representative and customer service on Monday, but they will ship out the phosgene you need on Sunday. Or if you are a restaurateur and you forgot to order specialty pasta you will need for this evening's dinner menu and it's 3 p.m. and the delivery truck has already come and gone, what would you do? Just call a SYSCO marketing associate, and he will personally deliver it to you, in time for you to serve pasta that evening. These and similar other rapid-response behaviors of our Most Admired companies make up the yarn from which the fabric of personalization ValueSpace is woven.

Relational Nurture

Easy access and rapid response will go a long way. When companies can provide true rapid response, they will have built a good measure of personalization ValueSpace—a solid ground for long-term customer retention. The real builder of personalization ValueSpace is, however, *relational nurture*, and it can be built only after the first two blocks are in place.

Relational nurture refers to the relationship the company builds with the customer. Now *relationship* is an elusive term. What should a company do to build a relationship—send greeting cards? Send flowers? Wine and dine customers? None of that, actually. Not by themselves, anyway. The core ingredient of a relationship is trust. A customer has to be able to trust the company. In his or her interactions with the company, the question the customer asks is, Can I trust this company? Would the company take advantage of the situation where I might be vulnerable? Would the company act in a professional manner, doing what is right, and safeguarding my interests, or would it sacrifice them for personal gain? Is the company interested in just selling me the product or service, or in ensuring that my need is met on an enduring basis? The need for such trust is more directly evident in some situations, for example between clients and professionals. Clearly, as individuals as well as business customers, we need to trust our doctors, lawyers, car mechanics, and our market research suppliers. We need to feel assured for example that our personal primary physician will interrupt a game of golf to return our emergency call, and that the marketing research company would hold our information in confidence. But even where less evident, the need for trust is implicitly present for *all* customers in *all* marketplace exchanges. When we buy a watch, for example, and it breaks down during the warranty period, we want to be able to trust that they won't do a quick-fix on the watch for it to merely survive for the remainder of the warranty period.

Relationship also takes mutual respect. As individual customers, we want respect. As business customers, we want to be treated as partners rather than as targets of impersonal sales pitches. We want to be treated as individuals, not as numbers or statistics. We can do business via automated transactions (for example, ATMs, voicemail, or the Web), but if we need to, we want to be able to speak to a human voice. Nothing substitutes for a little human touch. We want to know someone at the company by name and face, and we want to know that, in turn, he or she knows us, and that this person, and through him or her the company, understands us, our needs, and our desire to be treated well. We want to know that the company cares for our business, that it values us as a long-term customer. Knowing these things fuels our desire to stay with the company. Staying with the company, indeed longing for it—is the goal of the relationship from the company's perspective. Trust, respect, individualized recognition, empathy, a human face, personableness—these are the ingredients that make up relational nurture.

Xerox Business Services assigns a senior executive to be a *focus executive*, to establish a one-to-one relationship with a senior executive at the client company. 3M's roofing granules division executives hold a 2-day retreat with major customers. Call a travel associate at Rosenbluth International and experience a delightful dose of respect, empathy, and personal warmth first hand. As we describe in subsequent chapters, these and the rest of our Most Admired companies are creating unparalleled personalization ValueSpace for the customer.

ValueSpace Expanders

The three ValueSpaces are shown in Figure 2.1 as 3 sectors of a circular space, and 8 building blocks/components as subsectors. Surrounding them is an outer circle of value expanders consisting of value-added offerings. Value-added offerings are just what the name implies. They add to the value customers receive from the company's product or service per se. They expand the circle of ValueSpace outward. And they can expand it by stretching any one or more of the three ValueSpaces. They can add to customers' total gains or benefits from the product and thus expand the performance ValueSpace; or they can make the price even more attractive or affordable to augment the price ValueSpace; or they can further augment the customer's buying experience, enhancing the personalization ValueSpace.

For an airline, for example, value expander offerings would include the range of meal options, custodian assistance to juvenile solo travelers, in-flight entertainment, and so on. Airlines deliver many other

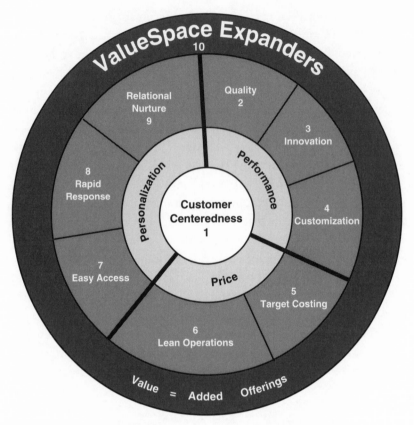

Figure 2.1 A framework for customer ValueSpace creation.

value-added offerings to their frequent flier customers—priority boarding, free upgrades, and free travel awards are familiar examples. Customized meal options or expanded in-flight entertainment are value-adds to the performance ValueSpace; free upgrades or free travel awards are add-ons to the price ValueSpace; and priority boarding or special customer service desks for frequent flyers expand the personalization ValueSpace.

Examples of ValueSpace expanders abound among our Most Admired companies. SYSCO will loan you, free of charge, one of its freezer trucks should yours go bust. Caterpillar will accept barter payments for its tractors. And UPS will offer you free seminars on the handling of hazardous materials.

Whether given free, or at cost, or even at a profit, value expanders can become an effective differentiator when there is little else to distinguish you from the competition. They can lift the customer ValueSpace to a new height.

ValueSpace Components in Perspective

We believe that there is a hierarchy among these ValueSpace builders. And companies *must* follow that hierarchy. Customers want performance first. If the product does not perform, if it does not do the job it is supposed to do, then a price is not a good price, no matter how low that price might be. Customers want to spend the least amount possible, but that is a conditional desire, not an absolute one—that is, it is conditional upon the product or service delivering the requisite performance. As we all know, nobody buys a $600 suit because it is cheaper than $700! They buy it because it, first and foremost, meets their expectations on fit, style, and looks, and then, among all such suits that meet these performance criteria, the one at $600 happens to be the best price value as well.

Likewise, when performance value and price value are deemed to be adequate, only then does the customer look for personalization value. A company cannot make up for a product or service's inadequate performance or for an unattractive price by going overboard with personalization. An airline has to provide on-time flights to desired destinations by safe planes, and offer them at a price customers can afford. Only then does the pampering on board even become relevant, let alone become a value to the customer.

Thus, performance is the foundation. Then, price and personalization can, in that order, enhance and build on that foundation. Companies have to build them in that order.

Next, we believe that there is also a sequence among the builders of each of the 3P's of ValueSpace. In the performance ValueSpace, companies must first offer quality, then innovation, and then customization. This is for two reasons. First, in any competitive space, a company delivering superior quality would be able to differentiate itself and offer the customer better performance value. Eventually, however, at least some competitors will catch up on quality, so the company would have to move to the next frontier of value-delivery, namely, innovation. Second, an innovation produced in a low-quality production system would simply offer the same negative value, only now in the form of a new product or service. That is, innovation would simply amount to one poor quality product being replaced by another poor quality product. The same goes for customization. Customers will prefer a good quality product that is a standard offering for a large market, rather than a customized product of shoddy quality. And they will prefer a mass marketed product of the latest generation (the result of innovation), rather than a customized product assembled from a previous generation.

In the price ValueSpace, there is a natural progression from fair price to value price, the latter being lower than the former. And among its two drivers, target costing should take primacy over lean operations. Products have to be *designed* to be within cost targets to begin with. Lean production can later tweak the costs, and tweak them substantially; however, the *price space* within which the product would compete is first determined at the product or service design stage. Among the lean production tools, automation, just-in-time manufacturing, and process reengineering take precedence over flexible manufacturing. The latter becomes relevant and imperative if the firm is offering customization-based performance value.

Similarly, the hierarchy among the builders of personalization ValueSpace is also intuitively obvious. Easy access is needed for personalization value to even be initiated. This must be followed, and followed inevitably, by rapid response. Lack of easy access would deter customers from dealing with the company; but an easy access without an adequate and prompt response would frustrate the customer. Once the company has established rapid response capabilities to solve all customer problems and meet their personalized response needs, they can then attend to the softer subject of relational nurture. This also takes a much longer time, as all customer contact employees (salespersons, customer account executives, customer service personnel) have to acquire the relational attitude.

ValueSpace expanders come last, literally mounted on a solid foundation of the three core ValueSpaces. At any point in time, given any specific levels of performance, price, and personalization values, an outer ring of value-added offerings can help. In this sense, the conception and delivery of value-added offerings need *not* wait until perfection is reached on the performance, price, and personalization fronts. At the same time, endeavors to improve on the three core ValueSpaces should not slack just because a ring of value-added offerings is in place.

In the chapters that follow, we will see how the world's Most Admired companies create these ValueSpaces for their customers.

Customer Centeredness: The Launching Pad for ValueSpace

"In the end, our customers will determine whether or not we have a job."

Joseph C. Wilson,
founder and former chairman,
Xerox Corporation

E VERY BUSINESS TALKS about being customer centered. Few walk their talk. Truly customer-centered companies are easy to identify. You will see it in their everyday behaviors. They show a keen interest in learning about their customers' needs and interests, and an obsession with delivering the best value to target customers. They make customer needs and interests the acid test for all company policies and procedures, and indoctrinate all employees into becoming customer advocates—being focused on doing the best by the customer.

Figure 3.1 Customer Centeredness and ValueSpace.

In customer-centered companies, a variety of customer research programs—formal and informal—are in place. Senior executives spend time with customers. Internally, they articulate the crucial role that the customer's point-of-view plays in how their businesses define themselves. In these companies, all strategy and core competence is dedicated to creating ever-growing value for the customer. All business processes are adopted only after the company has asked the question and answered it in the affirmative: "Does it add value to what we do for the customer?" In these companies, every employee and every manager knows that customers are the reason for all work and that therefore customers come before all work; that policies and procedures were invented in the first place to serve customers, not to obstruct serving them. In customer-centered companies, employees get rewarded if and only if they have served customers well; and senior executives preach and practice such customer orientation at every step. In other words, building customers' ValueSpace is the "be all" and "end all" of customer-centered businesses.

Several of our sampled companies exhibited just such a set of behaviors.

American Express: Building Customer Value Stories

American Express and its Establishment Services (ES) Division—the business unit we focused on—have invested significant money and effort in taking the pulse of the customer. Its focus on the customer shows up at least in four distinct endeavors. First, it conducts a comprehensive customer satisfaction (CS) survey twice a year. Second, it also conducts extensive customer research to find out what attributes and services are important to customers. Third, it makes what it terms *proactive calls* to learn of customer experiences first hand. Fourth, it explores customer ValueSpace with the rigor of an archeologist!

Its customer satisfaction survey is one of the most comprehensive surveys we have seen. Some 30 pages long, the survey explores, in a side-by-side comparison with its leading competitors, an exhaustive list of attributes ranging from point-of-sale transactions (for example, credit authorization) to reconciliation of charges for payment, to dispute resolution, to the usefulness of the marketing support that merchants receive from the company. The data are analyzed with sophisticated statistical models, and findings are closely reviewed by senior management. Customer satisfaction is a key goal at American Express. A considerable share of everyone's performance ratings depends on customer satisfaction ratings. And this means literally everyone, from the customer service representative up to the president!

American Express: The Financial Services Giant in ValueSpace

American Express is a diversified worldwide travel, financial, and network services company founded in 1850. With 2000 net revenues of $23.32 billion and a net income of $2.80 billion, it ranked #71 on Fortune 500 in the year 2000. Its slate of wide-ranging financial services include consumer charge and credit cards, corporate cards offered to employees in organizations, corporate purchasing cards to business and government organizations, financial planning and investment, insurance, brokerage services, and banking services to corporations. Its charge card is perhaps the most recognized card worldwide, made famous by its long-running slogan "Don't Leave Home Without It" and an advertising campaign featuring celebrity cardmembers who popped up from magazine pages, asking "Do You Know Me?" It was rated #1 in the

Continued

"diversified financial services industry" in the *Fortune*'s list of Global Most Admired (2000) as well as in America's Most Admired Companies (2000), the latest years for which these rankings are published.

An important revenue generator for the company, besides the income from its card members, is the fee the company charges from merchants who accept its credit and charge cards. These merchants, large and small, account, in fact, for nearly one-third of the company's growing revenues. Overseeing the complex operations of its vast and expanding network of merchants is Dave House, group president of the Global Establishment Services, the unit we studied. Dave House honed his marketing and managerial skills at Pepsi and at Reebok International Inc. With American Express since 1993, House has pursued an aggressive program of merchant expansion—recruiting more and more merchants to accept its cards. One recent noteworthy victory: Costco Wholesale Club, the warehouse club, which began accepting American Express for the first time in August 1999 and now exclusively accepts American Express!

Costco and thousands of other merchants around the world accept the American Express card, even though its fee is often higher than what Visa and MasterCard charge their merchants. Its basic but significant value proposition to them is that it will direct their way a special class of customers—customers with higher annual spending. This basic appeal is enhanced by its suite of merchant-specific, customized marketing program support services, designed to grow a merchant's business. In the pages to follow is the story of how this financial services powerhouse, one of the world's Most Admired companies—on Wall Street and Main Street alike—does it.

In 1998 the Establishment Services Division launched another major initiative to learn from its customers first hand—it established a program of proactive outgoing calls to merchant customers across various merchant segments. The conversation covers the areas of concern to the merchant, particularly those identified from the merchant's past interactions with the company. The purpose of the calls is not to generate sales, but rather to understand how merchants feel about their relationship with the company. The calls are recorded for careful expert analysis later. "We measure satisfaction twice a year," says Dave House, group president of Global Establishment Services, "but we want to know on an everyday basis, what is going on, what is on merchants' minds, and how our relationship is faring."

The Value Story

The final and perhaps the most important customer focus endeavor is its exploration of what it calls the *value story*. Most businesses understand that to earn and keep a customer's patronage, they must deliver significant value. They identify what customers want and then work to meet those wants. If customers express satisfaction and return to buy again, the companies conclude that the customer is receiving value. This inference of successful value delivery is usually implicit and intuitive.

Not at American Express. Here, customer value specification is a science. It is diligently researched and carefully documented. The nature of its business model demands it. The higher discount rate that it usually charges merchants is a significant initial barrier to getting merchants to accept the American Express card payment. They need strong reason for accepting the American Express card. That strong reason comes from the *value proposition* it makes to merchants. "Yes, our discount rate is higher," the company salesmen will explain, "but we bring more business to you, business that would otherwise be lost." To support that argument, American Express salespersons come prepared with a presentation on their laptops, detailing the value story.

The value story is developed and maintained by a group that regularly surveys both American Express and competing cardholders to quantify their spending patterns. For each merchant group, it estimates the additional business the merchant would get from his or her trading area by accepting the American Express card. These estimates become the principal arguments in the carefully crafted value story. Thus, an American Express salesperson will proudly declare, for example: "Among the American Express cardholders who shop at retail stores, 23 percent carry only the American Express card; 82 percent of them say that American Express is their card of choice for business retail purchases." The salesperson can point out that customers who pay by American Express card spend, for example, "40 to 60 percent more on their retail purchases than those who pay by competing cards."

A distinguishing feature that separates American Express from MasterCard and Visa is the fact that American Express is also the issuer of its cards, and moreover it is also the processor of its merchant transactions. In comparison, the ownership and control of MasterCard and Visa is vastly diffused among thousands of card issuing banks and still other thousands of transaction processors. Thus, a merchant might accept, in a single given day, Visa cards issued by 20 different banks, for example. Consequently, there is no way for Visa and MasterCard to know how their cardholders spend their money, and, even if they did, they in turn have no way to communicate this information to merchants.

In sharp contrast, American Express has information on the spending patterns of its card members and a direct link with its merchant customers. The company can therefore work with its merchants to develop cooperative-marketing programs designed for targeted groups of cardholders. "We show our merchant customers how they will benefit from a relationship with American Express. We tell them, 'when you accept American Express cards, you are not only getting new customers, but you are also getting the resources of American Express to plan and grow your business,' " says Ritu Clementi, the manager of the Value Story Library. (The library is virtual, stored on CD-ROMs and downloadable to the laptops of its salesforce.)

Clementi talks about the value story with unflinching enthusiasm. There is pride in her voice both for the substantive value she believes American Express offers its merchant customers and for the painstaking documentation her group has created for use by its salesforce. A tour of this virtual library is an eye-opening experience of what it means to contemplate, create, and document a customer value proposition.

"Our big challenge in delivering customer value," says House, "is constantly being aggressive in finding out what is important to the customer and then tailoring everything we do to meet those needs."

Xerox Business Services: Seeking a DNA Match

"A business enterprise works on knowledge. Knowledge lives in documents. Our basic customer value proposition is that we will manage the customer's documents more effectively and more efficiently. We can do more with the document than any other company in the world!"

William R. McDermott, senior vice president, XBS

To understand how XBS creates ValueSpace for its customers, one must understand the nature of its business. It offers two broad but related categories of services.

First, it offers a range of on-site document management services to business customers. These services range from maintaining copying machines or running a mail center to operating a full-service document center on customers' premises that stores, prints, copies, and distributes, both to internal and external customers, documents and information statements and/or collateral materials ranging from letters, faxes, manuals, reports, presentations, billing statements, and so on within and across digital and paper media. XBS manages these document services as an outsourcing supplier, operating mostly on client premises.

Its second service is more comprehensive and more centered in the so-called digital world. This is enterprise-wide management of a client's digital documents. XBS considers itself to be in the "knowledge management" business; and knowledge in an organization lives, according to XBS senior management, essentially in documents, more and more of which are in the digital media. XBS views its forte as helping companies share and use this digital knowledge efficiently and effectively across their organizations, on a global basis. That is its principal customer value proposition.

To deliver on that value proposition, XBS seeks a total alignment between its competence and resources and it's clients' needs. It begins at the beginning—when XBS acquires a client. That's when XBS looks for what, Bill McDermott, senior vice president and head of XBS, calls "a DNA match." He explains: "Most companies are still in the selling mode; they go out there, and sing their song. We have what I call a 'reverse executive communication exchange dialog.' We like to explain our services *after* we have listened to what the client does, what their definition of business process improvement is, and what they are really trying to achieve on a short- and long-term basis. When we ask these questions in an efficient manner, we know up front if there is a *DNA match*."

Again, McDermott explains, "I have that conversation directly with the clients' senior management. One of the things the senior management at the client company appreciates is 'candid disclosure.' So I share my business model with them. That we want to do business with those customers whom we can retain and whom we can grow. We want clients who are interested in our value proposition—effective management of the document—and for whom we can add value, for the long term." This "DNA match," this alignment, marks XBS's operations all along. (McDermott has since moved to Gartner Group as its president.)

Xerox Business Services: Building Customer ValueSpace in Document Management

Xerox Corporation is a global company offering products and services that help customers manage their documents. Its array of products includes copiers, printers, fax machines, scanners, desktop software, digital printing and publishing systems, and printing related supplies. Its growing services business offers comprehensive document management services—from running in-house production centers to creating networks.

Xerox was founded in 1906 in Rochester, New York, as the Haloid Company. In 1947 Haloid bought the rights to develop copying machines from Battelle Memorial Institute, Columbus, Ohio, which had, three years earlier, bought the basic technology invented in 1938 by Chester Carlson, a patent attorney and part-time inventor. Haloid coined the word *Xerox* for the new copiers and the company became Xerox Corporation in 1961.

Since the early 1990s, Xerox has been boldly reinventing itself from a predominantly black-and-white, light-lens copier company to a digital, color and document solutions company. With 2000 revenues of $18.6 billion, income of $117 million, and 94,600 employees worldwide, Xerox Corporation ranks #87 on the *Fortune 500* list.

For our study, we focused on one of its business units, Xerox Business Services (XBS). XBS has been providing document services to customers for more than 40 years and today is the world leader in outsourced document management services. Once focused primarily on managing customer copy centers and mailrooms, XBS has expanded its portfolio to include the complete range of industry-focused document solutions. Today, it provides outsourced document services and solutions to more than 5200 client companies in more than 50 countries. XBS is the winner of the 1997 Malcolm Baldrige National Quality Award. (Xerox Business Products and Systems had won it in 1989.)

How good is it in creating customer ValueSpace? For the last several years, its customer retention rate has exceeded 90 percent—almost all of its customers renew their contract with XBS! For an insight into how it carves out that ValueSpace, read on.

Putting Customers at the Center, Literally

XBS uses a chart to think about its management processes, and at the center of this chart is a box labeled "customer and market focus." To implement its customer focus, the company is constantly "tuned in" to its customers' changing needs. A variety of *listening posts* are in place: focus groups, formal invited reviews of site operations and performance by customers, post install surveys (customer surveys taken immediately after a new site operation is put in place), annual customer satisfaction surveys, and, most importantly, the army of its on-site associates in daily contact with client personnel.

Mention *customer focus* to McDermott, and his eyes light up as he collects his thoughts. "Customer focus is in fact one of our corporate values. That is the #1 goal of every Xerox employee around the world. Our founder and first chairman, Joe Wilson, said it best: 'In the end, our customers will determine whether or not we have a job.' And we live by this value everyday. When you go to a senior management meeting, people refer to Joe Wilson. This company is deeply entrenched in this value."

Such zeal for being customer centered runs through the entire senior management team. Mike Ruffolo, then president of Document

Solutions Group, wanted every employee to be focused on the customer's needs. " 'What's keeping our customers up at night?' That is the question I have asked myself many times," says Ruffolo. "It requires," he continues, "that they (our employees) make an effort to gain a deeper understanding of exactly what their customers are thinking. It means talking to their customers about their business. Spending time with them, observing their work processes. It only makes sense to organize everything you do around solving that customer's problems, making yourself a valuable part of their business, and cultivating their loyalty." (Ruffolo has since moved to EMC Corporation as its new president.)

Another senior executive we talked to, John Lawrence, vice president for quality at XBS, showed almost a cultlike dedication for customer focus. "This is the only company I know," says he, "where we ask, 'did you do the right thing for the customer?' "

Customer First

At the heart of being customer centered is a program XBS calls *Customer First*. The program is the result of a soul-searching internal analysis by Xerox top management in 1994 to 1995, in the wake of a 3-consecutive-year slide in customer satisfaction. In 1996 chairman Paul Allaire announced Customer First as an umbrella strategy to be adopted by every business unit within Xerox.

As part of the program, every employee has received a weeklong multimodule training. "Under the program," says Rick Anderson, manager of Customer First, "we want our people to be 'passionate customer champions' whose top priority is doing what is right for the customer; who are relentless about listening to customer's requirements and understanding customer's business processes in order to translate that acquired knowledge into actions that create value for the customer."

Does this corporate value survive as it travels from the boardroom to the field worker? And as employees go from the training suite to the work floor? You bet. XBS associates live it every day. Take Evelyn Taylor, the team leader of the XBS client site at a professional organization based in Washington, DC. The XBS team runs the company's mailroom, fax, and copying units. One recent year, the client company's director of operations, to whom the XBS team reports, nominated the entire XBS team for the Customer First Heroes award. How did the team do it? Evelyn Taylor says when she joined the team a few years ago, she "told everybody their job wasn't making copies or delivering mail. Rather it was to meet the needs of their customers and leave them with a positive, memorable experience." She and her team never reject a customer's request. "Whenever a customer asks us something, our answer is always a 'Yes,' " explains Evelyn. "Then we find a way to get it done, whatever it takes. We ask ourselves, 'If I were a customer, what would I want?' " It is customer centeredness like this—total dedication to the customer—that is at the core of the superior customer value XBS creates, as we shall describe in the chapters that follow.

3M: Deep into Customer Operations

3M makes and sells a large number of products to business customers, that is, other businesses who buy 3M products for specific applications. These business customers select and buy 3M products mainly on technical and economic criteria. Therefore, 3M defines customer Value-Space in very rational and economic terms: specifically, the total costs to a customer running a process or application in which 3M products are to be used.

3M is creating this ValueSpace for the customer with a systematic organizational process. "We set up cross-functional, transnational teams," explains Ernie Maier, 3M's director of corporate development, "and we do process mapping for a specific application. Then we identify, with client help, 'what the critical process variables are, and what sources of value opportunity exist in that process.' From this identification proceeds a search for 'lower total costs' solutions."

Minnesota Mining & Manufacturing Co. (3M): From Innovation to Customer Solutions

Minnesota Mining & Manufacturing Co. (3M)—is among the world's most innovative companies. To millions of consumers around the world, the company is perhaps most known for its Scotch adhesive tapes and Post-it Notes. It is, however, a manufac-

Continued

turer and marketer of more than 300 product lines for industry and home use. Its products range from pressure-sensitive adhesive tapes, abrasives, and specialty chemicals, to electrical and telecommunication products, medical devices, automotive parts, and office supplies. Its 2000 revenues were $16.72 billion (up 6.5 percent from 1999) and net income was $1.78 billion. Compared to others in its industry, 3M has consistently earned significantly higher return on assets (ROA) and on investment (ROI): For the past five years, it's average ROA was 14.23 percent versus 4.62 percent for the industry, and the average ROI was 16.84 percent versus 9.32 percent for its industry.

3M invests heavily in new technologies and product development—upward of $1 billion annually over the last three years, for example. For a long time, one of its strategic mandates has been that 30 percent of its sales should come from products no more than four years old. A recent refinement is that 10 percent of sales should come from products barely a year old! Currently, about 30 R&D projects have been placed on what it calls *Pacing Plus*—a program where innovative projects receive priority access to corporate resources.

In our study we focused on the divisions that produced industrial tapes, bonding systems, and roofing granules. Roofing granules is in an established industry while industrial tapes and bonding systems are in growth segments where growth is fueled by identification of new applications, especially in the transportation and construction industries. The principal means of stretching customer value in the roofing granules division lie in helping customers reduce total process costs in the application of roofing mineral and in servicing current customers responsively. In the industrial tapes and bonding systems divisions, customer value challenges reside in engineering new applications and in establishing more efficient—from the customer's standpoint—interfaces with the distributor as well as end-user markets. In the pages to follow, we describe how these three divisions of 3M create performance, price, and personalization ValueSpaces for their diverse customers.

The search for low-cost solutions takes 3M deep into customer operations, deeper sometimes than customers may actually be themselves. Textile mills provide an example. One of them is a 3M client for a bonding material that holds a rubber sheath to a roller. 3M determined the total cost of running this machine including the setup cost for replacing the rubber sheath at periodic intervals. That is what the customer didn't quite know; that is what 3M tried to figure out. And 3M set out to reduce the total cost of this operation. Its solution: replace the bonding resin with a hook and loop system. That method takes less time to replace the rubber sheath; it consequently reduces machine downtime; which reduces the total cost of operation. What will be the price of the new system? It is set at a level so as to equitably share the gains from the improved solution. The client saves money; and 3M makes more money. It is a win-win situation. This is what Maier means by "delivering lowest total cost."

Understanding customer costs and customer operations becomes quite an involved process. Sometimes, the cost savings of a proposed solution are not in the department that will use the product, but in the next department in the value-chain or with the customer's customer downstream. Or the costs are indirect or in overheads. For example, in one customer plant, $1 million was being spent in health costs. By using a specific application from 3M, the machine operator no longer needed to perform a certain repetitive hand movement; this reduced the incidence of carpel tunnel syndrome, which reduced worker downtime and health care costs. Understanding the customer processes to this level of detail requires a strong customer focus. And in developing alternative, better value solutions, it takes partnership. The hook and loop solution for the textile mill client, for example, took 20 months to develop. That kind of solution development requires a total immersion into customer operations—and a relationship of mutual trust in which the customer can share process and cost information.

PPG Industries: Staying Close to the Customer

For PPG, being close to customers is very functional—it allows PPG to differentiate its product performance from competitors, and to deliver a better price value. Explains Tom Von Lehman, PPG's vice president who heads its specialty chemicals division:

> We now spend a lot of time with the customer to make sure what the actual customer requirements are. A lot of our emphasis is on how efficiently you produce that product. And we look at the internal processes that drive the performance of that output. We say that to be successful, the quality of those processes—the time and cost metrics for it, have to be efficient. In the new product development process, for example, we now have what we call a "gatekeeper process" that outlines step-by-step that the customer requirements are well understood. And, all different elements of business decisions are brought together at certain key points—marketing, manufacturing, environmental, IT—all are aligned. We are using that process to manage our new product development process.

In other words, what PPG does is to develop a well-defined product development process closely aligned with customer requirements. This is doubly effective. The final product closely matches customer requirements; and the process is more efficient, keeping costs under check.

PPG Industries: Differentiating by Doing It All

PPG Industries, Inc. is a global manufacturer of coatings, glass, and chemicals. The coatings business includes protective and decorative finishes (such as rust protection and body paint) for automobiles, airplanes, appliances, and industrial equipment, and paint for architectural applications. Its glass products include automobile glass (for example, windshields), and flat glass for construction, industrial, and residential applications (for example, windows, mirrors, etc.). Its specialty chemicals division includes optical products, silicas, and fine chemicals. The optical products unit produces monomers, photochromic dyes, and ophthalmic plastic eyewear— its eyewear lenses are sold under the well-known brand name, Transitions. The silicas are used in the manufacture of tires, as flatting agents in paints, and as abrasives in toothpaste. Its fine chemicals unit produces phosgene derivatives for the agricultural and pharmaceutical industries.

With headquarters in Pittsburgh, Pennsylvania, where the company started as Pittsburgh Plate Glass manufacturer in 1883, the company now operates more than 110 manufacturing facilities around the world. Its revenues in 2000 were $8.36 billion and earnings were $620 million. With a market capitalization of $8.046 billion and some 33,800 employees, PPG ranks 227 on the Fortune 500 list, and fourth in the chemicals industry on *Fortune*'s "America's Most Admired Companies" list for 2000, and #5 on its "Global Most Admired" list.

The company has a strong program of new product research. Over the last three years, it achieved about 35 percent of its sales from new products. In each of the last four years, it also received an R&D 100 Award, an award by *R&D* magazine, recognizing "the world's 100 most significant technology breakthroughs in products and processes."

Like the rest of PPG, its specialty chemicals division, the unit we studied, operates in an industry where success requires simultaneous creation of all three ValueSpaces—performance, price, and personalization. To have any chance at all for success, a firm operating in fine chemicals has to meet the user's product requirements to tightly defined technical specifications; it has to prove its price value in a highly competitive and price-sensitive buying environment; and it has to make the buying process smooth and pleasant for the customer. PPG does these and then more. And rather than simply complying with these imperatives of the market, it strives to make each of these a distinctive, differentiating feature. Read on.

PPG tries to study even its customers' customers, although it does so only where the customer's customer is also its customer for some other product. Jim Faller, the commercial manager, describes an illustrative case:

There is this customer who buys from us a particular type of chloroformate which is used to make a certain organic peroxide which in turn is used by PVC manufacturers. So our customer's customers are PVC manufacturers. However, these PVC manufactur-

ers are also our direct customers for another product **PPG** makes, namely, a monomer called **VCM**, which is a precursor to **PVC**.

Anyway, in talking to a few **PVC** manufacturers, we discovered that the amount of chloride left in organic peroxide is such that it causes a critical problem in the **PVC** manufacturing process. So we went back to our direct customer of organic peroxide (who is our strategic customer with a long-term contract) and initiated a project to lower the chloride levels in organic peroxide that they make. Our research told us that if our customer would be willing to accept a higher level of alcohol in our chloroformate, then the chloride levels will be lower. In the end, this worked out very well. It didn't increase anybody's costs, and our customer's customers were happy.

The important thing is that when we meet with our customers of **VCM** monomer, we would be asking them not only about what we ourselves sell them but also about organic peroxide, which is our customer's product; we would ask them what is important to them in organic peroxide? We do this because we want to find out ways of improving our customers' business.

Such customer centeredness does not develop overnight. It has to be embedded in the company's very culture. Explains Von Lehman: "We have a history of being close to our customers; our technical process people who deal with customers absolutely believe that the customer is king—a belief honed in by our quality process. Sometimes, we in fact spend too much time with our customers, and wonder if it is cost-effective in terms of ROI. But ultimately, that is the only way to win the customer."

Rosenbluth International: Customer Orientation a Second Nature

While most companies accept customer orientation as a guiding principle for managing their business, few embody it as deeply as does Rosenbluth International (RI). In everything RI does, it is guided by how best it will serve the customer. Moreover, it does not pontificate about it;

rather it is just there, like its second nature, inseparable from its strategic planning and day-to-day operations alike. In fact, as far as RI is concerned, to be anything but customer oriented is not even an option. It doesn't know how else it will recruit new customers and keep current ones satisfied, except by ensuring that it offer them and serve them as well or better than anyone else could. By offering them excellent customer value, in effect.

Take recruitment of new customers. In order to pitch a new account, its painstaking groundwork includes interviews with a large cross-section of travelers in the company, assessing their needs and preferences. Then it considers the budget constraints imposed by the client's corporate financial requirements. Based on a close understanding of client needs, gained with painstaking groundwork, RI writes a proposal that is as customer centered as they come.

Rosenbluth International: The Contrarian Leader in ValueSpace

Rosenbluth International, Inc. is the third largest travel management company (measured by revenues worldwide), with headquarters in Philadelphia, Pennsylvania. It was founded in 1892 by Marcus Rosenbluth, an immigrant from Hungary, to bring other immigrants from Europe to America. Marcus would not only provide a steamship passage from Europe to New York, but also help travelers with immigration paperwork, and arrange transportation from Ellis Island to Philadelphia. The immigrants who came wanted to bring their relatives, so they gave Marcus their savings, nickels and dimes at a time, until the sum grew to $50. This was the unusual customer value Marcus provided. Today's Rosenbluth is a global travel service agency boasting more than $3.5 billion in annual revenue. But to this mega-agency, customer value remains as poignant a goal today as it was to its founder.

The company has always believed in a contrarian philosophy—do the opposite of what others in the industry are doing. To make that point, it uses a salmon as its mascot—a salmon always swims against the current. More than once, in search of greater customer

Continued

value, it has stood conventional industry practice on its head. At a time when travel agents made money on commissions paid to them by the airlines, Rosenbluth started the practice of returning its commission earnings to clients and charging them, instead, a performance-based fee. And currently, it is redefining its work as a *business interaction management.* Mere semantics? Hardly. The redefinition frees it to identify alternate means of arranging business interaction for the client so as to reduce the need for travel. Now, what travel agent would think of encouraging reduced travel among its clients? But, then, Rosenbluth is no ordinary travel agency. Indeed, it is no ordinary company. Also reputed to be one of the most desired employers, Rosenbluth International is an object lesson in how to create new customer ValueSpace in a chaotic industry with cutthroat competition, and, at the same time, have fun doing it!

To retain current customers, RI must ensure that its traveling clients receive the travel packages they request, at the least cost to their companies, and in an interchange that is not only efficient but also pleasant. To keep its current customers satisfied, it systematically measures their satisfaction, and uses that measurement as a tool for continuous performance monitoring and improvement.

The RI's customer focus is reflected in the very organization of its operations; its field business units are organized as independent business operations with profit and loss responsibility. Each unit is headed by a general manager (GM) who is responsible for serving all client needs in the unit's jurisdiction. The GMs know that the very existence of their unit (and indeed, their jobs) depends on their ability to satisfy and retain their clients.

From time to time, the company holds joint planning sessions with its individual clients. Their purpose is to identify the clients' growth plans that would impact their future travel needs. These meetings, which take two full days, are spearheaded by the account leader and the business unit's GM, although often a senior executive from headquarters (for example, a vice president of Business Development) might attend the sessions as a facilitator. From these meetings, Rosenbluth can forecast and plan for its own resource needs so that it is ready in scale and capability when the client comes calling with his or her expanded scale and scope of travel needs. Such dovetailing of the organization's developmental plans with the customers' future needs is an epitome of being customer centered.

Hilton Hotels: Immersion into Customer Research

At Hilton, customer focus thrives through organized, systematic customer research. Behind every strategic move, every new marketing action, lies extensive customer research. "Everything we do at Hilton is customer research driven," says Bob Dirks, Hilton's senior vice president of marketing. Linda Immer is the director of marketing research, and her enthusiasm is barely contained as she says, "we are constantly studying our customers—via surveys, focus groups, comment cards, and direct observations."

The topic of this research? Almost everything on which customers could have an opinion. The company researches new products, reconfirms current products and programs, and pretests changes in existing guest room amenities. Around the time of our visit, Hilton was testing a new upgraded amenities kit for guestrooms. And they had just finished testing their new advertising campaign, "It happens at Hilton." They also research their training efficacy. And, of course, they research the customer experience. And when they research, they sweat the details. Certainly, customer research forms the basis for setting brand standards. As Bill Brooks, vice president of quality and brand standards, puts it, "we do research into customer needs and into what our competitors are doing; and into what our customers are willing to pay for and then we write those things into brand standards."

Hilton Hotels: Leading in ValueSpace by Guest Technology

Hilton Hotels Corporation is a globally recognized brand in the hotel industry. Founded in 1919 by the legendary Conrad Hilton, Hilton Hotels have become the most desired address for discerning business and leisure travelers. It owns, manages, and franchises,

Continued

under the Hilton banner, 45 resorts, 50 first-class properties at various airports, and over 200 first-class hotels in city centers and suburban areas throughout the United States. Conrad International®, its international subsidiary, operates nine hotels in various international destinations including Europe, Asia, and South America. Today, Hilton's expanding portfolio includes Embassy Suites Hotels®, Doubletree®, Red Lion Hotel & Resorts®, Homewood Suites® by Hilton, and Harrison Conference Centers®, and the midpriced Hilton Garden Inn® and Hampton Inn®. Among its 1800 plus hotels are such well-known properties as The Waldorf-Astoria®, Hilton Hawaiian Village,® and Palmer House Hilton in Chicago. With 2000 revenues of $3.451 billion and net income of $272 million, Hilton ranks 644 on the *Fortune 1000* list. It also ranked #3 on the 2000 *Fortune* list of America's Most Admired Companies, up from #5 in 1999.

Hilton is known for its innovation in the hospitality industry, with a long list of "industry firsts" to its credit. It was the first coast-to-coast hotel chain in America by the early 1940s. With the opening of the Caribe Hilton in San Juan, Puerto Rico in 1949, it became the first international hotel company. It pioneered the concept of airport hotels with the opening of San Francisco Airport Hilton in 1959. Hilton also developed the first centralized reservation system, HILTRON, in 1973. In 1997 Hilton installed electric vehicle recharging facilities in its California properties, embracing a forward-looking proenvironmental innovation. Today, it is a leader in guest technology with an award-winning Web site (the first in the industry), high-speed Internet access in guestrooms, and *virtual* person-to-person meeting rooms.

Hilton is an artist in blending the historic character of its landmark properties with the state-of-the-art amenities and technology; the local culture with universal service; and the functionality of the high-flying business traveler with the creature comforts of the leisure vacationer. Such artistry earns it, indeed, the right to be called "A Contemporary Classic."

In the pages to follow, we describe how this outstanding hotel company commands its customer ValueSpace.

At the strategic level, customer satisfaction is integral to measuring the organization's success and in monitoring and rewarding property managers' performance. Hilton uses a *balanced scorecard* approach to drive organizational performance. Along with financial and productivity measures such as REVPAR (revenue per available room), the balanced scorecard utilizes the customer experience measured both through guest satisfaction surveys and mystery shoppers (independent market research firm investigators visit and stay, under cover, at the hotel properties as regular guests). Daniel Dinell, vice president of operations strategy and planning, who helped design the scorecard, is proud of this tool. "It integrates Hilton's entire value chain—from employee satisfaction, to shareholder value, to customer experience. It has helped put the customer on everybody's mind."

SYSCO: Where Customers Are Really Everything

SYSCO gives its customer centeredness a name—C.A.R.E.S. C.A.R.E.S. is an acronym for "Customers Are Really Everything to SYSCO." Launched some 18 months ago, C.A.R.E.S. is corporate shorthand for rallying all corporate resources for a single goal—to bring value to customers.

SYSCO Corporation: America's #1 Wholesaler

SYSCO Corporation is the largest foodservice marketing and distribution company in North America. A member of the *Fortune 100* for the fourth consecutive year, it had 2000 revenues of $19.3 billion and net earnings of $454 million. While the foodservice industry grew an average of 3 percent, the company's revenues grew by 11 percent and its profits grew by 25 percent over the previous year.

Every day, white truck trailers with the blue SYSCO logo fan out in cities around the country, carrying food products to restaurants and other foodservice operators. With its fleet of more than 7300 delivery vehicles, the company serves more than 356,000 business customers, supplying them with about 3 million cases of some 275,000 food items every day.

Continued

Among its customers are such national powerhouses as Wendy's, Hilton Hotels, and Aramark as well as local landmark restaurants such as the New York Stock Exchange Luncheon Club, Fried Green Tomatoes of Galena, Illinois, and Mike Fink's in Cincinnati, and of course, thousands of mom and pop restaurants. To these foodservice customers, SYSCO's principal customer value proposition is that it will offer them food products that are fresh and wholesome, deliver them at the time promised—in time for the busy lunch hour or for more leisurely evening diners with discerning tastes—and offer them at a price that would deliver them greater value than they could obtain elsewhere. In actuality, however, its value to customers goes further: It offers them counsel and help in growing their business. It acts, in other words, as their benefactor, their mentor, their coach.

In 2000 SYSCO was named as #2 on *Fortune*'s list of America's Most Admired Companies in the Wholesalers category (and #1 among food wholesalers).

SYSCO/Cincinnati, the unit we visited, is one of the nine original companies that founded SYSCO Corporation. One of the 101 operating units of the SYSCO Corporation, it services about 3800 customers with more than 9000 foodservice products.

SYSCO is in the business of delivering food ingredients and related materials to the foodservice industry, including restaurants, hotels, and institutional food kitchens such as cafeterias in hospitals and schools. Its principal customer value proposition is to offer high quality food products to foodservice customers, deliver them dependably, at the time they are needed, and in a cost-effective manner.

To deliver that value, it has embraced *customer centeredness* as its way of doing business itself. It is convinced that the only way it can sell more and more products is to help customers grow their restaurant business. That's the first thing every senior executive would tell you about the company's business model, about its mission, or about customer value.

"We look at our customers' business the way we look at ours," says Richard J. Schnieders, president and COO of SYSCO Corporation. "If we can grow our customers' business, then we ourselves grow." That realization makes everyone at SYSCO deeply customer centered. From its army of more than 7000 marketing associates to the presidents of its 101 operating units, to the senior executives at SYSCO headquarters and indeed to its CEO, everyone is constantly engaged, mentally, with its customers' businesses. As we describe in Chapters 4 through 7, SYSCO aggressively builds ValueSpace for its customers. From the corporate level to individual marketing associates, SYSCO people are constantly shuffling customer databases to identify customers whose business can be grown, evaluating the fit of products that customers might add to their menus, reengineering delivery routes to accommodate the needs of specific customers, teaching customers' chefs new dishes, helping new restaurant owners learn the ropes, visiting with customers, and getting to know them—as a business and as individuals, one-on-one.

AutoNation: Creating Customer Experience

"In our industry, there is this ocean of mistrust between car buyers and dealerships. We are trying to bridge that gap. We are trying to create a wholesome and trusting car buying experience for our customers."

Michael J. Jackson, CEO, AutoNation

"Just want you to know that our thrill began when we walked through your doors and we are still talking about how much fun it was!"

From a customer letter, dated December 1, 1999, received by John Elway
AutoNation dealership in Denver

In a world where car salespersons are about as trusted as a seasoned opponent in a game of poker, CEO Michael Jackson and president and COO Michael Maroone want to install a trustee whom you would entrust some $20,000 to $40,000 every three to five years with the same confidence with which you would entrust your life to a heart surgeon! " 'Open, honest, and transparent'—that is how we want to communicate with our customers who walk into our dealerships," declares Jackson, who recently assumed the reins of the company as CEO. Confirms Maroone, a second-generation car dealer who was among the first to sell his stores to AutoNation, "The opportunity for the company is really to redefine the buying and owning experience for the customer. We are a 100 years old industry. The system in the industry has not satisfied the customer to a level so as to encourage their repurchase. Our goal is to build a better business model through improved in-store customer experience."

AutoNation, Inc., America's Most Admired Automotive Retailer

AutoNation, Inc., is the largest automotive retailer in the United States. Headquartered in Fort Lauderdale, Florida, it owns and operates more than 400 new vehicle dealerships located in 26 major metropolitan areas spread over 19 states. The core brands of vehicles it sells include GM, Ford, DaimlerChrysler, Toyota, Honda, and Nissan as well as luxury brands such as Lexus, BMW, Mercedes-Benz, and Porsche. With 2000 annual revenues of $20.6 billion, the company was ranked #63 on the *Fortune 500* list in the year 2000 and was ranked #3 among Specialty Retailers on the *Fortune Global 500* in 2000.

Until recently, the company operated as a business unit of Republic Industries. Under the leadership of legendary businessman H. Wayne Huizenga (who also owns the NFL Miami Dolphins), Republic Industries was a conglomerate of such disparate businesses as waste management, car rental, and home security. In 1999 the company divested these other businesses to focus on its core business of car retailing. With Huizenga as the chairman, the new company brought in new management, snatching Michael J. Jackson from Mercedes-Benz, U.S.A., where he was CEO and president and who now serves in the same role at AutoNation. Also newly installed is president and COO Michael Maroone, one of the company's original automotive retailers, and unarguably the company's most dynamic insider, responsible for unifying the company's more than 400 dealerships with a common sales and service approach.

During 2000—the first year of the new leadership—the company's revenues rose by 7 percent, and operating income rose by 16 percent. In 1999 the company also entered e-commerce, selling cars on the Internet. In 2000 its Internet sales accounted for $1.5

billion of revenues (up 50 percent over the previous year), making it the largest automotive retailer both online and in the physical world. Its goal is to create an online national brand backed by a network of bricks-and-mortar stores. The new leadership and such innovations earned the company first place on *Fortune*'s Most Admired Companies' 1999 list of automotive retailers.

At the heart of that improved in-store customer experience is a new sales approach. Explains Maroone:

We say that a salesperson's job is to give the customer all the information he or she needs to make an intelligent decision. Our job is not to persuade you or, to use an old terminology, "to stuff you in a car you don't need or stick you with payments you can't afford." Our job is to be first a good listener, listen to what the customer needs are, and then find a vehicle that would meet that need.

Sounds good. But does it bring business? Most certainly, senior management is convinced. Maroone argues: "In the traditional method, 80 percent of the energy is focused on 'out-negotiating' the other party. Now, in our selling model, we don't believe you have to be a great negotiator to get a good price or that your price should be tied to which salesperson you get or which door you walked in."

We wanted to get a taste of that new sales approach. So on the afternoon of September 11, two hours after we talked to Jackson and Maroone, one of us decided to do some windowshopping. About two miles away from the corporate headquarters, I (BM) entered the showroom of Maroone Ford of Fort Lauderdale. Quite a few salesmen were around, and the one who approached me was a tall, slim gentleman of (as I later learned) French origin, wearing the company tee shirt (bright yellow with a racetrack motif). Since a Ford Taurus was on a nearby display, I showed an interest in wanting to know more about the car. He began to show me the car, at first with a polite but impersonal demeanor, but soon he warmed up—to the car at least if not to me. Five minutes into the conversation, and he was telling me about the car's belt retraction, about its CD changer, about temperature control, about the trunk space, and about the cup holders—about the special features I wanted to know and the ones I didn't know enough to ask. I showed no impatience with the details and he showed no ceiling to his enthusiasm: "This is the only car to have received 'double five stars' rating for safety," he told me more than once. Then he asked something about me and I asked for the price. "You can have this car for $22,500," he told me (the sticker price was $23,650). We chatted some more and then, when I was about to conclude my visit, he invited me to his open-entrance cabin. He gave me a brochure and a credit application, explaining how to fill it out. We talked some more. I asked for a lower price. He repeated himself: "You can have that car for $22,500." I persisted in my bargaining effort, so he said, "our philosophy is that we won't sell at cost and we won't take you to the cleaners." Then he followed up with a small concession: "When you are ready to buy, leave your rental car here and we will take care of your rental car." (My cover story was that I was moving to South Florida in about a month and he assumed that then, as now, I would be driving a rental car.) Then he offered me other intangible benefits: "When you buy a car from me, there will be a service rep I will assign to you and it will be one of the two best we have." "And at 3000 miles," he continued, "you come in for a free service and while the car is being looked at, we will go for breakfast; it will be on me." I didn't have any more heart to bargain. So I took his leave. His parting words were *not* "goodbye." Instead they were: "Welcome to South Florida; I want to introduce you to a unique experience of buying and owning a car. I want to introduce you to a friend. My name is Andre Deland."

Later that evening,, I was at another Ford dealership in the area (not owned by AutoNation). An elderly salesman met me in the lot and walked me to a row of Fords. There were four Taurus models and we looked at them briefly, identifying differences. He showed me a feature or two I didn't ask for, but if I didn't already have a preference for Taurus, he would not have changed my enthusiasm (or the lack of it) a bit. I asked for price and he said he would give me the best price in the area but that he would talk price when I was ready to buy. I thanked him and took leave. In fairness, I must add that he was laid back, easy to get along with, and I liked him for not being overbearing and pushy. He also left me with the impression that I would get a good price and that if I had a lower price from somewhere else, he would probably match it.

Now I must tell you my bottom-line conclusion, albeit necessarily biased. If I were really looking to buy a Taurus, I would definitely buy it from Andre Deland. And even if I were not looking for a car, and if I moved to South Florida, I would definitely drop in on Andre just to say "Hello"!

This "experience" was hardly unique to us. Hundreds of delighted customers write glowing letters to dealerships. Here is one example, taken from the company's database library:

> **As you both [salespersons] know it has been many years since we have purchased a vehicle and we both dreaded the thought of having to learn all over and get through the pain of long hours in the showroom and not feeling good about the whole event.**
>
> **We understand that there are people who like the "thrill of the hazzle [sic]" and that is OK. Just want you to know that our thrill began when we walked through your doors and we are still talking about how much fun it was.**
>
> **(Excerpted from a letter, dated December 1, 1999, from a customer who bought a Toyota Tundra from the John Elway AutoNation dealership in Denver)**

For AutoNation, creating customer experience *is* customer centeredness.

Customer Centeredness: The Launching Pad

These, then, are the behaviors manifested by our exemplary customer-centered organizations. They know their customers more than the customers know themselves; they beat customers at their own self-knowledge, diving deeply into their (i.e., customers') operations, validating with customer feedback every small detail of their offerings. Customer-centered organizations construct value stories with the rigor of an archeologist, describing in concrete detail what their products offer to their customers. Customer-centered organizations make sure that customer requirements are built into the entire product development process, researching the needs of their customers, learning to always say "yes" to customer requests, frequently asking themselves what's keeping their customers awake at night. Customer-centered organizations link every employee's and every manager's compensation to customer satisfaction, always asking "did you do the right thing for the customer?" Customer-centered organizations dovetail their own organization's developmental plans with the customer's future needs, making customer orientation second nature, inseparable from everyday operations; in effect, keeping customers, their interests, and the Value-Space that they seek always uppermost in the collective consciousness of the organization. These traits are the launching pad from which market leaders journey into ValueSpace.

Performance ValueSpace

"We at 3M make our living by developing products for specific customer applications. We view and present ourselves as a solution provider rather than product sellers. We go in, for example, and say to the customer, 'We are specialists in protection, bonding, masking, etcetera. How can we improve the way you protect, bond, or mask materials in your own production of goods that you make?' It is from such dialog that potential applications are identified. And what can be better performance value than products developed to precisely match a specific user's specific application need?"

Kevin Ries, *director of marketing, industrial tapes division, 3M*

As CUSTOMERS, WE SEEK products and services that will give us solid performance. We buy them with the hope that they will work reliably and effectively, that they will withstand the test of time, without deterioration in their performance. Companies create products and services that deliver superior performance value with three tools—quality, innovation, and customization. All of the companies we studied are focused on creating products and services designed and produced to deliver excellent performance value for their customers. They build these products to be of immaculate quality; they are constantly engaged in innovating new features to meet evolving customer requirements; and, wherever possible, they are increasingly acquiring the capability to customize the product or service to diverse groups of customers. In this chapter we highlight the efforts of selected companies from our study in creating performance ValueSpace.

3M: Quality, Innovation, Customization

Performance value is at the heart of 3M products for the three business units we studied—industrial tapes, bonding systems, and roofing granules. And these divisions, like the rest of 3M, offer performance value

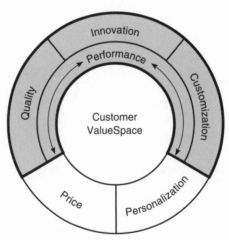

Figure 4.1   Performance ValueSpace.

by all three drivers in our framework: a first-class quality, a thriving program of innovation, and customized applications.

Quality

Quality for 3M means that products fully meet the application specifications, and they do so consistently, every time, every batch. "Our 'brand promise' is consistency, quality, and innovations," says Kevin Ries, marketing director of industrial tapes division.

Consider 3M's double-coated tapes, which can be used to bond two surfaces. They have advantages over traditional fastening methods such as rivets, screws, or welds. For example, the body of a truck is made by riveting a sheet metal panel onto stiffeners; 3M is working toward replacing the rivets with double coated tapes. By eliminating any air gaps that inevitably remain between any two riveted surfaces, the adhesive tape will create a seamless joint. This would mean a good moisture seal and no vibration noise. Moreover, using adhesive tape instead of rivets or welding will save on labor and it will also give better appearance. And of course, the bonding is as strong as possible. (Just for fun, try pulling on a sample of its double-coated tape, called 3M VHB Tape. We did, and failed!) For the company that makes the truck, this is a great performance value. Not only is the functionality of the truck better (better appearance and quieter truck body), but the company also saves on production costs as it takes much less time and skill to apply a bonding tape than to apply rivets or welds. "We have the technology base that allows us to produce a tape with unequaled performance," says Rich Mills, sales and marketing director of the bonding systems division.

Consider quality at 3M's industrial mineral products division. One of its products is roofing granules. Rooftop shingles are made with flat fiberglass sheets (called "webs") that have been impregnated with hot asphalt on which stone granules are sprinkled. The granules stick to hot asphalt on the base web. The resulting product, when dried, is the shingles we see all around us on rooftops. These granules are made by 3M and sold to shingle makers.

Now, although granules are more or less a commodity and granules from various suppliers are difficult to distinguish, 3M makes sure its granules are of the highest performance standards. To ensure high quality, 3M owns its own rock quarries (four in the United States and one in Canada), which have mineral with specific chemical and physical properties. For example, this mineral effectively blocks UV light, which is a desirable property in roof granules. Beyond the intrinsic qualities of the rock, the granules are treated with a proprietary process and ceramically colored in about 20 color varieties. This coloring is a very expensive process: For example, colored granules cost $80 to 100 per ton compared to $20 to 40 per ton for uncolored granules. 3M color-coats its granules with a process that ensures highest quality color fastness. And the granules are designed to endure severe and varying weather conditions.

"Our quality is exemplary," says Robert Morrow, sales and marketing director of the industrial mineral products division. "Almost without exception," he continues, "we are better on quality than our competitors." As proof, Morrow offers the fact that their warranty work is nearly nonexistent. And so sure are they of their quality, that in an industry where no one offers any warranty, 3M does!

Innovation

3M is also a leader in product innovation. A well-known fact about 3M is that 30 to 40 percent of its revenues come from products invented within the last three years. In part, 3M brings out new products and product line extensions to fill the revenue gap caused by the normal price dip over a product's life cycle; but it is a fact that it is simply 3M culture to bring to market a constant stream of new products coming out of 3M's product development. An entire book can be filled with the litany of 3M innovations to-date. One in fact exists, documenting the "behind the scenes" history of some recent 3M innovations (*3M Way to Innovation*, Ernest Gundling, Kodansha International Ltd., 2000). Rather than enumerate these, here we focus on one that happened where you would least expect it.

Is there room for product innovation in such basic products as roof granules? It would be unlike 3M if it did not innovate, no matter how established the product category. So, the company's roofing granules division has developed a very innovative type of granule for special applications. It is the algae block copper roofing granule system. If you drive in Florida, you will notice a black streak on the rooftops there. For a long time it was believed to be fungi that possibly develops in humid climates. 3M researched this problem and found out that it is not fungi; rather it is an organism which, to protect itself from the sun's rays, secretes a black-brown-reddish pigment. It is this pigment that gives the roof shingles their undesirable streak. So, 3M set out to find a solution. With experimentation, its scientists discovered that copper is toxic to the organism. They created resistant granules by coating them with a layer of soluble copper (cuprous oxide) prior to applying the ceramic and color layers. This is done with a highly sophisticated proprietary process—the expensive process raises the cost of these granules to about $800 per ton (as compared to $80 per ton for ordinary granules). Fortunately, copper-granules need be used only in a 10 percent mix with regular granules, thus bringing this delightful innovation within affordable price range.

Customization

3M's customization comes from applications engineering and, in that context, increasingly, its innovations and customizations go hand-in-hand. While 3M has always been innovative, now there is a new twist: More and more of its product development work is driven by real assessments of market needs for specific applications rather than by basic R&D. If a customer needs a new application, would 3M invest in developing it? Here is how Kevin Ries responds: "We make our living by developing products for specific customer applications. We view and present ourselves as a solution provider rather than product sellers. We go in, for example, and say to the customer, 'We are specialists in protection, bonding, masking, etcetera. How can we improve the way you protect, bond, or mask materials in your own production of goods that you make?' " Increasingly, then, 3M is developing and customizing industry-specific product applications in response to needs identified through a dialog with specific customers. The use of double-coated tape to bond sheet metal on bus bodies, the application we spoke of earlier, is customization at a specific industry application level. The case of the textile mill for which 3M is experimenting with a hook and a loop system to bond a rubber sheath to a roller, which we described in Chapter 3, is an example of customization for an individual customer.

Xerox Business Services: Customer Amazer
in Performance ValueSpace

Xerox Business Services (XBS)—the division of Xerox we studied, offers business customers a range of on-site document management services—companies outsource to XBS their mailroom and copying and printing operations. The essential value customers seek for this service is that XBS meet their document needs effectively and efficiently—more so than customers could do for themselves. How well does XBS deliver this value? Amazingly well. Its customer satisfaction ratings and retention rates stand at a high of more than 90 percent!

Quality

XBS puts in place a service configuration designed to meet each client's specific needs for document management. Such custom-configured service is *designed* to meet customers' performance requirements well, at least in theory. Or perhaps only in theory. To realize the designed performance in *practice*, it must be implemented in a high quality operating environment.

That quality for XBS has its roots in the quality movement at its parent company, Xerox Corporation, where it began in 1983 with an initiative called Leadership Through Quality. At the core of this initiative was a philosophy about running the business—that all levels of the company had to practice quality. This *total quality management* (TQM) approach, and the success it gave Xerox is now legendary. TQM was responsible for Xerox's turnaround from declining marketplace performance in the early 1980s to reclaimed market leadership by the late 1980s, crowned by the prestigious Malcolm Baldrige National Quality Award it won in 1989. XBS has inherited this legacy of achievement from its parent company. Applying the same standards of quality to its service business, XBS won a Baldrige of its own, snatching the 1997 title for service industries.

How does XBS work quality in its day-to-day operations? "When the customer requirements are first appraised, these are discussed with the customer," says Ginny Craver, business excellence manager at Xerox's Document Services Group. "Built into these discussions is an agreement on the performance standards [for example, the copying machines will have an uptime of 98 percent; all copying work will be completed on time 96 percent of the time, etc.]. The process implementation then targets a 100 percent fulfillment of these standards." Any gaps are quickly diagnosed and corrections identified and promptly executed. XBS guarantees its performance. Its guarantee reads, in part:

> **Xerox will provide Services in accordance with the Performance Standards . . . and upon notification from the client, will then correct any such nonperformance issues identified within 30 days, failing which, the client may terminate Agreement without incurring Early Termination Charges.**

To deliver such guaranteed performance, XBS uses a number of quality tools (many are common across the entire Xerox organization). What are these quality tools? To begin with, there is Eureka! It is a *best practices* database on how someone somewhere in XBS or Xerox Corporation has solved a specific technical problem; the database is accessible by all Xerox customer service employees on all sites. Then there is the Operational Excellence program. Vele Galovski, vice president of U.S. customer operations, explains it: "Under the program, a site team, broadly self-propelled, reviews its site operations and identifies six to ten problem areas of high priority; the team then also identifies specific solutions and undertakes their implementation within a timeframe. Sites where these projects have been applied have renewed their contracts, often with enhanced activity volume, and sometimes even when competitors offered lower price bids!" Galovski illustrates his well-deserved boast with a recent example:

> **A client account in the financial industry was due for renewal and it was a vulnerable account. The current decision-maker was retiring and the new person wanted to put the account up for a bidding process. While he was not dissatisfied with the XBS performance, he did not see value for the price the company was paying. So the site team brain-stormed the situation and identified 10 problem areas and set out to rectify them. These included such problems as high internal rejects, lack of document control, and inadequate preventive maintenance. The team next brain-**

stormed the solution to each of these problems. To upgrade its preventive maintenance, for example, it decided to seek Docu-Care training for its associates (the training equips site associates with skills to perform simpler repairs on-site), establish a more stringent calendar for preventive maintenance, and devise a clearer machine status communication system to client personnel (for example, "red dot for copier down, service has been called"). Similarly, to address complaint handling, it set itself the goal of a "within 24 hour response" with a 7-day follow-up to ensure that the complainer was satisfied. To achieve and enable better document control, the team came up with such solutions as keeping the job requisitions for one year and providing job order copies by end-user to corporate services for proper charge-back. The team discussed these solutions with the client and put *themselves* on notice that they would deliver these solutions toward specific target goals. Six months after the plan was put into action, the uptime on equipment had improved 80 percent, the newly introduced imaging solutions had improved the productivity by 60 percent, its own profit margin improved by 10 percent, customer satisfaction scores reversed, client perception of "value for money" went up, and the account was renewed, and renewed at the highest bid price! Even more remarkable is the fact that the client now views **XBS** as a consultant for its document management needs.

Innovation

For Xerox, innovation takes two forms—innovations that happen in R&D labs and those that happen at its numerous sites in the course of day-to-day work. Stories of on-site innovations by local teams abound and are told and retold wherever XBS team members gather. One of these involves, for example, an on-site associate working for a health-care client. This particular site prints labels for the client. The XBS associate who works on this task identified a modification (the specifics of which the company would rather not divulge) in the label design which reduced the label design time from over 300 hours to a mere six hours! And mind you the associates' job is not the design of the label; rather his job was merely to run the printing machine to print the labels. But he was constantly focused on how he could offer more value to the customer.

A showcase of XBS quality and innovation is the company's site at a Fortune 500 high-tech company in the Silicon Valley. At that site, as at many others, XBS employees maintain what they call *The Customer Amazer Activity Book*—a journal of continuous improvement ideas implemented at the site. The August '98 edition of the *Amazer* at this client site contained 77 improvements! That year, the high-tech client gave its XBS site team the regional quality award.

Beyond the day-to-day operations and actual new products a company may have invented within the past few years, a company's innovation culture can be gleaned from the excitement managers feel about the future. John Lawrence, vice president of quality, can hardly contain his excitement as he says: "It is an exciting time. What is fascinating is that the very nature of work is changing. At PARC (Xerox's Research Center at Palo Alto), we are trying to understand the nature of work, and we are trying to bring technology to work for it. We can talk to our customers about the 'Office of the Future'!"

Customization

XBS begins work for its clients with the design of a site operation. Rather than offering an off-the-shelf, canned solution, XBS configures a custom solution for each specific customer. Thus, XBS deploys customization as a key driver of performance value for the customer.

For example, consider a manufacturing company that makes sewing machines. The machines come packed with an owner's manual. The current practice is to print it in bulk and enclose it with the product being shipped to retailers. This practice is slated to change for many of the businesses. Now, the manual can be stored and distributed digitally, and then printed by the dealer at the time of the product sale. The manual can even be customized for a specific model and/or for a specific customer. Now, as a supplier of this outsourced service, XBS can simply take over the current (traditional) manual printing service and run it more efficiently, or, it can print more model-specific manuals in smaller quantities, or, better still, it can distribute the manual to the retailer in a digital form, for the retailer to customize, incorporating its own value-added after-market services, and printing it on a just-in-time basis. This is in fact what it does for a number of clients.

Suppose XBS runs your company's mailroom services, and you wanted a certain category of mail distributed much earlier than currently delivered or even feasible. XBS can do it. One of its financial services clients, for example, wanted the mortgage applications distributed by 9 a.m. instead of the current delivery by 11 a.m. (Doing so would shorten the entire loan approval cycle by one full day!) So, XBS redesigned the whole document process for mortgage applications: It created a special return envelope that could be identified by sight, contracted with FedEx Corporation for a special 8:30 a.m. delivery of that envelope, and assigned an associate to deliver the envelope to the designated mortgage processing officer by 9 a.m.

Thus, from initial service configuration for a new customer site to subprocess redesign on an ongoing site, XBS offers customization to enhance its total performance ValueSpace for its clients.

American Express: Performing to Grow the Merchant's Business

For American Express's Establishment Services (ES) Division, it is especially important to create superior performance ValueSpace because its price (that is, the discount rate it charges merchants who accept American Express cards) is higher than the price Visa and MasterCard offer merchants. So it tries to create good performance value through all three avenues—quality, innovation, and customization.

Quality

Consider quality first. American Express is a service company, and like all service companies, quality for American Express translates as the quality of the operations that affect its customers. For the ES Division, it means that its network on which merchants seek credit authorization is up and running, credit authorization is quick, payment for charges is prompt, discrepancies in billing are few, disputes are resolved promptly, and so on. American Express wants to be as good on these operations as possible. And with an eye to improving these, it has benchmarked the "best in class."

"Quality," says Dave House, group president of the Establishment Services Division "is our creed. It is ingrained in the very culture of the company." One way American Express ensures quality is to zealously build and protect its brand equity. "The American Express brand stands for high quality, security, and customer service," continues House, "and we protect that brand image in everything we do." For example, a few years ago, the company purchased IDS, a financial services company, and rebranded it as American Express Financial Advisors. In the deal, independent financial advisors that represented IDS products could now use the American Express name. However, the company barred these agents from cold-calling customers; to do business with American Express/IDS, the customer had to be referred to the company by someone!

What matters, however, is the quality in the merchant's day-to-day transactions with the company. To upgrade this quality, the company's ES Division has recently launched a hugely expensive Six Sigma quality program targeted at specific customer transactions. The program is helping the company to eliminate mistakes most troublesome to its customers, and raise its transactions processing quality to a new level.

Innovation

Next, consider innovation. For the ES Division, innovation relates, again, to the processing of merchant transactions. It has placed technology in the hands of the merchants who accept its cards—for them to electronically handle all financial transactions. They can update their account information online—earlier they had to call an 800 number. Similarly, merchants used to have to send transaction documentation as paper copy, and also receive the financial information (a summary of the day's total charges) by mail; now the company sends this information electronically on its SE Workstations (front-end terminals that merchants use to read customer cards) or on the Internet. Also, merchants used to have to wait for an end-of-the-month statement or had to call their bank to find out if American Express has deposited the funds into their account; now, with newly installed technology, merchants can access this information on their SE Workstation or the Internet on a daily basis.

Most recently, the Company has also created an online business-to-business merchant directory. American Express Corporate, Purchasing, and Small Business Cardmembers can now easily search and access thousands of American Express merchants online.

Customization

American Express also pursues customization in a number of ways. For starters, as alluded to in the previous chapter, its value story is made as directly relevant to specific merchant categories as possible. Then, over time, it has refined its customer segmentation—targeting its offerings by geographic reach (national versus local), industry type (Internet versus bricks-and-mortar; travel versus retail), and industry maturity (whether the merchant operates in an industry where accepting credit cards is the norm versus where it is a new and growing trend). The sales and client support functions of the company are organized around these segments. Most national accounts, for instance, are managed out of the company's New York headquarters, whereas regional and local accounts receive dedicated support in the market where they are headquartered.

Customers in different industries receive different types of information and support. If you are an Internet merchant, for example, you have a number of unique needs and concerns distinct from the needs of a large restaurateur. American Express has sales representatives who are knowledgeable about your industry (and it has a different set of sales representatives who are knowledgeable about the restaurant business), and they will provide advice on your concerns such as online transaction security. If you were a restaurateur, on the other hand, the company's sales representatives would help you with advice on how you could, if you desired, branch out into catering, for example.

The company also has several value-added programs that are highly customizable. While these will be described in detail later (in Chapter 7), briefly, the company can deliver a merchant-specific aggregate profile of customers who shopped at the merchant and used the American Express charge card. And it can provide useful information on the total spending level of customers in the area, both with the merchant and his or her competitors. And, finally, to cardmembers (who do business with merchants), the company offers merchant-specific promotions custom-created by the merchant, using the American Express Web site.

American Express can offer such customization because, uniquely in the industry, the company processes its customers' transactions in-house (other credit-issuing companies outsource transaction processing), so it has access to all merchant data as well as its cardmember data. The company milks this information to help merchants grow their businesses. And what can be a better ValueSpace for a customer than that?

Rosenbluth: Performance ValueSpace in Travel Services

To Rosenbluth International (RI), performance value means meeting customer needs and making the customer happy: so happy in fact, that customers will look forward to doing business with it. Consider this backdrop: In many a company, until recently, individual employees could call any travel agent of their choice or call the airline or hotel directly. With increasing centralization of corporate travel, now they are required to call their corporate travel agency, such as Rosenbluth. So, although the corporate travel manager signs the annual contract, the traveling employees are the ones who have to deal with the travel management company on a day-to-day basis. With their freedom curtailed in the wake of centralization of corporate travel, they are not exactly thrilled to have to call their new travel agency. Rosenbluth strives to change this. "We want customers [that is, travelers] to call us not because they *have* to, but because they *want* to," says Ken Nardone, the company's general manager of customer satisfaction at the time of our study.

Quality

To get them to "want to," the company must deliver first-class quality travel service—it must find the most preferred travel itinerary, and book the travel quickly and accurately. To manage this process effectively, the company maintains and monitors high process standards defined by such statistics as the percentage of calls answered within 20 seconds, percentage of abandoned calls, the average speed of answering the call, the maximum time the caller is placed on hold, and so on.

To reduce error rate on reservations, RI has developed software that reduces by 75 percent the keystrokes required for each reservation. The fewer the strokes, the fewer the wrong key entries. Moreover, fewer strokes equals fewer demands on agents, leaving them much less stressed, and further improving the quality of their interaction with the customer. The company has also developed a proprietary quality assurance system that checks every reservation in real time. The system can check 2000 reservations an hour. The result: no wrong tickets will ever be mailed out to clients!

Innovation

Even more than quality, what would really impress the observer about this company is its innovativeness, vividly present both in its culture and in its products. As to its culture and attitude, RI's contrarian philosophy speaks volumes. So does the story of how, in the wake of airline deregulation when keeping track of fares became a nightmare, RI's chairman and CEO, Hal Rosenbluth, saw in it an exciting business opportunity! In that marketplace of fare chaos, he sighted a gaping customer need and an avenue of creating a new value for the customer.

Now to the actual innovations in products and services. Consider its early adventure in the use of computer technology, for example. When the airline industry became deregulated, keeping track of fares became a Herculean task. For a time, each airline leased to travel agents a computer system that would show its fare and flight schedules (or travel agents had to individually call the airline on the phone). Then, two airlines launched comprehensive systems that showed every airline's schedule on a real-time basis. As a result, most travel agents subscribed to one of them, either American Airline's SABRE or United Airline's APOLLO. And that did the job. Except for Rosenbluth. The snag with the system was that SABRE and APOLLO showed their own airline schedules at the top of the list and in a biased manner, often delaying the posting of a lower fare by a competitor. So Rosenbluth bought all of the airlines' individual systems, put them in a back room, connected them to its own mainframe with software that would integrate these fares from diverse sources and list them for Rosenbluth in an ascending order (lowest fare first).

This, an industry-first, fare finder has of course since been upgraded many times. The present-day system is called DACODA® (Discount Analysis Containing Optimal Decision Algorithms). It is a proprietary program that deciphers complex airline pricing to identify an optimal air travel program for a client company.

If a company is innovative, it will show in the new products it brings to the marketplace. What are Rosenbluth's plans for new products? For a business travel company that has never advertised in mass media, a foray into consumer markets would be quite a sea-change, but that is exactly what the company is successfully launching. It recently launched an online travel booking service, called Travelution.com, selling online, direct to retail consumers. And it is not going to be your usual online travel service. "We are working with some MIT researchers to develop a search engine that would find a fare we could guarantee to be the absolute lowest," says Justin Shaw, a Harvard Business School graduate and vice president and general manager of Rosenbluth Interactive, the company's unit for e-commerce. Among other "new business ideas" on his plate right now are a "gold concierge service" for business travelers—a service that could arrange a limo, purchase a theater ticket, or deliver chocolate to a traveler's hotel room—and a meeting planner service.

Finally, there is Continuum®—a futuristic laboratory to test new travel products and services in the travel industry.

Continuum: Travel Lab of the Future

The real showcase of RI's innovativeness sits on the fifth floor of its Philadelphia headquarters building. It is a futuristic travel laboratory called Continuum. This state-of-the art research and development laboratory houses a carefully assembled collage of prototypes of travel products and services. Continuum is a testing ground for new product ideas from a number of partner companies (in travel, technology, and telecommunications) that provide a variety of services to the traveler. Among its current list of partners are AT&T, British Airways, Continental Airlines,, Palm Computing Inc., Loews Hotels, Visa, and Lucent Technologies.

One of the exhibits is a cutout section of an airplane—a prototype interior design that British Airways wants to test. Another is a section of a hotel room by Loews Hotels that features a contemporary functional design for the business traveler. Yet another exhibit

Continued

is AT&T's smart card that allows customers to make and receive wireless calls worldwide. Finally, there is the video-conferencing technology, complete with an oversized smart-board, that is Rosenbluth's own invention.

These are not mock displays, mind you. They are fully functional, exactly as they would be when and if commercially launched. And they, or their modified versions, will be launched if enough positive customer feedback is received . . . from visitors to Continuum. To get the needed feedback Rosenbluth brings corporate travel managers and senior executives, who are themselves heavy travelers, to Continuum and asks them to record their reactions on an electronic keyboard as they tour the facility. This customer feedback is then analyzed and shared with the partnering companies. Not only are the tested travel products and services innovations-in-development, but the method to market test them is also innovative.

Customization

Rosenbluth has also developed distinctive competence in customizing its services. Every time it recruits a major new client, it custom-configures a service operation specific to that client's needs. There is a range of possible service configurations: an on-site office, a general reservation center or a call center (which may have about 100 to 300 associates), a specialized reservation center (which is like a dedicated offsite office), or a virtual office—a network of call centers located around the globe with capability to route the incoming calls automatically to the next available associate. Here is how Ira Greenberg, RI's vice president of strategy, explains it:

> We would customize an option according to the customer requirements. We can do it in terms of level of service. We can manipulate such tools as location (where to locate a service site) and the extent of technology. For example, we had a big client in a Metro area who was consolidating its corporate travel. We cus-

tomized it so that, for example, international travel requests and top executive requests would go to a business unit—which is staffed with dedicated travel associates; other travel requests would go to lower cost centers, called Res Centers. Almost all new substantial contracts would later require new hires; we have degrees of freedom on what level of staff to hire, for example, college educated, or not.

A second type of customization happens at the level of a specific travel ticket, with built-in technology that screens all travel requests against prespecified criteria. A good example of this is its reservation system installed on the client company's intranet, or on individual travelers' PCs. The reservation system takes into account traveler's preferences. For example, if to you as a traveler, shorter travel time is more important than a lower ticket cost, or coming back home even if it is late night is more valuable than a next morning flight, then the software on your PC can handle that. The company can even customize the software according to your company's travel policies and furthermore to such a detail as to whether the corporate travel office merely wants to suggest to the traveler a particular corporate travel restriction, or, in fact, enforce it. If the latter parameter (that is, "enforce it") is chosen, for example, then the software will simply not allow the display of the alternative travel itinerary. Consequently, the corporate travel policies are enforced and implemented seamlessly.

Lastly, travel services associates (TSAs), who serve specific client companies, customize for each traveler. On the surface, a travel ticket is a travel ticket, so how can one customize it? Explains a senior marketing executive:

It is all about knowing what customers want. We—our Associates—try to get to know you and know your culture. So when Mary makes her travel, we have to make sure these five things are available; and when John makes his travel, we have to check that upgrades are available, for example. With that level of knowledge about your environment, we come much closer to giving you what you want. So customization is all about knowing what customers want.

Hilton Hotels: Inventing Performance Value in Putting Heads to Bed

For hotel customers, whether business or leisure, performance value comes from the comfort and functionality of the hotel's property. Hilton offers this value both in the guest rooms and in its public areas. A case in point is its flagship hotel, opened September 15, 1999, at Boston's Logan Airport. This 600-room property has a unique design. The distinctive building is surfaced with two-color concrete panels textured with decorative patterns. Centered in the chevron-shaped building is a 104-foot circular frame and glass skylight, which serves as roof to the hotel's spacious lobby. Attached to the 85-foot lighted spire, which rises 200 feet above the ground, is a unique architectural feature in the shape of an airplane tail. Inside, the hotel is decorated with contemporary jewel and earth tones and accented with cherry hardwood details.

The guestrooms themselves are state-of-the-art. All guestrooms feature ergonomically designed chairs and contemporary amenities, dataports with high-speed Internet access, conference call capabilities, and on-demand movies. For relaxation, the hotel offers a 6600 square-foot, full-service European-style spa and fitness center. And of course, several of the hotel's 20 meeting rooms feature breathtaking views of the Boston skyline. With all this, who can deny the superior performance value this Boston landmark hotel delivers to its customers?

Quality

For Hilton Hotels, quality means meticulous adherence to brand standards—detailed standards on everything—physical property, processes, employee behavior, and so on. These brand standards are enforced via mystery shopper surveys, and field inspections from the headquarters management. Bill Brooks, vice president of quality and brand standards, has risen from the ranks, having worked as a hotel general manager himself. No brand standard escapes his keen eye, and when he points to some brand standard slipping at franchised properties, the property general managers respect his judgment, for they know that he knows what he is talking about. To keep the hotel's physical property at par with the brand standards, there is a rigid refurbishment schedule (for example, furnishing/soft goods redone every five years, and room furniture renewed every ten years). In recent years, the company has spent more than $1 billion in renovations at its flagship properties such as Waldorf-Astoria Hilton, Hilton New York, Hilton O'Hare, and Hilton San Francisco.

The ultimate test of quality is, of course, exceeding guest expectations. And Hilton ensures it by giving its Customer Satisfaction Tracking Study (CSTS) results some teeth. It compiles customer ratings at the individual property level and feeds them back to property management within 24 hours, along with some actionable analysis that points out, for example, which hotel and service attributes need fixing right away! Even more importantly, as mentioned before, these CSTS results are made part of a balanced scorecard and incentive program for each property management.

In any hotel company, the quality of its service can only be as good as the quality of its employees. Hilton makes a major effort in developing and investing in its human resources. It calls its employees *team members*—signifying how much it values loyalty in those who work for Hilton. Every employee is expected to show and feel the *Hilton Pride*. To nurture that spirit, Hilton invests heavily in training activity. Every new employee goes through an orientation program comprised of such modules as Brand Standards, Recognition & Rewards, Balanced Score Card, Continuous Improvement Process, Drug and Alcohol Policy, and so on. There is a segment on Valuing Individual Differences, and also on HR policies, paydays, schedules, code of conduct, telephone skills, and Service Recovery. Hilton spends more than a million dollars annually on training in out-of-pocket expenses at the headquarters.

Innovation

For a business in the hospitality industry, the most significant innovation comes from new product development. For Hilton, a recent new product was the Hilton Garden Inn, an engine of its growth strategy and a source of great value for its customers. Garden Inn was designed to fill a gap in its product line and indeed in its industry. It is targeted at the traveler who is cost-conscious but also seeks high quality functionality in lodging, and accordingly is willing to pay at the upper end of the midprice range.

Purported to serve the discerning traveler, the hotel is designed to be aesthetically pleasant as well as offer all the requisite services on the property. For example, all Hilton Garden Inn properties feature a signature glass-walled Pavilion that houses the reception desk; a Pavilion Pantry^{SM} with a selection of microwaveable packaged, refrigerated, and frozen items, and sundries; a comfortable lounge area with a television and fireplace; meeting rooms; a laundry facility; and a restaurant, of course. In addition to the indoor swimming pool and a whirlpool, a fitness room is standard. All guestrooms are equipped with office technology for the business traveler, and there is a 24-hour, complimentary business center.

Hilton has a rich history of innovation. It was the first coast-to-coast chain (established by 1943); and the first to offer such amenities as air-conditioning and direct dial in guestrooms. Hilton pioneered the concept of airport hotels with the opening of the San Francisco Airport Hilton in 1959. In 1973 it launched the industry's most sophisticated computerized hotel reservation referral and reporting system with uptime of 99 percent. In 1995 it pioneered the hotel industry's first comprehensive Internet Web site; and in 1999 it revamped its reservation system with a $30 million state-of-the-art central reservation system that links more than 500 hotels worldwide.

Hilton also makes considerable investment in guest technology. Currently, it is experimenting with the idea of Internet kiosks installed in the hotel lobby where (for a fee per usage) guests will be able to go online and send and receive e-mail. "Hilton wants to be the absolute technology leader in the hotel industry," says Bob Dirks, senior vice president of marketing. The latest in its technology explorations is a state-of-the-art video-conferencing facility called *telesuite*. Established in collaboration with IBM and Dayton, Ohio based Telesuite Corporation, the Telesuite networks enable virtual person-to-person meetings in fully synchronized audio and video environment that produces life-size images "across the table." We tested the one in its property at Beverly Hills. While the images do not pretend to replace the real thing, they come, with their life-size dimensions, as close as one can imagine.

Perhaps the apex of Hilton innovation is the development of its Sleep-Tight^{SM} rooms. The special rooms are designed in collaboration with the National Sleep Foundation (NSF), a nonprofit organization, and are currently available at such leading properties as the Waldorf-Astoria in New York, the Capital Hilton in Washington, DC, and the Hilton at Chicago's O'Hare Airport. These rooms are equipped with special amenities to help a traveler sleep better. If you check into one of these rooms, you will find a pair of earplugs and an eye mask, a specially designed mattress with extra pillow-top support, blackout curtains, and a minibar filled with caffeine-free beverages. You will also find some special-effects gadgetry: A heart and sound soother from the Sharper Image will create environmental sounds. A light source from Apollo will help realign your body's circadian rhythms. A set of CDs provides natural, environmental sounds and a sunrise clock gently wakes you with a soft simulated sunrise. If you are a frequent business traveler with an important meeting the next morning, you cannot but be amazed at the tremendous performance value these innovations offer you.

Customization

Hilton is also experimenting with a few avenues of customization. One of these avenues, now standard in the industry, is to manage a variety of properties—airport hotels, downtown business district hotels, suburban hotels, and the latest, the Hilton Garden Inns. Guests can choose what fits their need the best. A related variation is in the room amenities; some are Sleep Tight^{SM} rooms; others are equipped with extensive business equipment; still others with minibars and cordless phones. Hilton is also experimenting with a system to give guests hypoallergenic pillows—a most frequent special-request item. "If we know that 40 percent of our guests request hypoallergenic pillows, we can equip 40 percent of our rooms with those pillows. So we are trying to monitor our guests' special preferences more closely," says Daniel Dinell, Hilton's vice president of operations strategy and planning.

Its most prominent customization is for its frequent guests. Under a program called Hilton HHonors (HH), members are classified into Silver, Gold, or Diamond status, depending on the frequency of their stays. Diamond members are recognized with the highest level of service and quite a few freebies. Under what Hilton calls a "7 + 5 action plan—12 ways to win," Diamond members get accommodations in "the towers"—better rooms; they get special breakfasts; at many properties, they get special check-ins; the hotel eliminates the blackout dates (which apply to less frequent guest members); and they are guaranteed 48-hour reservations—if they call within 48 hours, Hilton will give them a room, even if it is sold out!

Hilton's customization takes yet another form. Uniquely among its competitors, Hilton integrates the local culture into its properties and services. Not only are its properties frequently part of local history, but they also feature local cuisine and host local festivals and functions. The Hilton Washington, for example, is the home of many large political events, in which the U.S. president is a frequent guest.

Yet another outstanding example of customization, albeit at the property level rather than the individual level, is Yokoso Hilton E—a special program for Japanese travelers to the United States. The program, designed to respond to Japanese customers' special needs, includes an extensive Japanese menu, double beds and alarm clocks, phone directories printed in Japanese, and Ryoku cha (tea service) offered at the hotel restaurants.

Most hotel guests want customization at yet another level—being recognized as a guest, and a frequent guest at that. Hilton's Bob Dirks, senior vice president of marketing explains:

> **Our guests have told us, time and again, if you could do just one more thing for me, it would be this: Recognize me for how important I am; know that I have stayed here, at the Waldorf, 25 times within the last six months; they beg us for recognition. We have had technology challenge, but in very short order, we are going to be installing the system that will give us that functionality, enabling us to recognize our guests and recognize their preferences from their previous stay, and give them those things without even their asking. That would be the ultimate customization, which we are striving for.**

PPG Industries: Fine Chemistry in Performance ValueSpace

PPG Industries, Inc., through its specialty chemicals division, is a leader in phosgene chemistry. It supplies phosgene derivatives and both starting and intermediate chemicals to a number of industries including pharmaceutical, agricultural pesticide, and artificial sweetener producers. For customers in each of these industries, but especially in the pharmaceutical, performance value of chemicals is of utmost importance. Not only should the intermediate chemical be of requisite purity so as to meet the finished product's desired quality parameters, but the process by which the intermediate chemicals are qualified should be of high and consistent quality. End-user consumers of pharmaceuticals, suffering from serious ailments, trust the pharmaceutical company for product quality and efficacy. The pharmaceutical company in turn trusts its suppliers for raw materials. The same is true with silica (which goes into tire manufacturing and in toothcleaning abrasives) and plastic that goes into optical lenses: the performance of phosgene derivatives, silica, and optical lenses should be impeccable. PPG understands the significance of meeting such strict performance requirements, and it delivers in such performance ValueSpace by all three means: quality obsession, innovation, and customization.

Quality

PPG specialty chemicals division operates in an industry where any chance at success at all requires an ability to meet the user's product requirements to tightly defined technical specifications. For PPG, its product quality means controlling the chemical processes by which those products are produced. The quality of these processes is what becomes its differentiating value. This is how Marino Feuntes, general manager for PPG's fine chemicals division, explains it:

> There are not many suppliers of phosgene. We are difficult to copy. Not so much in terms of the phosgene itself, but in producing the phosgene derivative—the specific application using phosgene. The technology to produce phosgene derivatives is difficult and differentiated—in terms of how you handle the product, the shipping of the product, having quality-associated systems in place.
>
> Our chiral reaction [chemistry to produce pharmaceutical products] is better for some derivatives. Customers want pure, single isomers. This kind of chiral reaction capability—we are known for it. We have a reputation for it. Our name is associated with it.

Innovation

Recall that PPG has a corporate goal to achieve one-third of its annual sales from new products. Specialty chemicals division more than meets its goals. Says Tom Von Lehman: "In Transitions Optical [PPG's joint-venture optical lens company], 100 percent of our products are new. In our fine chemicals business, it is at a maturity stage and there is a much longer product life cycle extending up to 10 to 12 years, so the ratio is only 10 percent—We are trying to spruce that up a little. In silica, it [new product/sales ratio] tends to be 30 percent. So my ratio overall is 40 percent."

Consider its Transitions Optical business unit. Transitions—the well-known photochromic plastic lens used in eyewear—tries to be at the cutting edge of performance. "For a while," says Rick Eilers, the Transitions president, "we were the only performance plastic. Now there are some new competitors, so we continue to differentiate by improving the product but also by advertising, which creates brand equity for the consumer."

One of its recent innovations was in the application of antireflective coatings on photochromic lenses. The company did a lot of customer research, talking to distributors, opticians, and consumers. Today, the antireflective lens, which makes the face behind the eyewear look almost as clear as without any eyewear at all, is one of the most customer-valued innovations.

Yet another innovation is Trivex™ lenses—made from a plastic material that is slated to replace polycarbonate, the current plastic used in lenses. Polycarbonate makes the lenses shatterproof and, for this reason, it is mandated for children's eyewear by the government. However, according to industry sources, polycarbonate has less than optimum "optics"—optical properties of the lens—particularly as the lens thickness increases. The new plastic in Trivex™ lenses not only gives the same safety performance as polycarbonate, but also provides excellent optics and is, in addition, a thin and light material. The combination of these three most important properties of plastic lenses in one product is unique in the industry. Being just introduced in the market at the press time, PPG's customers—lensmakers—are excited about Trivex™ lenses and about the great performance value they would offer end-users.

Customization

PPG also pushes its performance value by customization. At PPG's specialty chemicals division, customization occurs, in a sense, every time a pharmaceutical manufacturer wants to use one of its phosgene derivatives in its manufacturing process. Explains Marino Fuentes, the unit's GM:

We do a lot of customization—producing one product for one customer. For example, Cydex, a manufacturer of pharmaceuticals, came to us for a very special need. Cydex had just developed a technology to deliver drugs in a way more acceptable to the human body. For this, they required a particular type of molecule. They needed someone to do some chemical reaction with the product. A process that entailed putting a particular molecule inside a particular delivery system (a chemical compound). They wanted it done under GMP [Good Manufacturing Practice] conditions. And we did it for them. We set up the necessary special equipment.

PPG can also customize the molecule's specs for a customer. For example, the usual guaranteed purity level is 99.5 percent, but if a customer wants 99.7 percent purity, it can deliver that level of purity in the molecule.

Indeed, customization seems to be the modus operandi for the specialty chemicals division. For its silica business unit, for example, the product is individually manufactured for each customer's requirements. Says Dick Beuke, general manager of silica division: "We try to differentiate our performance by custom-producing each silica—we try to identify what is important to the customer in terms of performance criteria, and then we try to make it, rather than try to sell what we make."

SYSCO Corporation: Building Performance ValueSpace in the Foodservice Industry

SYSCO customers value product performance highly, higher than price value. In a national survey of its "gold customers" (customers who are most valuable to SYSCO due to their profitability), price was ranked dead last as a supplier selection criterion. At the top of the list, customers named five things they valued: (1) orders delivered exactly as ordered, with no substitutions; (2) on-time delivery as promised; (3) accurate invoices; (4) helpful salespeople; and (5) helpful delivery associates. To deliver that performance value, SYSCO is focused on quality and innovation.

Quality

For SYSCO, quality applies to both the products it sells and the delivery process. SYSCO has more than 180 quality assurance inspectors who inspect farms, factories, and field-sites to constantly evaluate products and processes for quality standards. Produce, like lettuce or spinach, provides a good example. SYSCO has mandated its suppliers of produce not to pack the produce from the first three rows planted by roadsides because road dirt and traffic pollution would get inside the vegetables. What about the produce beyond the first three rows? That gets inspected too. Indeed, the entire crop receives a random inspection. Every week, suppliers e-mail their crop cutting schedules to the company and SYSCO lets them know which crop sites must wait for its inspectors to arrive; only after the inspectors have approved the crop can suppliers pack the produce. "If some year we get a bad crop, we will simply not pack the inferior produce under SYSCO name, and we will simply not supply that produce to our customers," says Mark Mignogna, director of quality assurance. The same rigor of quality monitoring occurs at hundreds of factories that pack meat, poultry, fish, or canned goods under the SYSCO brand name. "We think we have done better than our competitors in product quality in SYSCO brands and we give our customers a lot of information, a lot of statistics on ingredients and quality, better than our competitors," says Larry Accardi, SYSCO's executive vice president of merchandising.

We all know that food products have to meet USDA standards. SYSCO believes that many of these standards are good, but not good enough, so it tries to go one better. Case in point: green beans. USDA grading for grade A requires a minimum score of 90 on a scale of 100. SYSCO's own standards exceed those of the USDA by at least one, and often by two, points. Does it cost more? Sure, it does. But that is just the way SYSCO works—an aggressive Quality Assurance program is a central plank in its endeavor to build performance ValueSpace for its customers.

SYSCO's own brands come in four quality tiers: Supreme, Imperial, Classic, and Reliance. Supreme is the highest quality, often uniquely developed for SYSCO. But all four SYSCO brands exceed the USDA minimum requirements. For example, canned fruits come in two USDA grades, Choice and Standard; USDA minimum score for these is 80 points and 70 points, respectively. SYSCO's equivalent of Standard is Reliance with a score of 75, and compared to Choice, SYSCO's Classic and Imperial score 80 to 85 and SYSCO's Supreme fruits score 87! For Grade A canned carrots, USDA score is 85 points but SYSCO minimum score is 90. "We attempt to specify our Classic, Imperial, and Supreme quality products *above* the minimum score points needed for top government grade," says Mignogna.

Quality is also built into the *processing* of food ingredients. Consider spinach again. "We cut out a lot of stems; then we triple wash it; and then we mechanically dry it," says George M. Sideras, executive chef at the Cincinnati operating unit. What value does this bring to the customer? "The value is two-fold," explains Sideras. "Dry spinach requires 20 percent less salad dressing, because water and oil don't mix and the dressing slides off wet spinach to the bottom of the bowl. And the customer asks for more dressing. Besides, the mechanically dried spinach tastes better because the dressing sticks to and coats the spinach leaf." Small detail? Hardly. These are the food details that help a restaurant business attract and retain more customers.

For food products, assuring quality in the production factory is not enough; equally important is how the food is held in storage and transportation. Here too, SYSCO has tight standards. For example, meat room temperature should be 29° F, and potato room temperature should be 45° F, and the ice cream room should be at 15° F. And to keep those standards, the corporate office hires external auditors (such as those provided by the American Institute of Baking). The auditors visit each operating unit twice a year, unannounced; there, they inspect storage and transportation facilities as well as practices; they inspect everything—the cooler and freezer temperatures, sanitation conditions, compliance with OSHA standards, safety requirements, and so on. They write a report to the corporate office, and corporate executives review it closely. "All 101 pass the inspection—the passing score being 750 to 800 on a 1000-point scale," says Tom Langford, executive vice president of multi-unit sales, "but we want them to score above 900."

SYSCO's quality effort even extends to packaging. Earlier, the produce used to be packed in big boxes that were stapled. Now they are packed in small boxes that have no staples; just the flaps that close easily or are glued lightly. Small boxes are easy to lift by restaurant kitchen workers—most of whom are hired for their cooking skills, not weightlifting power. And small boxes reduce the chances of back injury. And the staples could hurt, or worse, they could get in the food—a very real problem that has now been solved!

Moreover, in the small boxes, the food stays fresher. Instead of the 40-lb bags or boxes, SYSCO now packs chicken in 10-lb bags. And whereas the industry standard is to use 2-mm poly-bags, SYSCO uses 3-mm poly-bags. The bags are vacuumed and filled with carbon dioxide, which takes out all oxygen so there will be no bacterial growth. Now, when customers open a 10-lb bag instead of a 40-lb bag, smaller portions of chicken are exposed to the air. This allows the company to guarantee a shelf life of 14 days (compared to the usual 7 days).

Quality is also a matter of delivering the products as ordered (no substitutes and no missing items and no wrong items) and at a time as promised. For the corporation as a whole, "our fill ratio is 99.4 percent!—fill ratio defined as 'the item ordered is in stock and is delivered on time'," says John Stubblefield, executive vice president of finance.

Technology deployment also helps raise quality. One technology tool SYSCO uses is called SYSCO Order Selector (SOS). It is a hand-mounted scanning device connected to a small computer and a small printer; the screen shows where the next order item is, the selector (that is, the employee) then travels to the specific shelf location and shoots at the shelf label. If the item matches, the device beeps. The selector picks up that merchandise, prints a label to stick on the merchandise, and places it on the pallet. This has reduced mispicks dramatically, saving wasted labor as well as avoiding wrong fills. "Our customers are very particular about getting exactly the merchandise they ordered and getting it within the specified time periods. These technologies are a great enabler in meeting those customer requirements," says Rex Brough, vice president of finance, who oversees technology at SYSCO Cincinnati.

Innovation

SYSCO's product innovation shows up in the form of its private label—the product it sells under its own name. The company claims that its Supreme tier is unique to the industry in terms of quality and composition. Beyond such general quality superiority, some products are specifically formulated by the company. One such product is its special brand of fryer oil, Fry-On. It is a proprietary blend of corn and canola oil with natural vitamin E. Now although all oils contain vitamin E, the processing (that is, deodorization) of oil normally results in the elimination of vitamin E. However, the company has perfected a method where the temperature and processes are such that vitamin E will be retained at its natural levels. "The unique quality of this oil is that it inhibits flavor transfer, which means you can fry different foods in the same deep fryer," says John McIntyre, director, manufactured grocery, at the corporate headquarters. Imagine the advantage to a restaurant owner who would otherwise have to have two separate fryers for frying fish and chicken, for example. The oil also is more stable so it lasts longer after its first use. And, finally, it can be filtered cold. "Handling hot oil can be very hazardous, so cold filtering is a big plus," proclaims McIntyre.

A few other innovations are notable. One SYSCO brand product is Pasta LaBella. It has an interesting history. There is a company called American Italian Pasta Company (AIPC). It used to import pasta from Italy, but the pasta itself was made from wheat from America. Why is this wheat being shipped to Italy and then back in pasta form to America? Because the technology to make the pasta was in Italy. So AIPC bought Italian machinery and expertise, and set up a factory in Kansas, the wheat growing state, and started making pasta. The goal was to create a pasta that would surpass the Italian pasta and at the same time cost less. SYSCO saw this as an opportunity to create a new brand of pasta and acted on the opportunity quickly. SYSCO wanted this brand to be unique in quality, exceeding all existing brands, so it developed a new strain of wheat, stronger and more durable than anything on the market. The new brand—manufactured by AIPC for SYSCO—that resulted was called Pasta LaBella. Try it and see if this is not something unique.

If you liked the taste of the regular version of Pasta LaBella, wait till you try its flavored version. It comes in four flavors: Tomato Basil, Lemon Pepper, Chili Pepper, and Cracked Black Peppercorn. These flavors might be familiar to you, but on LaBella, they are something else, and here is why. Traditionally, flavored pasta was made for the most part by small cottage producers who were unable to consistently deliver the promised flavor profiles and adequate durability. To overcome this shortcoming, SYSCO sought the solution in new flavor technology, called *encapsulation*. Encapsulation takes the intended flavor and enrobes it in a protective shell. In the case of Pasta LaBella, that shell is designed to release the flavor only when chewed. Now SYSCO can offer its discerning foodservice clients a pasta that does not lose its flavor during cooking. It remains locked right until the minute the restaurant patron chews on it! Such is the performance ValueSpace SYSCO builds for its customers.

Customization

One way SYSCO customizes is by offering from its large repertoire a product that would best fit its customer's clientele. "Depending on the customer's demographics, we can support any quality level, such as a Select grade steak, a Choice grade steak, or the premium Angus Beef program," says Phil Trewhitt, senior vice president of the Cincinnati operating division. "Our center-of-the-plate specialist works directly with the customer to identify protein products that best meet that customer's operation's needs."

Customization also occurs through the company's decentralized organization—each of its 101 operating companies are free to carry whatever products the local market requires. "When I was in Indiana," says Mike Seamon, senior vice president of merchandising and marketing for the Cincinnati operating division, "we sold thousands and thousands of pounds of catfish; here in the Cincinnati market, we hardly sell any. Our corporate office doesn't dictate what we should sell; we respond to our customers' needs within the marketplace by making the decision at the local level to carry those products that would satisfy our specific customers' needs."

While its range of products would meet almost every customer's need, occasionally a customer would want something beyond the company's normal fare, and often the company will try to accommodate. "We would start stocking an item for a specific customer even if we are not making any money on it if the customer has been a significant customer for our other products. And remember the warehouse slot position holds a pallet, so if we stock only a few cases for a customer, it is occupying the whole pallet space, but that is okay," says Mike Wiedower, executive vice president of the Cincinnati unit.

What else can the company customize? "We would prepare invoices in any format our customers desire [for example, by manufacturer ID, by product categories, etc.]," says Joe Calabrese, SYSCO Cincinnati's president. "And we would customize delivery times and inventory stocking levels as well."

The real customization happens, however, at the informal level. One-on-one; in the trenches. Stories of what every employee at SYSCO will do to meet a special request from the customer abound. Here is one told to us by Sideras:

> **One customer, which is a 14-unit chain, they wanted a proprietary recipe for a blue cheese dressing. They had developed it in one of their restaurants and then tried it at other units, but they concluded that they could not really make it with any degree of consistency. We took that recipe to one of our vendors and worked with them to get it as close as possible. Note that the original recipe was for a fresh product to be refrigerated and we had to transform it into a recipe that could be shipped and stored at room temperature. It was a lot of work but we did it!**

AutoNation: Crafting Performance Value in Car Retailing

For AutoNation, Performance Value is in creating a new kind of car-buying experience for customers. That experience takes all three elements: quality, innovation, and customization.

Quality

In Chapter 3, did you notice that the dealership Andre Deland works at is called Maroone Ford of Fort Lauderdale? It's an AutoNation dealership, so why call it Maroone Ford? The scoop is that the company is striving to create customer loyalty through a network of dealerships that are given a common local brand identity. In Denver, that brand identity is John Elway and it ties 17 dealerships together there. in Tampa, Florida, it is AutoWay, uniting 13 dealerships there; and in South Florida, it is Maroone, unifying some 30 dealerships under a local brand identity. The dealerships are all company-owned and are integrated by common processes and consistent communications.

Consistency and common practices are essential to a quality customer experience. The local umbrella branding is the best of two worlds: it retains the local touch and it gives all dealerships in a region a common identity. And to customers, this common yet localized identity means a seamless experience. No matter which of its dealers customers go to, they can expect the same quality in the sales approach—and, even more importantly, in the service centers.

AutoNation has listened closely to customer concerns in designing its service operations. According to a recent JD Power survey, the #1 concern of consumers in car repair is that the car is fixed right the first time. Timeliness is the #2 consideration. And then they would like an alternative transport. "We have designed our service to respond to these considerations," says Maroone.

As proof, AutoNation has some of the most customer-centered guarantees in the industry. As one poster at its dealership reads: "Auto-Nation guarantees its repair work for 12 months or 12,000 miles, whichever comes last." Last? No, it is *not* a typo! AutoNation is explicit: "whichever comes last, not first," its brochure states loud and clear.

As to timely completion of work, AutoNation is rolling out a program under which it guarantees the speed (and costs) for 13 of its routine maintenance services. For example, currently at its Maroone stores in South Florida, it offers: Oil and Filter Change: $19.95 and within 30 minutes; Automatic Transmission Service: $69.95 and within 60 minutes; Air Filter Replacement: $10.95 and within 20 minutes; and so on. "If we don't finish the work within the specified time, you will receive the service for free," a brochure declares.

Innovation

What is innovative at AutoNation? Its very philosophy of doing business is! Its very business model is! Creating the whole new car buying experience for the customer is innovation. And its move in e-commerce is innovation.

In this day and age, when a considerable segment of customers want to shop for their cars on the Internet, AutoNation's stake in ValueSpace will be at considerable risk if it remained a mere brick-and-mortar store. Quite to the contrary, not only does it have a presence on the Net, but rather it is a dominant player in the virtual space. Its Web site is one of the coolest among all automobile dealership Web sites. Go to AutoNation.com, click on the "find a new car" menu, and then fill in your zip code, and select a model and make you like. The next screen lists all the cars of the make and model you requested. A product picture pops up. This screen also gives you an option to take a 360° tour of its interior. Move the cursor inside the picture frame anywhere and rotate the ball left or right or up or down and see the car interior from every angle. Press the X key and the picture zooms in for you; press the Y key, and it zooms out!

Actually, the site gives you three choices for finding a car: you can tour the site for all available cars, or you can help the site find you a car you need, or you can build "your own dream car." "Tour the lot" requires you to specify only a car's make, and your zip code, and the search engine searches cars within a 50-mile radius. You will get a list of the cars. Click on a car you like, and you can request a dealer price (you already saw the MSRP on the list); within 30 seconds, you will get the dealer's price. Yes, the price the dealer will sell the car to you for! (In one mock trial search, using zip code 33301 for Fort Lauderdale, for a Ford Contour model with MSRP of $23,265, we got the dealer price of $21,294, available from Maroone Ford of Miami.) Next, you can apply for financing online and also get price quotes on insurance and protection such as extended warranty and theft-deterrent. Finally, one more click, and you can make a date with the dealer to test-drive and buy the car.

The "Let us find it for you" option allows you to specify a few more options on "major features" (for example, four-door or two-door, transmission type, price range, and payment schedule) and it will then search the inventory and give you a narrower list of available alternatives. The most customized option is "Build your dream car." Choose this and you can specify as many features as you like, including the color and trim level. The site promises that relevant dealers will search for your dream car anywhere—including at a competing dealer.

This direct site is only one of the avenues of selling cars on the Net. The company also subscribes to a number of referral services such as CarPoint and Autobytel; when a lead is received from one of these referral services, it goes to one of the dealers who has the car. Who in AutoNation decides which dealer the inquiry should go to? The answer is, "No one; or at least no one who is a *person*." Guiding the enormous

Web traffic is the company's in-house self-built data-management system called COMPASS. COMPASS takes all inquiries, whether received from its own Web site or from referral services, and matches them against available inventory by distance, and automatically routes the inquiry to the nearest dealer. COMPASS also manages the database, tracking all leads. When a dealer logs on to the COMPASS Web site, accessible to dealers only, on his or her screen he sees all the leads, new and old. But COMPASS does more for dealers than simply send leads their way. It guides them every step of the way to respond to the customer. It has a built-in bank of e-mails that dealers can draw on and modify and customize; they can price any car and options they like; they can pull up technical specs on any car; they can store, track, and retrieve the history of the interaction with specific e-customers, and they can use preformatted bulk mail for communicating with their patrons on a regular basis.

"The difference between our way of doing e-business and others' is," says Randall Rahe, AutoNation's vice president of e-commerce operations, "that we want to give the customer the complete information all at once. We don't want to play games; we tell them, this is the vehicle you asked for, this is where you can get it, this is our price, and when would you like to come in."

Do customers see value in this approach? Here is one sample letter:

I wanted to take the time to make you aware of the most positive car shopping experience I have ever had.

First off, let me tell you that for me, buying a car is one of the most unpleasant experiences life has to offer. Unfortunately, I have had this routine many times. This time, however, I thought I would take a different approach. In addition to shopping the local dealerships, I also tried the Internet. . . . Fortunately for me, CarPoint referred me to your dealership and to Greg Irvin. Greg was just the type of professional I was hoping to find through this service (none of the other representatives online or in person compared to Greg). His prompt initial e-mail response was the only one out of the online dealers that actually provided me with the information I was looking for. On the telephone, he was extremely courteous and informative. Most importantly, he was

no-nonsense, no pressure, and to the point. There was no haggling or game playing. . . . In fact, based on my research, he was also just slightly the best price I could find. In the end, it was his honesty and sincerity that impressed me the most. These are two qualities that you rarely find if ever in the car business.

—A customer in Oak Park, California, in a letter dated December 30, 1999

What is its success in e-commerce? Last year, it sold 9 percent cars via e-commerce (10 percent new and 5.5 percent used). In 1999 its Internet-based sales were 46,049 cars at an average price of $23,200 for a total of $1.1 billion; in 2000 its goal was 68,600 cars, and by the end of September (when we visited the company), it had already sold 48,053 cars.

Customization

What can a car dealership customize? Certainly, it is not feasible for dealers to customize the car itself, except some dealer-added options common in the trade. And granted that because it has more cars in stock than anyone else, there is a very good chance that customers would more easily find a car of their choice here than with other dealers. Beyond that, in the selling of the car itself, one would not expect much opportunity for customization. We were not sure ourselves, and we actually thought the question would be silly, but we were interviewing CEO Jackson, so we asked him the question anyway. Contrary to our expectations, Jackson did not consider the question silly; instead he seemed convinced that AutoNation's selling approach and focus on relationship necessarily implied customization. "Customization is merely tapping into what the customer wants in a transaction. When you walk into our dealership, our salesperson is supposed to listen, and understand a customer's need, and then fashion his or her information around your concerns." And indeed, as we will see later, its approach is truly one of customization—or mass customization. It has an effective standard approach, which it is able to adapt to individual customers. It customizes its financial packages of credit, insurance and protection (more later); it customizes its salespeople's presentation of the car; it customizes its correspondence and e-mail to customers; it will search for the car of your choice; it will hold it for you for an appointment of your choice; and it will deliver the car to your home if you like!

Winning the Market Leadership in Performance ValueSpace

From 3M's double-coated tape, VHB, to PPG's phosgene derivative with 99.5 percent purity level, and from Rosenbluth's ticket-coding system that disallows a wrong ticket from ever being issued, to SYSCO's canned foods and meats that "meet or exceed USDA standards," customers of companies in our study all around the world enjoy an impeccable quality in products and services. And every three to five years, they can look forward to a new generation of products. From 3M's copper-coated granules that prevent black streak on rooftops to PPG's shatterproof Transition optical lenses, and from American Express' automated backoffice functions for merchants to Hilton's Sleep Tight rooms for travelers, products and services constantly spring out of the Global Most Admired Companies. And finally, from XBS's custom reengineering of customer document management to AutoNation's custom fashioning of its entire selling approach around individual car shoppers, and from Rosenbluth's technology that ensures that a travel ticket meets each individual client's preferences as well as his or her company's travel policies to Hilton's Yokoso Hilton E hotels for Japanese travelers, market leading companies are forever delighting their customers around the world. Quality, innovation, and customization: these are the building blocks of performance Value-Space. An unflinching obsession with product and service quality, a thriving program of product and service innovation, and growing customization of ones' offerings to individual customer tastes, these are the practices by which market leaders are building ever greater performance ValueSpace.

Price ValueSpace

"It's the Airlines' Number One Priority to get as much money as they can for seat 10C; it's mine to make sure my clients pay as little as they must."

Hal Rosenbluth, *chairman and CEO, Rosenbluth International*

WHETHER A BUSINESS SELLS a consumer product or a product that other businesses buy, and no matter how outstanding its performance value is, it cannot ignore the price value that those customers seek. Increasingly, companies must offer products that will deliver excellent performance value; but companies also must sell products at prices that customers consider both affordable and reasonable. Not only should initial prices be justifiable as good economic value for the delivered performance, but as products mature, the customer expects the price value to continuously improve. The pressure from competitors forces even the innovators to progressively offer more price value to customers.

Companies can create price value in two stages: *fair price* and *value price*. As described in Chapter 2, fair price is a price that customers believe is fair and reasonable. Value price is a price that customers consider more than justified by the total benefits they receive. Fair price is a price customers are *willing* to pay. Value price is a price customers are *happy* to pay.

To offer fair price, companies need to pursue target costing—a practice where product or service offerings are designed and produced within predetermined budgeted costs. To move from fair price to value price, companies need to adopt methods of lean operations, making all processes within an organization cost-efficient. In this chapter, we describe the efforts of the world's Most Admired companies to create superior price ValueSpace for their customers.

Rosenbluth International: Making Its Forte in Price ValueSpace

For Rosenbluth, low price has always been its principal value to the customer. In its early days, this value came from its high-tech airline fare data organizer, which listed all airline fares in rank order and allowed RI to guarantee lowest fares to its clients. In 1984 the company gained its first major client, DuPont, and saved it $150 million in travel and entertainment (T&E) expenses!

Subsequently, Rosenbluth launched a pricing system wherein it would return all commissions from the airline to the client in return for a

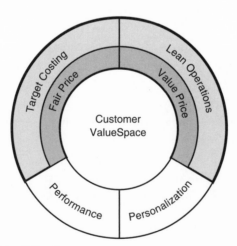

Figure 5.1 Price ValueSpace.

fee directly from the client. Clients paid the fee cheerfully, because, with RI's advanced fare database, they knew they would save on total corporate travel expenses. Next, Rosenbluth went to airlines and negotiated better rates for specific clients based on their annual travel spending.

Once a reservation is made, many travel agencies consider their work finished. But Rosenbluth monitors fares until the last minute, and should a lower-priced fare become available (still complying with the client's travel policies), they will change the ticket and send you a new one. The company considers it a mission to make a trip the least expensive for a client. Here is how Hal Rosenbluth, the company's charming CEO put it in a speech to corporate travel managers:

> **Do you really think that airlines are going to go out of their way to find a lower fare on a competing carrier if clients were to call them directly and inquire as such. . . . Hey, they are just doing their job for their shareholders and I am doing mine for you. It's their number one priority to get as much money as they can for seat 10C, and its mine to make sure they don't.**

Target Costing

Note that a corporate client's total travel costs have two components: the cost of tickets and RI's management fee. As already mentioned, RI assures lower ticket costs by using its high tech fare search engines; but to lower the second cost component, its management fee, it must use at least one of the processes in our framework. It uses both—target costing and running lean operations. When RI negotiates annual or longer-term service contracts with business clients, it faces one or both of the two cost benchmark hurdles—for companies that were hitherto managing its corporate travel in-house, the company must offer the service at demonstrated lower costs than the in-house costs; for others that are seeking to renew its travel management contract, the company must compete against other corporate travel service suppliers. Thus, prospective clients often present RI with a target cost figure to work with.

Now just as a manufacturing company would attempt to meet target costs by component redesign, materials substitution, productivity improvements, and so on, so does Rosenbluth strive to meet its target cost goals; it does so by configuring services to comply with given cost and budget constraints. Staffing is RI's major cost (accounting for some 60 to 65 percent of the total), and it can achieve different service configurations by use of different staffing levels (in terms of the number and skill of employees). For example, it can offer reservations through its call centers only, through a central reservation center, or staffed travel centers, or via its dedicated associates in an offsite office, or through an on-site dedicated reservation center. Choosing from one of these options or a combination thereof, RI is able to configure a client-specific travel service operation to meet the target cost.

Lean Operations

RI has also constantly sought to reduce its operational costs. It has done so by two means: automation of the reservation processes and low-cost location of its centralized services. One clear example of automation is its E-Res® system. E-Res® is an agent-free system useable by clients themselves on their desktop or laptop computers; it includes and automatically applies the client's travel policy constraints. U.S. giant retailer Wal-Mart is a recent RI client; Wal-Mart travelers use the E-Res system when they can, and the company estimates that it will save 10 percent of its $30 million air travel budget!

To reduce its operating costs, RI was the first travel agency to create a centralized reservation system in 1980—called IntelliCenters. Where would you think these centers are located? At its headquarters in Philadelphia? In some other metropolis? Near its major client clusters? No. In rural North Dakota, Delaware, and Pennsylvania; because the labor costs are low there. If clients use these centers, rather than Customer Service Centers (CSC) or dedicated offices, they can save 30 to 40 percent per ticket in booking costs! That is a tremendous value price.

SYSCO: Documenting the Price Value

Foodservice customers cite price as one of the last considerations in their choice of suppliers. "In a National Survey of our Gold customers done by Cornell University, price was not even mentioned," says Albert L. Gaylor, assistant vice president of marketing services at SYSCO

Corporate. Even so, the company is cognizant of the importance of price to the profitability of its business customers.

Fair Price: Target Costing

To offer its customers a fair price, SYSCO sources nationally branded products from diverse manufacturers at various price points to meet the price targets of its individual customers. Due to its buying power and large volume, SYSCO is able to secure attractive delivered prices from manufacturers for these national brands.

SYSCO's own brands come in four quality and price levels: Supreme, Imperial, Classic, and Reliance. Customers have the option of choosing from these four price levels, and these price levels are lower than comparable national brands. By targeting to develop, with its rigorous and creative merchandising programs, house brands that the company sources at significantly lower delivered costs, it is able to offer its customers better price than the price of national brands.

One remarkable feature of SYSCO's pricing is that it gives its marketing associates (MAs) virtually total control over pricing. The company publishes three levels of suggested prices based on volume categories, and each MA knows SYSCO's "salesman costs" (that is, costs to the salesperson, so to speak), and each MA is compensated as a percentage of the gross profits he or she generates, so they get to decide how much premium they must charge their customers. They have to achieve a delicate balance between their need to maximize total gross profits from a customer versus asking for a price that would cost them the loss of that customer altogether. The price they finally charge is therefore the one that is defensible and sustainable over the long haul and sustainable in the face of the constant barrage of competitor's pitches from necessarily lower priced (but also lower service level) competitors.

"Our customers know that we are not the cheapest. They would rate our price as "fair" because our customers have to be absolutely convinced—otherwise they would not buy from us—that our service levels require the price we are seeking," says John Stubblefield, executive vice president of finance at SYSCO Corporate. "If customers ask for a lower price, our MAs will tell customers," says Don Cowell, marketing vice president of the Cincinnati unit, " 'Do you like my service? Do you like the way we meet your delivery requirements? Do you like our merchandise? Then you have to understand that we need to support the costs of that level of service.' "

What if a customer wanted a lower price than what SYSCO offers? SYSCO works with customers to explore avenues of cost reduction. Larry Accardi, SYSCO's merchandising executive vice president explains it thus:

> **Take a national chain customer; if they want a better price, we**
> **would say that "you can help us give you a better price by helping**
> **our profitability, by bringing our costs down; bringing costs down**
> **by reducing the frequency of delivery, or by increasing the prod-**
> **uct cases per order, by changing the mix of products you buy, by**
> **buying a broad line of products, including nonfood items and**
> **equipment, by buying SYSCO brands which offer greater prof-**
> **itability to SYSCO as well as help customers gain more business."**

Price value to SYSCO customers comes not as much from the price they pay SYSCO for a certain quantity of product versus what they would have paid to a competitor. Rather it comes from how much actual food they can make for their patrons from the same quantity of ingredients—from the *yield* that is. "We have done many many actual, what we call, 'cuttings' that is, serving size strips of competing products and our product, and the results show that the yield, the number of servings that our customers consistently get is significantly higher than our competitors," says Stubblefield.

Can this claim be supported? Yes. SYSCO has documented *true value* to the customer for thousands of products. Here are two examples:

SYSCO sells its Supreme brand of canned prunes at $48.07 per case—compared to $45.56 per case of the leading competing brand Carbotrol—each containing six cans with a declared net weight of 102 ounces per can. However, the *drained weight* of prunes per can is 94.7 ounces for the SYSCO brand versus 83.4 ounces of Carbotrol. Consequently, SYSCO's cost for usable prunes is $1.35/lb compared to Carbotrol's cost of $1.45/lb.

A Packer brand of 50-pound whole onions costs $12.56. In comparison, SYSCO natural fresh-cut onions cost $14.44 per 21 pounds of sliced onion—nearly three times more expensive, pound for pound. But the usable product is only 31 (out of 51) pounds for the Packer brand versus 20 (out of 21) pounds for SYSCO's brand. Moreover, in-store labor cost is $28.96 for cutting 51 pounds of onions whereas that cost is barely seven cents for 21 pounds of precut onions. The net outcome: the cost per 8-oz. portion comes to 36 cents for SYSCO compared to 67 cents for the Packer brand!

Lean Operations

In order to offer such value price and still meet its targeted profits, SYSCO runs a very tight ship with constant watch on operational efficiency—lean production, that is.

To streamline its processes, SYSCO corporate uses some 20 indices ranging from shorts and "mispicks" to cases loaded per truck and quantity of product delivered per stop. Every week, the field level data are transmitted to Houston headquarters, and the corporate office goes at it, looking for trends and exceptions. It ranks the operating units into quartiles for each index. All companies are then required to catch up to the top 25 percent on every index. One of the current cost reduction initiatives is to reduce the SKUs (stock keeping units). In 2000, total SKUs were reduced from 614,000 to 597,000 (aggregate over 63 decentralized facilities nationwide, and from 9903 to 9629 per operating unit).

Each operating unit pursues an annual targeted cost reduction, based on how its current cost compares to the top quartile companies. The Cincinnati unit was right in the middle when we visited it, and so the corporate-given goal was a reduction by 2.5 percent in its current operating costs. Joe Calabrese, president of the Cincinnati unit had made definite plans to achieve these savings; he expected to squeeze some of it out of warehouse inventory shrinkage and out of better utilization of labor. A portion of the targeted cost reduction would come out of savings on "workers' comp"—specifically, workers' compensation due to injury—by giving its workers more safety education. Another interesting labor cost item targeted for cost reduction is *indirect minutes*. This is how indirect minutes work: When a selector (the person who selects items from the shelf to place them in the outgoing pallet) encounters a "short," he/she may go to find the item and record it as an indirect minute. In the revised process, the selector will have to write the exact activity and the supervisor will code it as an "indirect minutes job." How does it make the process more cost-efficient? Explains Calabrese:

> Now we know that the selector spent time finding the short item. He or she is *not supposed to*—there is a specific person just for that job, called "short chaser." So the new procedure will prevent employees from doing jobs they are not supposed to do, and allow them to concentrate on the jobs they are assigned to do, and save money by optimal utilization of labor.

3M: Price Value by Total Solution Costs

The customers of the industrial tapes and bonding systems—the divisions that we studied—are other businesses, be they the end-users or distributors. To both, price value is a very rational calculation: End users want to ensure that the 3M product will not raise the cost of their finished product beyond their own target costs; and for distributors, the overriding concern is that the products they carry and distribute give them the targeted profit margins. 3M meets these target costs as it inevitably must, but it does so not necessarily by always lowering its prices, but rather by finding applications and support services so as to reduce the overall costs of total solutions to customers.

Target Costing

To offer lower costs on total solutions, 3M investigates the manner in which its products are used in end-user applications and then it invents cost-saving modifications in those applications. "Using technology platforms," says Ernie Meier, director of corporate development, "sometimes we are replacing ourselves—we are replacing existing products—with lower cost applications produced with new technology platforms." In developing its applications, it employs customer-based tools such as Quality Function Deployment (QFD). QFD is used to assess the worth of individual product attributes to the customer. Indeed, then, "what it would be worth to the customer" assessment becomes the target price during the entire product development and production and sales cycle. Says 3M's Kevin Ries, "our salespeople never approach the customer with the product's price per se, but rather the value of the product considering how much it will save in application over the substitute process or substitute competing products." Since the proposed price is more than justified by the product's worth, this initial target cost lends itself not only to a fair price, but indeed to a value price.

Lean Operations

3M also has an intensive program of cost reduction. In 1995-1996 it launched a corporate-wide program called J35—a goal of 35 percent cost reduction in three years. When that goal was met, its cost reduction drive continued—as part of continuous improvement. One plank in the cost reduction strategy has been 3M's switch to what it calls *the focused factory*. Before this move, its factories were organized around broad processes such as coating a sheet—a sheet of whatever, that is. So the same production line put the required coat on plastic sheet, on a cloth sheet, on a rubber sheet, on a metal sheet, and so on. These identical processes were located in a number of plants around the world. Today, a single factory focuses on a single focused process such as coating a paper. If you want to coat a paper, come to this factory; to coat some other material, you have to go to a different 3M factory. Each factory is thus able to focus not only on a single process, but also on a single product, achieving both efficiency and quality excellence. And the site becomes a *center of excellence*, as 3M calls them. All of the coated aluminum foils are now being produced, for example, in its center of excellence in New Zealand. The efficiencies from such focused factories enable 3M to ensure that the price end-user customers get for applications is a value price.

Price Value to Distributors

Distributors are, of course, most concerned with price value (even more than end users are), being in business to make money. 3M managers realize the inevitable price pressure from distributors. As time goes on, distributors begin to demand better prices because after exploiting other vehicles of customer value (such as product application advice), price remains the only vehicle for these distributors to deliver value to their customers. 3M's bonding systems division's Rich Mills, director of sales and marketing, explains how price pressure could come from, for example, *integrated suppliers*—distributors who put together customized solutions for their customers, integrating components from different vendors:

> Tell you a story—a major Integrated Supplier makes a sales call on a large customer—a manufacturing company—but instead of going to the purchasing department they call on the COO, and say: "We will save you 5 million dollars a year, guaranteed. Interested?" "Sure." "Here is what you do. You eliminate your purchasing department; and outsource it to us. We will manage your procurement for you. We will have open book policy; you look at our books. And we save you money." Now what COO can resist such a proposition? And the savings are progressive, graduated. There is a forecast that 20–25% of the industry will be purchasing through some form of Integrated Suppliers.

How do integrated suppliers save customers money? What integrated suppliers do is put together solutions for their customers. For some end users, the actual product cost dwarfs in relation to the total acquisition costs, and integrated suppliers could deliver cost efficiency by managing the purchasing function better. But this works only for the first few years. Therein lies 3M's challenge. "In my view," continues Mills, "over time, the opportunities to continue to deliver value will become increasingly challenging to the integrated supplier. The time will come when many integrators will have difficulty delivering further cost efficiencies to their customers. They will then have to turn to manufacturers, like 3M, to either ask for better prices or use their help in delivering process cost savings or improved product performance."

3M strives to give its distributors a decent margin—that is, discount off the list price. Lately, the company is exploring ways of enhancing this value. For example, it is revising its system of discounts to make the discounts more commensurate with dealer effort and results. It wants to reward its distributors if they make selective developmental efforts to help an end user appreciate the value of 3M products in an application. A major move in creating more price value for distributors is the company's Pay for Performance program—a program of offering functional discounts. Under the program, distributors get discounts for specific activity and functions they conduct rather than merely on total sales. This is how Rich Mills explains it:

> Over the years, we have homogenized our merchandising plans, which have not really rewarded large volume distributors who invest significantly in developmental efforts. Our large distributors are saying that 3M is not rewarding them for those investments they have made on 3M's behalf. So we are looking at plans that reward behavior, investing the time to develop some of our applications; sometimes it can take up to one year. We are looking at a program we call, **Pay for Performance.**

Pay for Performance is like target costing, attaching a specific targeted cost for specific distributor performance.

Continues Mills:

> Let us take the bus example, where, instead of the panels being welded and riveted, we are now promoting 3M bonding solutions. Here, we don't sell the typical way—like, say, "throw out the riveting method." Instead, we have to capture the imagination of the design department, so that the thought of using the tape makes sense. When the customer becomes interested, then we get in a "prove it" mode. We may now do a prototype, and they would then run an obstacle course—run it over a railroad or so, expose it to cold and heat, and so on. Much is at stake here—if the tape on a bus fails, the bus company's own reputation is tarnished. So "proving the application" takes a long time. Our large distributors and partners spend that kind of time. Now suppose, [after the application is proven], the bus company puts the requisition out for a low bid; sometimes the whole assignment goes to the purchasing department which doesn't necessarily appreciate the project value as determined by the engineering department, so they put it out for bids. And the low bidding distributor would get the business, leaving the distributor who had put in the development effort unrewarded. So we are trying to find ways of rewarding this original distributor.

More than any other example, this one illustrates fair pricing—making distributor rewards equitable to their individual efforts.

The focused factories described above also lead to value price for distributor customers. The focused factory is able to produce in smaller lot sizes—that is a capability that enables just-in-time and lean inventory in its distribution channel. That reduces the cost of inventory for its distributors, which then constitutes value price for 3M's intermediary customers.

AutoNation: No-Hassle Pricing

The relationship selling approach we described in Chapters 3 and 4, this superior customer experience, must cost AutoNation more and therefore it must cost the customer more, right? CEO Jackson is under no illusion: "What we have learned is that you can create a clearly superior customer experience that the customer will like to have, but if you think you can charge for it, you are wrong. The consumer will not pay for it. You have to create a superior customer experience at competitive price points."

Fair Price

AutoNation is now on two pricing models. The first is the *no haggle price*, already in effect in the company's Denver and Tampa Bay markets. Under this approach, the company posts its best price on every vehicle, and that is the price you will get the car for. This is the ideal the company wants to move toward. But many dealers are not ready to give up the ways of the old world yet, and for these dealers the company has a second model, called the *no-hassle process*. "Under this process," says President Maroone, "yes, we will negotiate within a realm but you don't have to fight us to get that price."

The goal of the no haggle policy is: "We make it easy for you to find the vehicle that's right for you without ever having to haggle or negotiate." Stores with a no haggle policy have a sign posted that reads:

One Low Price: At AutoNation every new and used vehicle on display is sold for one remarkably low no-haggle price.

Stores that work on the no-hassle policy are called *Negotiated Stores*, and they carry the following sign:

Low Price: At AutoNation every new and used vehicle on display has a remarkably low price.

The company is able to offer market competitive low price because it has cost advantages due to its scale. "Our scale gives us the cost advantage," says Jackson. In South Florida, for example, the company owns 28 dealerships and buys media in bulk at significantly discounted rates.

Likewise, at its service centers, the company endeavors to offer good price value. "There is a perception of car dealers that they are slow and expensive. We are fighting that stereotype. We are working diligently to fight that perception," says Hank Phillips, vice president of fixed operations. He is fighting that perception by offering a good price value during the warranty work. "It is during the warranty work," says Phillips, "that we have to impress the customer with our quality work and with our service. The fact is that an average oil change at Jiffy Lube is $26; our price is $19.95!" For maintenance service, the company has identified thirteen commonly needed maintenance services, and for those services it guarantees to be "at or below the competitor's advertised prices." To ensure that its prices are a good value to customers, it employs a third party to price shop competitors' prices, once every quarter. Here are some signs a customer would find in its service centers:

We offer low prices at all Maroone Service centers. If you see a lower advertised price on the same maintenance service, bring in the advertised special or coupon and we'll match it.

No surprises. We guarantee to complete all repairs for the promised, estimated amount. If we fail to do so, we will gladly pay any charges above the estimate. No questions asked.

Do customers find its price fair? There is no hard data on it yet, but here is part of one customer's response:

I would like you to know that we appreciated the way we were treated and the efficiency of your staff. We purchased our new

**grand Caravan Sport without any hassle and with what we con-
sidered a *fair price* [emphasis added]. This was not the case at the
first dealership we visited. Carl was very helpful and made the
process painless.**

> **—A customer who bought a vehicle from
> an AutoNation dealership**

Financial Services Pricing: Open, Honest, and Transparent

Perhaps the most distrust customers have is about dealer financing and
the perplexing payment amounts customers are given after they have
agreed to buy a car. AutoNation is trying to overcome this distrust with
a menu approach. "We have a menu of services approach. We present
the customer with a menu of services with prices clearly identified for
each service. Our pricing for these services is 'open, honest, and transparent'," says Jackson.

Menu of financial options? What could that be? We asked to see a
demonstration, so we went down to the Maroone-Toyota dealership on
Sunrise Boulevard in Fort Lauderdale. Ric Gregson, director of finance
at the dealership, took us through the menu. Basically, the menu is a
form that offers four preassembled packages of a number of individual
services—services like the Vehicle Protection Program, which is essentially an extended warranty program; Vehicle Care Program, which
serves as a prepaid routine maintenance service; Theft Protection Program based on window engraving; Lojack Protection Program, which
activates a specially installed transmitter in coordination with the local
police; and Guaranteed Auto Protection (GAP), which makes up the
gap between what you owe the bank and what your insurance company
pays you in the event of a loss. The four preconfigured service packages
include these in what the company considers most desired combinations. And the price of each is clearly mentioned. How is this different
from the traditional practice. Explains Ric Gregson:

> **Traditionally what the dealers would do is to give you a single final
> figure that incorporates the basic financing payment. Let us say,
> you agreed to a 9-percent financing rate, so you will be given, say,**

a $600 monthly payment, and that payment included all the services and options, and you didn't know why the payment was so high. Then the negotiation process began, where the salesperson would delete a service here and a service there to come to a lower figure and you still didn't know how much your basic payment would have been.

In the menu we saw, there is a box right at the top left corner. It shows the base payment, which is exactly what you were told and what you agreed to when, a few minutes ago, the credit finance was discussed. And then in four columns, there are four different payment amounts depending upon which of the four preconfigured packages you desire. In one such demo sheet we reviewed, the base amount was $425 a month for 54 months. You can buy one of the four protection packages for a combined monthly payment of $460 a month, which includes the base payment of $425; or you can keep the payment constant at $425 (yes at the same amount as was the basic payment) provided you can accept a 60 month payment period instead of the 54 months, and still get all the protection. There was on this form one other slightly reduced protection option that would cost $445 a month for 54 months but in fact cost only $410 a month (less than the basic payment of $425 on a 54 month option) for a 60 month period. Don't like any of the prepackaged options? The next page has a column for a totally customized protection plan, including the two insurance options (appearance protection and credit insurance) that were not included in the preconfigured four packages.

Indeed, a menu of options! And a menu approach that is a far cry from the black-box approach of many other dealers (including perhaps some of the AutoNation dealers in their pre-AutoNation life). An open, honest, and transparent transaction indeed. Thank you, AutoNation!

"Thank you, AutoNation"? Says who? Customers. Here is one:

My wife and I both were very impressed with the honesty, thoroughness, and thoughtfulness of everyone there at Courtesy. . . . My wife and I both remarked that this is the first time we have had a 100% enjoyable experience buying a car. Even all of the paperwork seemed enjoyable.

THE SHORT AND SWEET OF IT—A super car, at super price, at a super financing rate and sold to you by super people—what more could a person ask for.

—A customer of AutoNation

Fair Price

"Our price (for financing and protection products) is fair because we look at our competitors' prices including third party insurance companies that provide protection," says Kevin Westfall, president, AutoNation Financial Services, the company's financing unit:

We consider competitors' prices and also our own costs of doing business. If we find that competitors' price is say $800, and if we feel that $800 is too much, unjustified by the benefits, and we can make a fair profit at, say, $300 then we are going to charge $300. Because then, the customer would be happy. And for $800 we can sell them many more services, and with those services the customer would be better protected and they would be more satisfied with their decisions, and that pays off in our long-term relationship. So we want to sell more—more services, and more cars to a customer over the long haul rather than charge more in any single transaction.

So mindful of the price value is the home office that they monitor individual dealer's prices on the protection services, and if they find some dealers selling at more than a fair price, they call them up and get them to refund the excess charge to the customer. "It doesn't happen often, but it has happened on a few occasions, and we have forced the dealer to refund money to the customer," says Westfall.

Value Price and Lean Operations

Such price value as the company is able to offer would not be possible if the company did not pursue *lean operations*. It pursues lean operations in selling, in service centers, and in financing. As to the selling process, the company believes that the no-hassle, open and honest and relationship approach is less time-consuming for the salesperson and more productive in closing the sale. Indeed, for AutoNation, better in-store customer experience is not a mushy, touchy-feely goal. Rather the senior executives believe that its results are quantifiable—"They translate into increased repurchase intention, in sales growth, and in margin expansion," says Maroone.

Advanced Production Structure

To repair the vehicle right the first time and at the same time to keep costs under control, service departments at AutoNation-owned dealerships have adopted what they call Advanced Production Structure (APS). To understand APS, first consider how the operations were organized under the old method. When you brought in a car, a service writer would write up the order, and then one of the dispatchers would assign the job to one of the foremen who would then assign a technician to it. And the technician would earn the hours he or she directly worked on, so when there was a specific job like air-conditioning or transmission, the technicians skilled in these tasks would vie with each other to get the job. And if there are five different problems to be resolved, the car will move from the parking area to the repair bay five times—and it is a different repair bay every time; every time the foreman would have to assign the next task to a technician. One can imagine how inefficient this process must have been. And if the customer called in the meantime, the service writer would have no idea as to the whereabouts and status of the car!

Under the new APS method, service writers are now called assistant service managers and each of them is directly assigned a team of technicians led by one of their peers. The technicians are cross-trained and are more versatile, and the team leader also works on the car (in the old system, the dispatcher was merely a paper pusher). And, for most service jobs, the car stays in a single bay throughout even as different technicians work on the car. And of course, the service writer is in a position to tell the customer anytime where the car is and what the car status is. This is lean production par excellence. And though the cost savings are necessarily inside information, the method clearly renders the repair service work more efficient as well as more effective due to better control.

What about protection services—where dealers handle work under extended warranties? Yes, even there, the dealers are expected to run lean operations. The protection programs are the company's own; that is, the company is the underwriter for these protection services. The home office monitors repair costs per car under protection, and ensures that dealers don't "over-repair" a car and claim high repair reimbursements from the corporate office. If a dealer is doing too many genuine repairs then maybe they did not prep the car properly to begin with, so they are held accountable for meeting the cost norms, and for charging a fair price and still return target profits.

And the new menu approach in financing? Is that an example of lean operations? According to Ric Gregson, "It speeds up the process; it involves fewer dealership employees for a single transaction; it is more customer-friendly. And we close more deals." The dealership has 28 salespersons and 5 financing people whom Gregson supervises, and they close on 350 cars a month. "We couldn't have done it under the old approach," confirms Gregson. A true win-win proposition, indeed.

E-Commerce as Lean Operations

E-commerce itself is both a better performance value to customers as well as a lean operations method of selling. That is, the cost of doing business on the Web is lower than handling the in-store walk-in traffic. But what gives AutoNation further cost advantage (that is, lean production) is its sophisticated data management capability. Recall the message bank that the dealer salespersons can draw upon; and the history and details on the leads that they can pull in. Besides, the corporate office monitors and analyzes the database for continuous performance improvement. It knows, for example, the closing ratios for leads coming from different referral services, so it can negotiate cost-effective deals with them. And it monitors each car dealership's performance record in terms of closing rates, profit margins, and even transaction history. Dealer e-salespersons who experience lower success receive training help. And more and more of its leads now come from its own sites (up from 20 percent in 1999 to 52 percent in 2000), cutting down on referral service fees.

PPG: Price Value through Tight Process Controls

For PPG's fine chemicals business unit, cost control processes and quality processes move in lockstep. Because the production process determines certain specs and quality levels, it becomes necessary to clearly specify and tightly control the process. A tightly controlled and well-specified process has cost and time metrics; and the process must adhere to the technical specifications. Such adherence achieves both the product quality and efficiency in terms of the time and cost metrics.

Explains PPG's Feuntes, "We come from a company that prides itself on GMP [Good Manufacturing Practice], and on being very cost conscious. In the future, cost containment will be very important for the pharmaceutical industry. We are not taking it for granted that technical superiority or government regulation would protect us from the necessity to be very cost-effective." In addition to tight process control, PPG attempts cost reduction through better catalyst systems; through better ways of purifying the material more systematically; and through extracting a better price support from its suppliers.

For PPG, target-costing takes yet another form; instead of limiting itself to target costing its product per se, it works on technical improvements in the product so as to reduce the cost of the product's application at the customer's plant. Take its silica division. When it proposed to its tire manufacturing customers (who use silica in making the tire) to produce "green" tires—the tires are designed to have lower roll resistance and consequently be more energy efficient—one barrier to its adoption by tire makers was the higher process cost of using green silica. Working with the Goodyear Tire Company, PPG's silica division worked to make Goodyear's process more efficient. Goodyear adopted it when modification in the silica brought the applications process within cost targets.

American Express Establishment Services: Being Prepared to Meet the Price Pressure

For American Express, the market pressure to reduce its discount rate is constant. While it does not want to compete on the basis of low price, and in fact it strives to deliver better performance and personalization value to justify its premium price, American Express recognizes the need to be prepared to meet the constant price pressure in its markets. To achieve this preparedness, American Express is pursuing a rigorous program of achieving world class economies. Back in 1992, the company set a cost reduction goal of $1 billion, and achieved that goal in three years. To date, since then, the company has cut another $1 billion through process reengineering, waste reduction, and automation. The

ES Division itself was able to cut its transaction processing costs by 50 percent, realizing savings of more than $200 million within the last few years. A big source of these cost savings was the drive to get more and more merchants to adopt electronic processing for its transactions. This not only saved money for American Express, but it also resulted in a lower discount rate for these merchants.

At American Express, cost cutting does not come at the expense of performance or service value. Every reengineered process that will reduce costs is first tested on a small group of merchant customers; the process is adopted only if it is proven to have no adverse effect on customer satisfaction, at the least, and increase value to customer whenever possible.

Xerox Business Services: Focus on Value Pricing

Like other companies in our sample, XBS delivers price value to its clients through both target costing and lean operations. Like Rosenbluth, XBS also custom-configures its site operations to meet the needs of specific clients. Incorporated into these configurations are customers' cost parameters, that is, target costs. For XBS, customization is not a choice but a requirement of site configuration. However, such customization does not cost XBS much. In part, this is because of its long history of experience at putting together customer-specific document site solutions.

However, target cost for XBS does not mean the lowest price, as it does not compete on that basis. Typically, in fact, its price would be somewhat higher than competitors. But it seeks to offer good value for what it charges. At the same time, it knows that its price premium cannot but be small, and that in order to offer the appropriate price value, it must keep a lid on costs. The Xerox Corporation as a whole has targeted cost reductions of $1 billion in nonproduction spending over a period of several years. XBS shoulders its share of responsibility. One of its major cost items is employees, and the nature of its business (that is, fluctuating activity levels at customer sites, or short term contracts) necessitates hiring temporary employees. To reduce its cost of temporary personnel, it has worked diligently with its temp supplier firm to streamline temp costs.

Another means of cost reduction is automation and XBS uses it wherever it can. Its salesforce was recently armed with automation tools; one of them, called X-Sellerator, has market or industry information that a salesperson can access, a pricing tool for pricing a proposed service, and a customized proposal writer. For its sales managers, it has a territory assignment program. In addition to reducing the cost of selling via its direct salesforce, Xerox and XBS are also exploring other channels such as telemarketing and the Internet.

What also helps is its perspective on price value. Its core strategy for business growth is to grow the *same-client-revenue;* this requires expanding the scope of its services within a given client's operations. It offers value price by offering a more effective document solution at a lower total cost (lower than the current in-house implementation) in a new domain (expanding from the printing shop to, say, invoicing, or bill payment, or customer service, etc.). The client gets a cost saving, and XBS gets increased revenue. Thus, it works on a win-win principle. "At the end of the day," says McDermott, "our focus is not on reducing the costs to clients; our focus is on adding value in terms of what we do for their document management."

Hilton Hotels: Eyes on Value Price

The senior management at Hilton Hotels has a special perspective on price value. Before we visit that perspective, let us first recount the usual price value avenues Hilton does follow. For starters, it maintains its rates to be competitive in its class, and it offers a slate of special rates for various traveler segments—business travelers, AARP members, military or government employees, leisure travelers, for example. One of its popular promotional rates is called Value Rate, which can be up to 50 percent off its regular rate, depending on occupancy at a particular hotel.

In part, its price value offerings are fueled by one of its key performance measures, REVPAR (revenue per available room). Written into every managerial evaluation, for every owned property or franchise, REVPAR is incentive enough for every property general manager to put every available room for sale. Consequently, Hilton participates in inventory clearance on the Web, offering rooms at substantial discounts for the immediate forthcoming weekend.

Besides, the chain often runs special promotions. For example, late last year, it was offering four- to seven-day packages at its Hawaiian resorts. This package was especially attractive because the Hilton Hawaiian Village located on the Waikiki beachfront is the official resort hotel for the cast and crew of the popular syndicated television show *Baywatch*. Hilton Hawaiian Village itself will be featured in 7 out of the 22 shows, to be broadcast internationally. The *Baywatch* Hawaii package was priced at $800 to $1200 per room, and included roundtrip airfare, five-nights accommodation at Hilton Hawaiian Village, roundtrip transfers to Waikiki, and a special gift set including *Baywatch* beach towels, caps, and so on. Promotional programs like these constitute a considerable price value to leisure travelers, and they also enhance performance value, especially for those who consider themselves fans of *Baywatch*.

Now to the special perspective its senior management holds on price value. Customers define value as the ratio of what they get over what they pay. If the numerator is increased, customer satisfaction increases, leading to higher price value for the customer. This perspective was best articulated by Dennis Koci, Hilton's senior vice president of operations. We asked him, "How does Hilton work at cost reduction in its operations so that it may offer better price value to customers?" "Our goal is not to focus as much on costs," Koci begins in a passionate voice, almost questioning the wisdom in our question. "Competing on price tends to commoditize the product; we prefer to offer the experience and on the value of the benefits. Our stance is, 'find out the individual wants and preferences, and then deliver individualized products and services to meet those needs.'" We probe, inquiring about a recent cost-saving measure adopted by many hotels (but not at Hilton)—these hotels ask their guests whether they would like their linen to be changed every day or prefer to reuse it as an environment-friendly action. "For Hilton," says Koci, "cost savings would be a wrong reason to adopt that practice. Hilton would not do it if it detracts from customer value; conversely, Hilton would do it if it is of value to its guests." This singular focus on customer value rather than cost savings is noteworthy in a milieu where lesser corporations would often go on a short-sighted cost-cutting spree.

Price ValueSpace: A Double-Win Strategy

The amazing thing about the world's Most Admired companies is that at the same time that they are creating a first-rate performance Value-Space in their markets, they are also inventing unbeatable price value for their customers. Rosenbluth International assures "never a wrong ticket" and also has the search engine to find the lowest ticket price. 3M creates new performance value in new customer applications but also "gain-shares" in the resulting cost economies. SYSCO offers food products that exceed USDA standards, and at the same time it offers documented value price when compared by final usable yield. AutoNation offers a no-hassle price that customers find fair, at the same time that it is crafting a wholesome car-buying experience for the customer.

These and other market leaders are able to accomplish this *double-win*, because they find a formula that works for them. They implement practices or technologies that simultaneously produce better performance and reduced costs (as in E-Res, an automated customized reservation software by Rosenbluth). Or they sweat the details to reduce costs (via target costing, lean operations, low cost sites). Either way, they build price ValueSpace without nibbling on the performance ValueSpace. This simultaneous accomplishment in two ValueSpace components, this double-win, we think, is a key secret to winning the battle for market leadership.

Personalization ValueSpace

Gary Moss is a Marketing Associate at SYSCO Food Services of Jacksonville, Florida. One of his customers works a full-time job during the day and runs a restaurant at night. The customer is pleased with SYSCO products, but there is only one snag: the restaurant does not open until 6 p.m. whereas the latest the SYSCO truck can make delivery in that area is 3 p.m. What should Gary do? What did Gary do? He volunteered to come and wait at the restaurant every Thursday at 3 p.m. to accept the delivery. The customer gave him a key and the checkbook—and every single bit of her business!

Customers seek performance value, and they seek price value. But they want more. They want their suppliers to be easy to do business with. Suppliers should be easy to access; they should show responsiveness to all customer concerns and problems that may arise in product acquisition and use; and it would help if the company employees were pleasant and nice in dealing with the customer; if the customer felt welcomed, respected, and cared for. This is what personalization ValueSpace is all about. Let us see how our sampled companies fare in this ValueSpace. If the tales of their accomplishments in performance and price ValueSpace amazed us, wait till we see their play in the personalization ValueSpace.

Personalization is our label, mind you, not theirs. They call it customer service, which we consider to be a catchall word. In personalization, we include a few things they call customer service and then a few more that companies variously call relationship building, value-adds, personal touch, partnership, and so on. The true character of personalization is that whether it is in accessing the company, or in getting a problem resolved, or in day-to-day interactions, customers feel personally cared for.

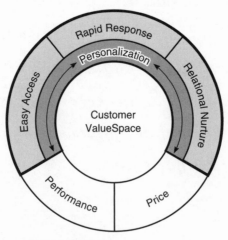

Figure 6.1 Personalization ValueSpace

SYSCO: Building Personalization ValueSpace
One Customer at a Time

If you visit SYSCO offices, at its headquarters in Houston or at any of its 101 operating companies, everywhere you will see signs and posters with five letters inscribed on them: C.A.R.E.S. As we mentioned before, C.A.R.E.S. is an acronym for "Customers Are Really Everything to SYSCO." At SYSCO it is more than a slogan. It is being put in practice, every day, by every employee and by every manager. By marketing associates like Gary Moss who doubles up as the receiving agent for one of his customers, gratis. And by district sales managers like Andrew Sterner who took over as chef for a customer and cooked a 13-course meal identical to the one served on the *Titanic* (see the third opening vignette in Chapter 1). To call these individual acts "service" (as SYSCO and most companies do) is not doing them full justice. They are the kind of stuff that personalization ValueSpace is made of. And SYSCO builds it "one customer at a time." And it builds it through all three of its components in our framework: easy access, rapid response, and relational nurture.

Easy Access

In terms of access, what SYSCO customers look for is an easy way to place an order. The order placement procedure is different for two classes of customers—national or program customers (these are multi-unit operations who sign contracts with the corporate headquarters) and street or retail customers that each operating company recruits. But both categories have easy access for order placement. To place the order, program or national customers call customer service (CS) in the local operating unit. In the Cincinnati unit, there are seven customer service reps (CSR), and each is assigned specific national accounts, and each national account is given a 1-800 number that rings on that CSR's desk. And the CSRs recognize most customers by name. They are able to pull up the caller's account on their computer instantly and are able to take a new order, read status on an existing order, and make any changes the customer requests, all within minutes. "There is no voice-mail or automated phone menu here; we don't feel it is necessary and we don't feel it gives the personalized service we want to give our customers," says Flo Halterman, manager of customer service. And each call is picked up by the CSR within three rings, and there is a 100 percent compliance of this standard!

Street customers place orders with their marketing associate (MA) during the MA's visit to the account, or later, by calling the MA, leaving a voicemail message, or paging the MA for a callback. Occasionally, customers will call their CSR who will then relay the order by phone (or pager) to the MA. For street customers, only MAs are authorized to place orders—the company considers it important for MAs to be intimately involved with their customers.

Rapid Response

For SYSCO customers, rapid response really becomes valuable when they place a last-minute order. What happens is that customers don't always place all the order they need to. They discover at the last minute that they forgot to order something. That is when SYSCO's rapid response machine swings into action. It will handle the request in one of three ways: (1) Each operating unit maintains some vans for special delivery, so one of these vans will deliver the order within a 90-minute window (a time standard always followed); or (2) the customer may offer to pick up the order. They are given a time (usually about an hour after they call). They will pull up at the "Will Call" area, and their order will be ready. (CSR keys in the order and sends it to the warehouse from where the merchandise is sent to the "Will Call" area.); or (3) the MAs will be informed and sometimes they may decide to carry the order themselves in their car. They often do, just to see the customer one more time!

Sometimes, a customer will call to inquire why the delivery has not been made by the scheduled time. Let's say it is 11 a.m. and the delivery should have been made by 10 a.m. In such cases, the CSM will page the driver, inquire the status, and report it back to the customer immediately. If necessary, with the consent of other customers next on the route, the routing will be modified in minutes. In any case, the CSM will apologize and see that the delivery is made ASAP. Later that afternoon, the CSR will call that customer to follow up.

The company's responsiveness really gets tested when customers make special requests in desperation. "There was this restaurant client," says Sideras, executive chef in the Cincinnati operating unit, "who called me around Christmastime last year; he had put a particular chicken item on his menu which we had discontinued. So I went to our merchandiser and got him to order 10 cases just for this customer; then in January, when it came time to change the menu, we offered the customer new items that we stocked."

The greater and more serious the emergency, the more demanding the need, and SYSCO rises to the occasion, every time. Here is one example: A customer in Cedar City, Utah, had his fryer break down on a Saturday. In panic, he called Jerry Clayton, a SYSCO equipment merchandiser. Jerry called a local supplier in Salt Lake City, found a fryer, went to pick it up personally, and delivered it to Cedar City in time for the weekend business.

Such is the rapid response SYSCO delivers!

Relational Nurture

Bobby Wallace is a delivery associate in the Dallas unit of SYSCO. One of his customers is a church. On one of his delivery visits to this customer, Bobby noticed that the church's freezer was not working. He notified the church's kitchen manager, and insisted on taking the food down back to his truck, four difficult flights of stairs away. Then he redelivered the product later in the day when the freezer got repaired.

Now, why would a delivery driver go through such trouble? Because the importance of building a relationship with the customer is honed into every employee. The foundation for SYSCO's relationship with customers comes from the very way it looks at its customers and at its own role for them. It views its role as one of helping the customer manage his or her restaurant business better. And customers seek this relationship because the marketing associates who visit them have experience in their business, and they have great product knowledge. Says Phil Trewhitt, Cincinnati unit's senior vice president:

> **Sometimes our MAs are loved by our customers, because even though we sell to them at higher prices, we help them reduce waste, we help them save on their food costs, we teach them better ways of running the restaurants. Lots of our MAs have restau-**

rant experience and some of our very best have gone to culinary arts schools.

To help its restaurant customers improve and grow their business, SYSCO marketing associates are being trained to act as *consultants*, able to advise customers on menu design and presentation. SYSCO believes that by serving new and high quality *branded* entree products (what SYSCO calls *center of the plate* items), restaurants can brand their individual establishments. President Rick Schnieders explains: "Last time I was in Minneapolis, I went to a restaurant, I was served Minnesota Red Deer, presented with a 'little bit of romance'; next time I am in Minneapolis, I would look for that restaurant. So, restaurants should serve branded products that can be unique to them and of unique quality, such as SYSCO brands." This advice is self-serving, admits Schnieders, but he is very proud and very confident of the quality of SYSCO brands and of the market edge that quality in turn gives its customers. "To our foodservice customers, we are constantly promoting the idea that they have to aim at increasing the 'share of stomach' of their patrons. And this they can do by expanding their menu, and by serving consistent quality SYSCO brands," says Thomas E. Lanford, executive vice president, merchandising and multiunit sales at SYSCO Corporate.

Chef Sideras recalls an incident: "I got a call one day from one of our marketing associates that one of his customers was losing $10 to 15k per month. This was a guy new to restaurant business. So I went down with the MA, looked at his inventory, his menu, even his books. We put together a business plan for him, wrote him a new menu. This was a year ago, and now he is making money."

"There is this one particular account I visit every month," continues Sideras. "I set up a meeting, bring three new products-recipes, every time. I know him very well, and I know what he is buying so I bring him recipes built around the ingredients he is already buying or I bring a new item that will complement his other items. I prepare those dishes for him, teaching him everything, and I show him how much the food will cost and how much he should price it."

"Some of our major customers, we bring them here to our facility," says Joe Calabrese, president of the Cincinnati unit. "We do a slide show. Various executives will talk about their functions within the company. We would tell them a little bit about our operations, about our computer system, about our warehouse, transportation, and delivery system, about our SYSCO brands, about our quality standards, and about our MAs and delivery associates, about our safety procedures and about our value-added services. Our chef will present some key products such as meat and produce items. He will do a menu analysis, show the customer the economics of using our products." Does this sound like your typical selling? Hardly. Rather it is an in-depth self-disclosure, a no-holds-barred tour of company operations; it is the foundation for an open and enduring relationship. "Our goal is clear," says Calabrese. "We are focused on SYSCO's mission statement: 'To help our customers be more successful.' "

One plank in SYSCO's relational nurture of its customers is its program of Executive Rides. Each of the senior executives of an operating unit rides with an MA for a day (occasionally with a delivery associate—the driver) to visit customers. In the Cincinnati unit, for example, they have 15 districts, and each has an average of seven MAs, so each of its six senior executives rides with at least one MA every three to four weeks throughout the year. Calabrese describes these visits thus:

> **I would go in, and talk to the chef or kitchen manager or the restaurant manager, whoever is available—sometimes the customer would know I am coming, so they may plan on meeting me. I talk to them about how is our service to them, are they happy with our products, our delivery, our drivers, and our marketing associates; I will talk to them about the products they are buying and other related products they could buy (I will have reviewed the account prior to the visit); sometimes we will do lunch together so we can get to know each other more. They have to feel they can approach us, the senior executives any time. Know that our relationship goes beyond mere selling.**

Beyond it must surely go, because we went for lunch to Embassy Suite in Cincinnati, a recently acquired SYSCO customer, and Calabrese walked in through the kitchen, not the front door. "Do you mind going through the kitchen? . . . That way I can say hello to whoever is there," he tells me. For some reason, neither the chef nor any of the managers was there; just the shift supervisor and the waitstaff. So we were seated, and the waiter brought us beverages and took our order. A few minutes later, with an order for a neighboring table in hand, he stopped by our table, and pointing to a dish on his plate, he says, "Hey Joe, this fish here. . . ." How many other companies do you know of where a customer's nonexecutive staff can address the supplier company's president by name?

American Express and Personalization ValueSpace

As we said before, *personalization* is our label. American Express, like most companies, calls it *customer service*. American Express's customer service is one of the best in corporate America. "Among its customers, the company has a reputation for bending over," says Chuck Aubrey, vice president of quality and strategy. "Bending over backwards" means, of course, that it accommodates customer requests. So how well does it manage the three components of personalization ValueSpace? Very well.

Easy Access

Merchants can reach American Express customer service centers 24 hours a day. The routing switchboard makes sure all calls are promptly answered—in 1999 the company's customer service centers received more than 1.9 million calls. More than 82 percent of these were answered in 20 seconds or less; only less than 1 percent of callers were abandoned. Once answered, the well-trained, very personable, and highly motivated customer service representatives seek to resolve problems promptly. Customers can also reach American Express online, of course. But a human voice is available 24 hours, 7 days a week!

Rapid Response

But rather than merely being accessible when customers call, a real value to merchants would be a system that eliminated the need to call in the first place. The ES Division has gone the distance to make this a reality. First, its electronic charge card authorization system works with high reliability. But even more important is its innovative automation of merchant-specific financial data. Instead of merchants sending paper documentation or receiving financial information (such as daily or monthly summaries and deposit information) by mail, the company sends it electronically on its SE Workstations (front-end terminals that merchants use to read customer cards) or on the Internet.

One constant burden all merchants have to bear for accepting any credit cards is having to deal with disputes (the charges cardholders have disputed with the card company). Instead of receiving the dispute notice by mail and having to send a copy of a customer-signed receipt by mail, the entire dispute correspondence is now done electronically on the SE workstation or online. The built-in software even prioritizes disputes so that a merchant can, for example, list them by days left to respond to an inquiry, by charge amount, or by kind (for example, merchants can isolate and eliminate "no reply" chargebacks, where the merchant accepts the error). Needless to mention that this automation of financial information and disputes saves the merchant precious time and makes bookkeeping less of a grind.

Relational Nurture

The division has reengineered its customer service process so that now there is a single point of contact for a merchant. When merchants call, their service needs are met by the customer service associate who receives the call. To achieve this, the company has trained and empowered its frontline employees and has made sure they have all the technology and all the information they need to solve that customer's problems.

So much does the company value a relationship with customers that a customer can rest assured that if he or she calls a senior executive of the company, his or her call will always be taken and/or returned, often the same day. Says Dave House, "I always return phone calls from customers, no matter how small or big. I personally visit our customers. And I am in contact with customers on a regular basis."

PPG: Treating Customers Well

We saw how PPG offers performance and price value to its customers. PPG is also very conscious of the importance of making it easy for the customer to do business with it.

Easy Access

PPG facilitates customer access by establishing lines of communication between customers and each of the various PPG functional areas and departments involved in the transaction—the lab, manufacturing, quality assurance, and marketing, for example. And these links are established early, while customers are still evaluating PPG and its offerings for their needs. PPG deploys a crossfunctional team coordinated by a commercial development manager, who handles account development during the qualifying process. Thus, a customer's R&D person can call up PPG's R&D directly if he or she has a question. And the customer's manufacturing department can directly call PPG's customer service to discuss a shipment.

Rapid Response

However, these open lines of communication would be only half as useful if the people the customer communicates with were not empowered to fulfill the customer's request. At PPG, all customer service employees are indeed authorized to do what's needed for their strategic and key customers. For example, illustrates Jim Faller, fine chemical unit's commercial development manager, "One of our strategic customers can call one of our plants directly on a Saturday night for an emergency shipment, and the plant will ship it as soon as it is technically possible. Sales and accounting will be notified on Monday but the plant won't hold the shipment for approval from sales." This is rapid response, par excellence!

In fact, the company prides itself on being responsive and deems it as its differentiating feature. For example, initially in an RFP situation (where it answers a "Request for Proposal" from a prospective buyer), when the customer is trying to qualify its process, it is very quick with product samples, process data, and in helping the customer move quickly toward commercialization of its own new product in its end-product markets. This level of responsiveness is epitomized in a slogan PPG uses in its advertising: "We make it difficult for you to know where your business stops and ours begins"!

To drive its customer response level higher, it measures what it calls "customer action incident reports" (CAIRs). Every time a customer problem gets recorded, it gets into a system that analyzes the problems by categories; how and when the problem was resolved is also recorded. Management reviews the CAIR summaries regularly.

Another point of excellence is its service response. The company can customize delivery time. It can even customize on package size. For example, a customer might want three 400-lb drums of a chemical that PPG normally ships in 441-lb drums (so that the customer will not have to split a drum for a process that requires 1200 pounds of the chemical). "Can you do that?" the customer asks. "We sure will," says Faller.

Relational Nurture

PPG's interface with its customers always takes the form of a partnership in which both parties explore new avenues of value. Let us hear Fuentes, fine chemical's general manager, explain it:

> **We have done supply chain meetings to identify cost-reduction strategies. In these meetings, we ask questions like, why is a certain purity level needed; why are you specifying a certain drum; can you plan longer; can we reduce freight. In this case, we identified ways of reducing freight. We now have a dedicated driver; we charge them the cost of the driver but it is a lot cheaper than using a commercial freight company. This customer buys from us $8–9 million worth of product and we saved him $50,000 in freight, which is important to him. The result [of such meetings] is that the customer gets committed to us and sees no reason to look for someone else.**

And Von Lehman, specialty chemical's vice president, is pleased with what that relational nurture does for PPG:

> **Our customer relationship management and service levels are so good that they make a mark on the customer. A major customer**

of ours was dealing with three suppliers. He wanted to reduce to two suppliers. After closely studying us and the other two suppliers, he saw no need even for two of us—he decided to make us the *sole* supplier. He figured, for the future, we were the horse to ride!

3M: Pushing ETDBW Higher

Making it easy for the customer to do business with has been a longstanding obsession with 3M. A few years ago, all 3M executives and salespersons wore a lapel pin with the insignia "ETDBW" ("Easy To Do Business With"). Now, ETDBW is being pushed even higher.

Easy Access

First consider "access" as a component of personalization value or ETDBW. Easier access takes on a different meaning at 3M. Its industrial end-user customers are increasingly demanding that they be able to buy via a range of channels, and 3M is making those channels available. 3M's intermediaries now include big category-killer distributors, catalogers, specialty houses, and integrators (such as Granger) who manage the total materials management for end-user customers.

For its distributor customers, likewise, it is offering more efficient ways of doing business. Fully 60 percent of its product volume is now sold to distributors who are EDI (Electronic Data Interchange) capable. EDI makes it very convenient for distributor customers to maintain their inventory, and in addition, it reduces the monetary cost of ordering, thus adding to the price value as well.

What about the 3M salesforce? How easy are they to do business with? Can they respond promptly to customer problems, for example? Do they have the skills? Are they well equipped with resources? Do they have the right attitude? To address these issues, 3M is doing two things: reorganizing and training.

Not so long ago, customers (both end users and distributors) had been confused and burdened with visits from a multitude of 3M salespersons from its various autonomous divisions. So now 3M is consolidating some of the sales calls. For a group of divisions and their salespersons, 3M is designating a leader who will coordinate the activities of various salespersons calling on the same client and will act as a single point of contact for the client. A single point-of-contact greatly simplifies access.

Rapid Response

In technical sales, responsiveness really depends on salesforce competence. 3M is investing in sales competence and training. Salespersons are paid 80 percent salary and 20 percent performance bonus—and performance is measured on a team basis. Most of the 3M salespersons are 3M veterans, with a lot of training behind them. To advance their competence level even further, 3M is launching a more systematic skills assessment program. Here is how Rich Mills, 3M's sales and marketing director for the bonding systems division, explains it:

> We have just developed a competency model and we have pilot-tested it in our division. The system is graded as S1, S2, S3, S4—S stands for Sales—the first level of sales competency, the second level, and so on. It is job-based, basically; they can move from one to the other and get paid more. It outlines some skill sets, and in the future we will be augmenting it with some courses they can take. We will have training on the Internet which they can self-study and self-test.

Beyond technical competence, salespersons also need control over 3M resources so as to be responsive. In this respect, they are fully empowered to access whatever resources they need in order to demonstrate the value of its products. They can bring in specialists, an area manager, even the company president (going through proper channels, of course). Another sense in which the salesforce is empowered is to give them a voice. Explains Rich Mills:

> We have sales councils to gather the collective voice of the salesforce. These councils meet regularly and discuss issues of import to the salesforce, discuss three or four things of priority to them, and then we ask them (the salesforce) to come up with recom-

mendations. We have done it for the last three years. Generally speaking, we have embraced those recommendations.

Relational Nurture through Information Technology

3M is also exploiting the digital technology for easy access, rapid response, and customer relationship management. Indeed, its Web presence, when completed, will be a showcase of customer-centric e-commerce sites. Alan P. Norton heads the IT services division at 3M; he views the #1 goal of 3M's Web presence as to make it easy for the customer to do business with 3M. Indeed, the ETDBW theme guides all of 3M's IT endeavors. Consider its still-evolving Web site, the company's electronic gateway to its customer network (end users and distributors). Because 3M divisions function autonomously, they have developed their marketing and communication programs independently and as "stand alone," and this includes not just the salesforce and distributor management, but also product information in catalogs and on Web sites. This means a customer looking for industrial coatings should know, for example, which division sells industrial tapes. Why should a customer have to know that? That is a question no one at 3M asked before; but now that question is receiving concerted attention. In response, Norton is creating integrated Web sites, organized by customer groups, or what he refers to as "Communities of Interests."

This configuration will be two steps ahead of the curve. The simpler and obvious solution would have been to replace the division-based organization of information by product-based organization. The new Web site will be able to search information by products of course, but what is remarkable is that a customer would be able to start his or her Web access from his or her vantage point, based on his or her community of interest. If you are a carpenter, for example, you would access a site called "woodworking," and on that site you will find ALL of the products 3M offers with applications in woodworking! "We are creating, in effect," says Norton, "virtual organizations built around the customer." 3M calls them—the new Web sites—*Customer Centers.* For now, ten such customer centers are planned—for example, architecture, office, automotive and marine, graphic arts, manufacturing, health care, and so on.

An important part of 3M's Web access to end-user customers is the integration of its channel members into the net. When customers access the 3M site, they have the facility to choose a distributor of choice in their area. This is important because 3M typically does not sell to end users directly, and it would hardly be of help to the end user to find the product application on the Web and then not know where to order it from. Now end-user customers can find the application information and order the merchandise at the same time from a distributor of their choice.

Relational Nurture as Social Bonding

Personalization is also strong at the industrial minerals division, the division that makes roofing granules. Customers can call its national account manager anytime, on a 24/7 basis. If they need the product in a rush, they can even call the plant directly and the plant is authorized to fulfill their need. The national account manager and other service reps even develop a relationship with the customers they deal with. At least once every six months, they will visit their customers along with the area sales manager and the plant manager. The division encourages discipline-to-discipline communication—that is, the customer's plant manager can talk to 3M's plant manager, logistics can talk to 3M Logistics, and so on.

What 3M's roofing granules division does particularly well is build a relationship with customers—one-on-one, person-to-person. The relationship develops through sharing ideas, business plans, joint applications research, and even some social time. The high point of the latter, for example, is an annual retreat of its major customers (usually about six to eight) at 3M's Wonewok Conference Center. The invitees are all CEOs or presidents of their organizations, who bring their spouses. From 3M, the division's senior management including the division vice president, technical director, manufacturing director, and marketing director, and all national account managers are in attendance; every one of the hosts is invited to bring his or her spouse, too. "It is a three-day event," explains Robert Morrow, the division's marketing director. "We kick it off with a dinner in St. Paul and then we all fly to Wonewok.

"Once there, we begin the meeting with a presentation of the economic forecasts. Over the next two days, we discuss a range of business issues of mutual interest." Because many of the customers are direct competitors of one another, the company even has a 3M attorney at hand, just to make sure no discussions take place that would violate any antitrust laws. Interspersed with these business discussions are social activities—fishing, hunting, golfing, and other sporting events. Some of the guests are the same group of customers every year—consequently, participants develop a good relationship with their hosts. "We get very close to our customers," says Morrow. "We have fun, we have games. And, they look forward to it, every year. Specially the wives!" According to Morrow, the division is a benchmark for the entire company for developing strong relationships with customers.

Rosenbluth International: A Maestro in Personalization ValueSpace

Rosenbluth International takes great pride in its customer service, and the quality of its customer service positions it as a leader in personalization ValueSpace. It has the technology and the infrastructure that enables customers to access the company easily; it has procedures and systems in place to be very responsive to customers' transaction needs; and its employees have the legendary reputation for extraordinary relational nurture. Let us look at each.

Easy Access

Certainly, Rosenbluth offers its customers easy access. Many of its travel operations are located on client premises and work seamlessly with client organizations. Its reservation and customer service centers are accessible 24 hours a day, 7 days a week, and state-of-the art equipment routes the calls to the next available representative anywhere in the world! Customers have also been given the ability to make a travel reservation themselves, using its E-Res® system on their PCs. A more recently launched system also allows customers to access the company online and complete travel reservations with a few simple mouse clicks.

Anywhere you live in Europe, no matter which country, you can reach Rosenbluth International by dialing a local number, and your call will automatically be connected to the recently installed Intellicenter in Killarney, Ireland. And don't worry about whether you will be able to follow the Irish accent of the service associate—the associate who answers your call will speak in your native language, because the automated call routing system automatically routes your call to an associate who speaks your language and knows travel in your country. Such is the access value Rosenbluth International provides its customers.

Rapid Response

When quality gaps come to light (for example, an expression of discontent from a specific customer), the corporate quality team (formally called Center for Organization Effectiveness) swings into action. For example, recently, the center got a call from a business unit in Vienna from a client who was not happy with turnaround times. So the quality team quickly flowcharted the process, and made the requisite modifications.

The company also has a very sophisticated complaint management system. Actually, what customers bring to the company are not as much complaints as inquiries—inquiries about a past bill, for example. A typical inquiry may relate to a discrepancy between the rate quoted for, say, a hotel, and the price actually charged by the hotel. Since most such queries require a communication with independent suppliers (for example, airlines, hotels, etc.), the company has to necessarily "shelve" the inquiry for some time as opposed to resolving the problem in one call. To manage this process well, the inquiry is researched by an associate in the company's Total Client Satisfaction Center (TCSC) located in North Dakota, where all records are kept, including paper copies of all tickets. As soon as all the information from various vendors involved in the dispute has been assembled, a customer service agent proactively calls the client to resolve the matter promptly. The associate who receives the inquiry initially tells the caller that "our Customer Service Center will get back to you within seven days." What is its record? "Eighty percent of the 'history inquiries' are handled within seven days; many within forty-eight hours," says Ken Nardone, Rosenbluth's general manager for global quality and operations measurements at the time of our study.

Relational Nurture

RI sends periodic communications to its clients. One such communiqué is e-mail alerts. The second is its quarterly newsletter, called *Directions,* which is mailed to all clients every quarter. It contains items of useful information, travel industry news, and happenings at Rosenbluth that will impact (mostly favorably) the travelers in the client companies. One recent issue of this newsletter featured, for example, a news story on the newly inaugurated Heathrow Express, the rail link that connects Heathrow Airport to Central London, cutting down the trip time from one hour to fifteen minutes, and costing about one-fourth of the taxi fare. The same issue also carried information on DACODA, the company's own patented decision support system that will recommend the most optimal solution for the client. These are the issues that corporate client travel managers find very relevant to their responsibility. "The objective of these client communications is," says Alicia Klosowski, Rosenbluth's internal/external communications manager, "to keep our customers informed, and also to educate them about our industry and about our practices. For example, if the traveler does not use certain air-lines, it can erode their company's travel policies or they might lose their special negotiated rate with an airline. In short, to educate them about how to be a wise traveler."

What distinctly serves relational nurture at Rosenbluth is that, for all employees, *being nice* is a credo. When customers call Rosenbluth, no matter which of its hundreds of associates they reach, they get a very personable, courteous, and joyful voice that handles their problem with caring and professionalism. Their goal is nothing short of bringing happiness to the caller. What Rosenbluth's customers find is that not only it is so easy to do business with this company (remember its easy access and digitized customer records accessible worldwide), but that it is indeed a *pleasure*.

Hilton Hotels: Personalization through Hilton Pride

How easy was it to check into the hotel? And out of it? You found your room spic and span, and all amenities prim and proper, but how good was the room service? When you buzzed them for an extra set of tow-els, for example, did they deliver the towels within a reasonable time, just as you expected? And did the hotel staff—from the check-in clerk to concierge to the valet—deal with you with a human touch rather than mechanically? Beyond the functionality and the aesthetics of the physical property, beyond the high-tech wired guest rooms, and beyond the state-of-the art acoustics of the meeting rooms, your "take away" from your stay at the hotel is the memory of those faces who wore the hotel uniform. Were those faces happy—happy to be doing their jobs and happy to be doing them for you? Happy, in other words, that you were there, staying at their hotel, being their guest. Hilton wants your answer to these questions to be "yes." This is the experience Hilton aims to give you—through easy access, rapid response, and relational nurture by employees who are indoctrinated in guest service by what the company calls "Hilton Pride."

Easy Access

Easy access is a given in the hotel industry. You can call them all 24 hours a day and also contact them online. What is noteworthy about Hilton is the quality of its Web site. On a single site, you can do business with all of its brands—ranging from Doubletree to Hampton Inn. It is a "Top Rated Web Site" by *USA Today*. Hilton's frequent guest program, HHonors, which provides a dedicated (800) toll-free line for reservations and other services is now also available on the Internet. Don't worry, the Web site is a breeze to navigate. After all, not for nothing does *Inside Flyer Magazine* call it the "Best Website."

Rapid Response

No matter how meticulously one monitors the service delivery system, things do go wrong every once in a while. When they do, that is when rapid response gets tested. Hilton's rapid response is reflected in its comprehensive *Recovery Process Manual*. The manual clearly (1) articulates the recovery *philosophy* (for example, that it is an "opportunity" rather than a burden), (2) specifies a process (for example, acknowledge—>listen—>apologize—>empathize—>explain action—>solicit feedback), (3) specifies organizational support and responsibility (for example, training), (4) incorporates an "unexpected personal service touch" (for example, free drink coupon, room upgrade, etc.)—a very important element in the recovery process, and (5) provides for diagnosis and learning. The document directs its *team members* to resolve problems within their level of empowerment or to seek quick resolution from their superiors when necessary.

Relational Nurture

For service companies, relational nurture happens through customer contact employees. Hilton drills its employees in what it calls "Hilton Pride"—a *can-do* attitude. To prepare employees to acquire and display the competence and attitude reflective of such pride, Hilton runs intensive training programs for them—some of the most intensive in the industry. Orientation for new employees includes a digitized video (called "I am Hilton") on a fully customizable computer program. (We described Hilton's intensive entry-level training programs in Chapter 4.)

In 1992 Hilton established a training institute at its headquarters, from where it directs its intensive and extensive training activities on-site at properties as well as at offsite locations for general managers and other senior property executives. Hilton spends more than a million dollars on training as direct costs at the HQ level; system-wide, the cost is about three times as much. Then there are also hotel-specific programs at large hotels; for example, Hilton New York has a dedicated training department for its 1800 employees.

Constantly then, team members (that is, associates, supervisors, property managers) are undergoing training and recertification, honing on their skills to do the job right the first time, practicing a can-do attitude, displaying the customer welcoming behavior day in, day out; in effect, offering its guests superior personalization value.

XBS: Personalization through Partnership

XBS runs on-site document service operations for clients. The sites operate to serve clients' document needs on a day in, day out basis, and right under the nose of the client personnel. Such proximity is a mixed blessing: the client can observe up close both the high points and the low points of the service. Such a setting warrants a client who understands the vicissitudes of such operations, but also a provider who appreciates the importance of being responsive to customers' "requirements of the moment." More than anything else, this requires mutual understanding and open communication. XBS strives to attain this by establishing a partnership with clients—a formal and informal arrangement that gives client personnel easy access, rapid response, and a relational nurture; which gives, in other words, a great *personalization* ValueSpace. Here is how XBS does it.

Easy Access

Most of the XBS associates are on-site, so for a client getting access to XBS is a nonissue. Xerox has also launched and will continue to bolster its e-business, where customers will be able to get product information and order Xerox products online. Such a move is doubly effective: it gives customers the avenue to do business anytime anywhere; and it reduces, for Xerox, the cost of doing business.

Rapid Response

A document site is a document site—with machines that will occasionally jam, an employee that will occasionally call in sick, or a job that will occasionally go awry. "It can happen in any business company's self-managed office," observes Vele Galowski, vice president of U.S. Customer Operations. "Only when it happens in an outsourced document site, it suddenly doesn't look all that normal to the customer." Such insight about customer behavior has served XBS management well: They understand the importance of a prompt response to client problems.

Because XBS personnel work on-site—keeping their eyes and ears focused on the customer—they are able to sense early warning signs of potential customer defections. And they have put in place a rapid response system. Indeed, XBS calls its rapid response (that is, prompt problem resolution) just that, *Rapid Response*. It entails the deployment of a special task force from the headquarters to study the situation and identify corrective action. Matt Henrichs was, when we visited XBS, the leader of one such headquarters team that worked on a problem resolution for a major financial services company. (Currently, he is national accounts operations manager.) Here is how he explains it:

Here is what we did for a client, one of the Big Five accounting and management consulting firms, for whom XBS manages its mailroom, copying services, and document preparation operations

**(for example, preparing graphics, reports, etc.). When the rapid
response team arrived at the client site, the nagging problem it
identified was that each of the functional areas within the client
company felt that their document job orders were being given a
lower priority than their counterparts'. The team reengineered
the process to reduce the cycle time. But it did something else: It
devised a time-based scheduling process whose openness would
dismiss any suspicions of favoritism. XBS applied what it knew—
technical efficacy is important; equally important is integrity—in
the eyes of all the end users in the client organization.**

Relational Nurture

Relational attitude is the foundation of XBS's business model. Its
three-part business model is "retain the present customer, grow the
same-account revenues, and gain new customers." And XBS knows
you can't retain and grow a client unless you develop, maintain, and
grow a relationship with the client. Bill McDermott puts it thus: "I
think that for Xerox to transform itself to a knowledge-based company,
it has to be very much in partnering, in nurturing, in symbiotic relationships where both parties strategically need each other to get the
job done."

The partnering relationship with clients begins at the very outset.
XBS management outlines for its strategic clients (that is, clients who
seek enterprise-wide document management services) what kind of
relationship XBS is seeking, and how it works to build that relationship.
The "retain and grow" objective colors all of XBS's behavior and all of
its attitude toward how it approaches specific industries and specific
clients. Bill Patterson, XBS's senior vice president of marketing, sums
up that approach:

> **First, we understand the document intensity and document tech-
> nology requirements by industries. Next, we move to under-
> standing the client's critical success factors, and mission critical
> documents, and then we sort that out through conversations
> with the client. We absolutely ensure in the selling process that
> we have captured the requirements of the end users. And with
> our existing customers, we spend a lot of time getting their feed-**

back and ensuring that we are constantly building our capabilities to serve the client's long term and emerging needs.

From Day One, when you identify a client as part of your target market or part of served market, you plan the things you would take to that client, and how you would grow that client over the years. We have the goal of converting the prospect into a customer into a client into a strategic partner. We believe that our growth, our success, has been the result of what we do *after* we get the client.

Partnership and relationship with clients was a theme that emerged again and again as we spoke to various executives separately. Vele Galovski, vice president of operations, put it thus: "We have three-to-five-year contracts with our clients. Three-to-five-years contracts means *partnership*. To this partnership, we bring a level of expertise to the white collar arena, which is, as of now, untouched by competitors!"

A key pillar for fostering a relational mindset, and indeed of implementing that mindset in actual behavior, is XBS's *Focus Executive* program (a practice common across the entire Xerox Corporation). Under the program, now in effect for more than ten years, an XBS Focus Executive is assigned to build relationships with the senior management of two or three major clients. This Focus Executive is different from the account manager, field general manager, or account supervisor. The latter are in place to manage day-to-day client operations. The role of the Focus Executive is to identify a senior executive (or executives) at the client company who would act as a strategic partner. The Focus Executive also serves as the point of highest contact within XBS if any problems need to be resolved. Says Patterson, himself a Focus Executive for a few clients: "The client knows he or she can always reach a member of the senior management should there ever be a problem. I meet my counterpart in the client organization regularly. There develops a relationship at the management level—person to person, one-on-one, that is invaluable. To both the parties."

The same intensity of relational nurture is found in the trenches—at the associates level. XBS account associates make it their goal to develop a relationship with clients. Ricky Owens is an account associate at the same Washington, DC-based professional organization client we mentioned before; he is always stopping by people's offices (in the client company) to see if they need something or if he can do anything for them. And he always has a big smile on his face. The client employees are delighted to see him. He has a big stack of "Thank You" notes from them.

Another client who appreciates XBS employees' relation-building attitude is one of Oklahoma City's largest distributors of groceries. "They have taken care of everything so well here in Oklahoma City," says the manager of office services at the client company. "They care as much about what is good for our company as we do. They really look out for our interests 100 percent."

AutoNation: Retooling the Car Buying Experience

You log onto a car company's Web site and ask it to find the exact model of the car you want, and the answer, addressed to you personally, comes back in less than a minute, complete with the price quote. You walk in for maintenance service on your car, and the company performs it within 30 minutes, guaranteed. Customers write letters to this company to share their thoughts: "Your salesperson made the process not only rewarding, but painless and refreshing," writes one customer; "I was so impressed with your [salesperson's] approach that I intend on referring him to friends," writes another. To customers well-worn with the usual hassle of dealing with car dealers, these descriptions seem fictional. But AutoNation is making them real. Its goal is nothing less: it is to completely "retool" the customer's car buying experience—through easy access, rapid response, and relational nurture.

Easy Access

Car buyers and owners want to be able to reach a dealer at convenient hours and via convenient means. For AutoNation, its strategy of combining brick-and-mortar stores with a strong Web presence gives customers the freedom to search for a car on its Web site anytime, anywhere. Unlike other car Web sites, such as Autobytel and CarPoint, that merely act as information transmitters between customers and subscribing dealers, the company's Web site is linked to its real store inventory, so the customers can get online real-time information on available cars.

The company has recently expanded its Web presence by acquiring the AutoVantage site's dealer contracts and by forming an alliance with AOL. Now, when you search AOL for automobiles, and if you click on "buying options," AOL AutosDirect (which is a version of AutoNation.com) appears as the default choice. Choose it and you are instantly taken to "AOL AutosDirect Powered by AutoNation."

Of course customers can walk into its bricks-and-mortar stores, typically open from 8 a.m. to 9 p.m. on weekdays and Saturdays; its service centers are open from 8 a.m. to 7 p.m. on weekdays and from 8 a.m. to 3 p.m. on Saturdays. This much is in common with most (though not all) other car dealers; what is different here is the large number of dealerships available to you. The company acquires and owns dealerships market by market, with a dominant presence in a market. So if you live anywhere in the South Florida area, for example, you have more than one AutoNation dealer for the same car and some 30 dealers combined for all makes of car. The company is also experimenting with seamless car service. Explains Hank Phillips, the head of fixed operations at the corporate office:

> **Since we have multiple locations and we deal with a vast range of models and makes, we are able to provide locational convenience. In the Denver market, we have instituted a system whereby all dealerships service all cars, so you could take your car, regardless of the model and make, to any of our dealerships. We hope to roll out that model nationally.**

When this program becomes available nationally, it would raise easy access for car service to a new height.

Rapid Response

For AutoNation, rapid response becomes relevant on two occasions: first, when it receives a customer inquiry on the Web, and second, when customers call to make a service appointment. On both counts, its response is exemplary.

First let us look at its response on the Web. How does a dealer respond when an online lead comes in? Fast. At each dealership, there is one (often two) salesperson dedicated exclusively to Internet sales.

The dealership's goal is to respond within one hour; that includes e-mail inquiries that come in the middle of the night. What is its accomplishment? The company has endeavored to bring it down from 48 hours in August 1998 to about 2.5 hours in August 1999, to one hour or less by August 2000! In September 2000 (at the time of our visit), the average response time was 52 minutes! Yes, in a recent month, Auto-Nation's e-salespersons received and responded to a total of 55,000 inquiries and they answered them all on an average within 52 minutes. When they are in the office, the e-mail alert gets them into action. What happens when they are away from the office? They carry a pager and the e-mail alert goes there, automatically. They get on their laptop or home PC and attend to the inquiry. No, they don't get up in the middle of the night to answer the e-mail pager alert. But during business hours, inquiries are answered almost immediately, maybe within ten minutes. So, combining their daytime responses with their responses to dead-of-night inquiries, they can still maintain a less-than-one hour response time, on average.

This less-than-one hour average response time is an important milestone. But that is only the beginning. The other part of a response is how helpful that response is. AutoNation's Internet sales guides write a response that is fully informative, honest, and personal. That full disclosure includes the no-haggle price, quoted right in the first e-mail response. Here is one such response, written by Talbott Summers of Maroone Ford of Margate in South Florida:

Hi ——:

Thank you for giving us the opportunity to serve you. In order to achieve our commitment to the highest level of customer satisfaction, we have developed a process specifically designed for Internet users. This allows you to avoid the usual car-buying experience by having most of all the information you need in advance of meeting with me in person and by appointment. I work exclusively with Internet users. I have been with Maroone Ford of Margate, formerly Mullinax Ford South, since November of 1995. I am a career employee that will be here to serve you through the years. Whether with sales or service, you will be able to count on me as a reliable and trustworthy friend when you need me. As Florida's

largest automobile dealership, Maroone Ford of Margate does not have dealer prep fees, hidden charges or any pricing games. Just add tax and tag to our no-haggle selling price. This is why we are the 2nd largest Ford dealership in America and the largest Mustang dealer in the world—we make it easy and haggle free. The Mustang we discussed is VIN# 1fafp4043yf_____. It is a white v-6 coupe with a/c, pw, pl, tilt, cruise, am/fm cass/cd Mach audio system, rear defrost, floor mats, rear spoiler, 16″ machined aluminum rims, dark charcoal leather seats, leather wrapped steering wheel and 6-way power driver's seat. The selling price for this vehicle is $17,995 after a $1,000 rebate from Ford. The 3-year/36,000 mile Ford Red Carpet lease program for this vehicle will have a monthly payment of $317.84, including tax, with a total out-of-pocket expense of $1,500. This money represents your 1st monthly payment, tax, tag and $858.22 capitalized cost reduction (down payment). No security deposit is required. There are no acquisition or disposition fees.

If you have any questions, I may be reached directly at the phone number below or by return e-mail. I will personally ensure that your car-buying experience is your most pleasant ever. Thanks again for the opportunity to serve you, I look forward to hearing from you soon.

This is a sharp contrast to the industry norm: A *Consumer Reports* study reported in its April 1999 issue that in a survey of 1056 Internet car shoppers, only 35 percent received a price quote within two days; others were told to visit the dealership to discuss pricing.

As to the responsiveness of service centers, the company's scope (multiple dealerships in a ten-mile radius, and its plan to make service available at all dealership locations regardless of the make of the car), position it to offer service appointments nearly on-demand. Once in the store, the repair work itself is handled expeditiously and on the promised time. As already mentioned, a menu of 13 routine maintenance services are currently available at certain dealership locations on a "fast or free" guaranteed time. For tire rotation, for example, the service time is 30 minutes. Guaranteed. And for cooling system fluid replacement, it is 60 minutes. Guaranteed.

Relational Nurture

Relationships are something every executive talks about at AutoNation. Says CEO Jackson, "We can do what has not been done before. It is to take a relationship approach. Every transaction is a moment of truth and also an opportunity to build a relationship."

For AutoNation customers, the seeds of relationship are sown in that first encounter with its salespersons—whether in the showroom or on the Web; in the painless purchase experience, that is. How painless is it? Let its customers explain it in their own words.

Dear Mr. Miller:

I have been purchasing GM automobiles for about 30 years and have always found the experience frightening, frustrating, intimidating, and most unpleasant. I actually dread the idea of having to deal with salespeople at car dealerships. Everything they say about lawyers goes double for salespeople at car dealerships. Most car salespeople I encountered over the years were pushy and obnoxious, especially toward women.

Recently I began investigating purchasing a car on the Internet since I would not have to deal face to face with a salesperson in the showroom. To my surprise and delight, I encountered Dennis Greenwood of Steve Moore Chevrolet . . .

Dennis made the process not only rewarding but painless and refreshing.

—A customer

Likewise, relationship is the goal at the financial dealings stage. The company wants to make sure that the financing and protection products are presented to the customer in a professional manner—that the whole slate of services is presented so the company does not forgo an opportunity and that it is presented in an open and honest way. Says Kevin Westfall, president of AutoNation Financial Services, "We spend 8 million dollars a year in training of F&I—Finance and Insurance—people."

The company also sees its extensive scope (covering all makes and models of cars) as a tool to build a relationship with customers. Explains Phillips: Our new focus is not only the share of repairs on your one car, but on the "share of your garage." We want to service all your cars and our scope and multiple locations allow us that. We are able to have a relationship.

What can be better testimony to the company's relational nurturance posture than a favorable word of mouth from noncustomers. Here is an excerpt from a letter from a customer who visited the dealership but did *not* buy the car from it (and yet took the trouble to write):

The only regret that I have is that your dealership did not have the car that I wanted (Blue Odyssey EX), and my wife was not willing to settle for another color. I realize there was the possibility that you could have located the car for us but due to personal circumstances we could not wait for that to happen.

I was so impressed with your dealership and Greg's approach, that I intend on referring him to friends and family who might be looking for a car as opposed to the dealer whom I bought the car from.

—A customer in Oak Park, California, in a letter dated December 30, 1999

Personalization ValueSpace: Delighting the Customer Galore

Personalization value begins with easy access. All of our sample companies have it: their customers know whom to call and how; their Web sites are user-friendly; and they have high standards of phone access (for example, calls answered within three rings). Increasingly, more and more companies, including many market followers, have paid attention to easy access. Yet, easy access is by no means universal in businesses around the world.

With easy access as a given, it is in rapid response that the mettle of our sample companies shows up. From PPG's fine chemicals division that will jump through hoops to get you product samples and test data real quickly, to AutoNation's "open, honest, and detailed" less-than-52 minutes average response to e-shoppers; from 3M's roofing granules technical reps who will fly out the next morning to inspect the latest shipment, to XBS's rapid response teams who arrive at client sites to reengineer troubled work processes; rapid response is the hallmark of our sampled companies.

And finally, relational nurture is the ValueSpace component that gives personalization its name. That is where market leaders gain a sustainable advantage over market followers. From SYSCO's marketing associates who act as business counselors as well as a "friend-in-need" to their customers, to XBS's Focus Executives who build partnership with customers' senior management; from American Express's senior executives who talk to customers every day, to Rosenbluth's travel service associates who serve as ambassadors of the company's "be nice" culture; our sample companies are building commercial relationships of lasting mutual value. On top of the superior performance and price ValueSpaces, our market-leading companies' play in personalization ValueSpace is delighting customers galore!

ValueSpace Expanders

"We sell roofing granules to roofing manufacturers. But as a value-add, we also give our customers an annual economic forecast. For years, it has been the economic bible for the industry. One of our customers has even used it to get a bank loan."

Robert Morrow, *director of marketing, roofing granules division, 3M*

VALUESPACE EXPANDERS ARE like icing on the cake. Without the more substantive core inside the cake, the icing has no base to sit on. But once a firm has baked an enticing customer value cake with performance, price, and personalization as its three main ingredients, value-added offerings can do wonders in making that cake irresistible. Here is how our sampled companies do it.

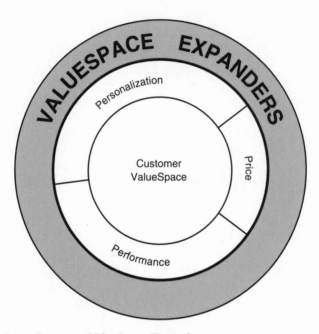

Figure 7.1   Customer ValueSpace Expanders.

ValueSpace Expanders at 3M

For 3M's distributor customers, perhaps the greatest ValueSpace expander comes in the form of 3M's missionary-like selling force— salespersons who will go out to end users and educate them; and then, when they are ready to order, turn them over to the company distributor in the area. Another significant ValueSpace expander is its program of sales and operations planning. Under this program, 3M offers its distributors advice and assistance in supply chain management—order quantity, timing, demand forecasting, on-site consulting, and help in market development. Yet another important value-added service 3M gives its distributors is relevant and useful information about the business. Says Alan P. Norton, 3M's director of information technology and customer relationship management:

> **We give a wealth of marketing information to our distributors.
> We are very good at isolating—we are very good at applications,
> so we are very good at identifying what those applications are,
> and predicting who can use them. And we have got literally thou-**

sands and thousands of applications on CD ROMs—for each application, we put graphics together, benefits story, provide directions to distributor partners, we have SIC codes and names of current users and then map similar other companies in the SIC code.

3M's roofing granules division offers another good example of a ValueSpace expander. Every year, the division prepares an economic forecast for the roofing industry and shares it with its customers. The forecast uses a 20-year database, and is based on historic trends and factors that affect new constructions and reroofing. So every January and February, the 3M roofing granules division's marketing director and his economic forecasting manager go from customer to customer, and make a one to two hour presentation. This is so valuable to its customers that one of them even used it successfully to get a bank loan. "For years, it has been the economic bible for the industry," says, Robert Morrow, marketing director.

Rosenbluth: Helping You Manage Your Travel

Rosenbluth's ValueSpace expanders help you manage your travel better. One of these is called *en-route service*—available 24 hours a day, 7 days a week. As a RI client, you can call this service if you need any help while in transit. And you can call it en route even if you booked your travel with a local office. Then there is the Electronic Messaging Service: You get e-mail alerts if there are weather emergencies, and you will be advised to call your corporate travel agent to reroute any trips that may be affected.

Some ValueSpace expanders benefit travel managers rather than travelers. One of these comes from the company's information consolidation capabilities; the company compiles information on total travel spending across all travelers in a client company, comprising air, hotel, and car rental, and can make that information available on a regular basis to the client company's travel managers. The travel managers can then use this information to negotiate favorable rates with specific suppliers (that is, hotels, airlines, etc.). And RI also offers consultancy help in the analysis of that information for clients to use for internal cost control.

Finally there is *e-Vision*. E-Vision is a PC-based program that gives you, the client, a peek into your entire travel records—past or pending. You can access your travel data and produce pre- and post-travel reports. If you are a corporate travel manager, then you can access your company's records kept by Rosenbluth, and download the data onto a floppy or a CD-ROM. You can use them to prepare your expense and other travel reports. This can save you a lot of grunge work. Besides, with this complete vision over your entire travel activity, you gain a much-needed sense of control.

Hilton Hotels: Frequent Guests Can Have It All!

Consider the following news item:

> **BEVERLY HILLS, Calif.—(BUSINESS WIRE)—Oct. 4, 1999—** Hilton Hotels Corporation, headquartered in Beverly Hills, CA, has announced that Hilton HHonors(R), one of the world's leading guest reward programs, and Virgin Atlantic Airways have formed an exciting program partnership. HHonors members will earn 1000 miles in the Virgin Atlantic Airways' Freeway frequent flyer program with every business-rate stay at a participating Hilton hotel. These miles will be accrued in addition to HHonors points, via HHonors' unique Double Dip® feature, which allows members to earn both points and miles with every qualifying stay.
>
> With Virgin Atlantic's Freeway participation in the HHonors Reward Exchange, members may also now convert Freeway miles into HHonors points and also may convert HHonors points into Freeway miles.

Although most hotels offer frequent guest programs, HHonors is the only hotel program that allows its members to simultaneously accumulate both airline miles and hotel points with each business-rate stay—a benefit Hilton calls Double Dip® earnings. Moreover, it is the industry's only two-way exchange of hotel points and airline miles; you can convert the miles you earned on airlines into hotel points and vice versa. It is because of such flexibility that *InsideFlyer* magazine has noted: "[It] has changed the world of frequent travel by removing most of the limits on airline miles and points."

If you are a HHonors member, Hilton also offers you a number of extra services, free of charge. For example, in each of its hotel properties, it has designated one or more entire floors as HHonors floors. Stay on one of these floors and you will sleep better—for the hallways are quieter. You can also get a daily newspaper, a special lounge, free room upgrades, and so on. As an HHonors member, then, you can have it all! Well, almost all.

American Express: Growing Merchants' Business

American Express ValueSpace expanders are designed to help merchant customers manage their back-office better as well as grow their business. For starters, the automated transfer of financial information on the merchants' SE Workstations is in a format suitable for export into a spreadsheet application, allowing the merchant to do additional financial analysis of his or her business. Secondly, the availability of up-to-date information on a daily basis about funds deposited to the merchants' accounts helps merchants improve their cash flow management.

There are a number of other value-added services. One of these is called *SE Insight*, a software-based information product. Merchants install *SE Insight* on their desktop computer equipped with a modem, and the company will send periodic aggregate analyses of customers who visit a specific merchant. Representative information includes where customers come from and what cardmember segments are most represented. For example, what proportion of the customers are local versus out-of-town, international or domestic, and whether they are using the personal or the corporate card. What makes these data useful is that the merchant-specific aggregate customer information is compared against the aggregate customer information from the merchant's competitors. Thus the subscribing merchant knows which segment of customers is undertapped by his or her business relative to the competition. At the press time, the company was preparing to launch an Internet version of this program, to be called *Merchant Edge*.

If you are a merchant accepting American Express cards, the company also offers you valuable assistance in planning and implementing your promotional programs. One program is called *Custom Extras*. For a fee, American Express will place your customized promotional offer right on the cardmember's monthly statement! Consumers receive a lot of promotions in the mail and never even open much of what they perceive to be junk mail. But everyone opens a bill, so your promotion would never go unnoticed. A related promotion program is Web-based. As a merchant customer, you can go to the company's Web site, and from the available menu options create a "merchant exclusive"—a set of promotional deals to customers that customers can get only from you. Cardmembers also have a Web site where they may register and visit to review any promotional offers from merchants in their area. What is more, to redeem these offers, neither the cardholder nor the merchant have to handle any coupons, punch any keys, or make any modifications at the time of the transaction. The redemption is automatically credited to the cardmember's account and debited to the merchant's account as the transaction is processed! Moreover, unlike other promotional vehicles such as coupons in the mail, the promotions are highly targeted by customer profile and help merchants to attract new prospects and bring back current customers.

ValueSpace Expanders at SYSCO

SYSCO has a long slate of value-added offerings. One of them comes in the form of foods that are further along in their processing. The less the restaurant workers have to work on them, the more value it is to the restaurant—value both from labor savings and from food consistency. This point is explained vividly by George Sideras, executive chef at the Cincinnati unit: "Let us say a restaurant is buying a whole New York strip, and the cook there cuts 12 strips out of it. No matter how experienced the cook is, the 12 strips will not be of the same size. And the customer would get a different size strip every time. To these customers, we are now selling 'portion cut meat'—precut strips of exact same size."

A number of ValueSpace expanders are directed at its Gold—top profit generating—customers. For starters, Gold customers get a preferred delivery schedule. Then Gold customers are invited one hour early for a preview at food shows that SYSCO organizes twice a year.

Within the food shows are seminars delivered by outside experts. These are heavily attended and restaurant workers can get credit for continuing education.

SYSCO will also help customers in emergency situations. For example, it will loan them a truck for food storage (with cold storage) for, say, a company picnic. If a customer, say a hospital, has its freezer broken, it will loan them a freezer. It even loans its meeting facilities.

One of its more notable value-added offerings, available to all customers, is its *ServSafe* training. It is a 16-hour course on how to prepare and serve food safely. SYSCO charges a nominal fee of $90 for the course. (Similar training from the Restaurant Association will cost about $200 to $250.) Normally done at its headquarters, SYSCO occasionally takes its training on the road, offering it at customer sites.

Another great ValueSpace expander is its in-house trade magazine, *SYSCO Serve Smart*. This quarterly magazine features "Business-building ideas and trends for the foodservice operator." One recent issue carried the following short articles: "Dealing with Difficult Employees," "Maximizing Technology in Foodservice Operations," "Adventures in Recruiting," a guide on proper "internal temperature" for various food items, and a guide on "handling cheese." There is an article highlighting two menu trends, one on egg dishes and the other on ice creams. To be sure, the two trends feature restaurants that are SYSCO customers and they feature dishes based on SYSCO brand ingredients, but the stories are helpful menu guides from successful peers such as the 24-hour chain of Kerby Lane of Austin and the News Cafe of fashionable Coconut Grove, Florida. And the stories are far from commercial speech—they are fun to read and exciting to implement. Here is an excerpt (on the popularity of hand-dipped ice cream) from Kathy Pallette, manager of the Southland Snack Bar in a popular Atlantic seaside vacation destination in North Carolina: "People taste it with their eyes before they taste it with their mouths. Everyone's tastes are different, but when they look in the case, they are bound to see something that appeals to them, and I think that is what makes them decide." Here is a sampler of exciting ideas to implement:

Turn heads with shake garnishes as fun to look at as they are to eat. Add frilly chocolate curls, fresh fruit, small candies or cookies, or whipped cream and a cherry for presentation pizzazz!

Dress up mug rims by dipping the edge of the frozen glass in chocolate. Store dipped items in the freezer until use for added convenience.

Bigger is better. Try upsizing fountain shakes to 22 ounces or larger to capitalize on the traditional popularity of shared sippers—and watch these oversized treats draw couple crowds!

The excitement—and a new food recipe certainly is excitement to chefs everywhere—continues in a feature article on a historic restaurant—Fried Green Tomatoes, of Galena, Illinois. Its chef manager Craig Joos delivers a secret gem, Bistecca All' Espresso: "We take ground espresso coffee beans and roll a 6-ounce aged Angus filet mignon in them and then pan sear it and serve it with garlic roasted mashed potatoes and a caramelized shallot-and-port wine sauce. It's amazing—the combination of the bitterness of the coffee and the caramel-like port sauce!"

Finally, let us come back to the food shows. For all customers, Gold or otherwise, the two annual food shows provide useful business information and assistance. But just as important is the social aspect. These are big events where communities of SYSCO people, foodservice operator customers, food brokers, and manufacturers come together to show and tell, to learn and teach, to ask and give, to negotiate and motivate, and to have fun while doing business.

Another community building event is its annual cruise excursions. In May 2000, SYSCO's Cincinnati unit celebrated what it calls its largest marketing promotion program, the Customer Incentive Promotion (CIP). Under the program, customers who increased their share of SYSCO brands earned random-drawing chances. Winners, 300 of them, won an all-expense paid seven-day cruise to the Caribbean! The hosts included the winning sales managers and several members of the executive staff. This is SYSCO's way of saying "thanks" to its customers; and of further strengthening its relationship with them.

ValueSpace Expanders; Many Roads, Same Goal

It would be ironic to confine ValueSpace expanders to a finite list. Even so, for the sake of understanding, we suggest some broad categories of ValueSpace expanders:

First, and most obvious, are memberships or frequent patron rewards. These can range from cash-back bonuses to free service upgrades to free future products. The best example of this among our sample companies is Hilton's HHonors programs.

Second are those offerings that customers generally don't actively seek or may not even be aware of at the time of patronage decisions. These come as surprise value-adds. Examples include annual spending reports from some credit card companies, Rosenbluth's E-Vision, 3M's annual economic forecasts for the roofing industry, SYSCO's help in menu design or its ServSafe training, American Express's sharing of merchant-specific aggregate clientele information, and so on.

Third are those ad hoc things company employees do for you occasionally. These differ from the second category in that those have now become regular and systematic offerings from the company. These occur, in contrast, on a more spontaneous basis, flowing out of a general company attitude. Examples include the SYSCO marketing associate standing in for an absent cook in the customer's hour of need, or loaning a freezer when a customer's freezer breaks down.

There is virtually no limit to the value-expanders one can conceive. Our broad categorization is intended to stimulate brainstorming—the more ValueSpace expanders you can dream up, the more you can stretch your ValueSpace. But many do cost money, mind you, so their true value to customers must be closely assessed. Even more importantly, they should not be used to substitute for core value builders—the eight ValueSpace components discussed in the three preceding chapters.

CHAPTER

8

Caterpillar, Inc.: Rock-Solid ValueSpace from Yellow Iron

"Our single focus will continue to be helping customers all over the world succeed in their businesses. When we do that—when we make them winners—then employees, dealers, and stockholders win as well."

Donald V. Fites, *former chairman and CEO, Caterpillar*

"Under the '16X Quality Improvement' program, we literally eliminated repetitive product failures. Now we are attacking

*random failures with Six Sigma methodology,
continuing to drive defect rates so low that no
competing machine will even come close.*"

James E. Despain, *vice president,
Caterpillar and general manager, TTT division*

WHAT DO HOOVER DAM, the English Channel tunnel, and the Three Gorges Dam in China have in common? They were built—all three of them—with significant aid from Caterpillar earth-moving equipment. If you look around, wherever some earth is being moved—in the mines of Africa, at construction sites of future skyscrapers in cities from New York to New Delhi, at dams and bridges in the third world, on roadbuilding sites, and on farms around the world, you are likely to find, hard at work, *Yellow Iron*, as Caterpillar's equipment is fondly called.

Caterpillar Inc., or CAT, is a global manufacturing company with headquarters in Peoria, Illinois, on the banks of the Illinois River.[1] Its products include tractors and combines for harvesting, hydraulic excavators, mining shovels, motor graders and off-highway trucks for mining and construction industries, and gas and diesel engines and gas turbines for diverse industrial applications. Its customers are builders and contractors, miners and oil diggers, farmers and loggers, and truckers and utility companies. It employs about 65,000 employees worldwide (about 40,000 in the United States) and is the market share leader and the "best in class" in its industry.

In 1999 Caterpillar's revenues stood tall at $19.702 billion; profits stood at $946 million. The company is the undisputed market leader both in terms of market share and brand reputation. Three times in a row (1997, 1998, and 1999) CAT has been ranked as number #1 in its industry (industrial and farm equipment) on *Fortune*'s Most Admired Companies List.

The forerunner of this modern day Fortune 500 corporation was created with an observed customer need. Daniel Best, one of the two founders, working on his brother's California ranch, noticed area farmers hauling their grain long distances and paying hefty fees for cleaning and preparing it for the market. Best set out to build an affordable machine that farmers could use to clean grains on the farm itself. The "combined harvester" as the machine was called, combined the operations of cutting and threshing grain, increasing the farmer's productivity twofold. Increasing customer productivity was the customer value proposition then; increasing customer productivity, indeed, making progress possible around the world, is its customer value proposition now, a century later. Here is how CAT, or more specifically its Track-Type Tractors (TTT) division, the focus of our study, does it.

Customer Centeredness

Customers of Caterpillar and its TTT division are farmers, miners, construction contractors, and so on, looking for ways of moving earth. Caterpillar is so focused on delivering value to the user that it constantly asks its customers, "How can we help you move materials in a better way?"

CAT is very customer centered in at least two ways. First, it has systems in place to be intimately knowledgeable about its dealers; second, it uses dealers as instruments of knowledge about its end users. Dealers are its direct customers, who in turn serve end users. CAT chooses its dealers for the reputation and respect they hold in their respective communities where they live and operate, and CAT values their knowledge of end users deeply. To tap this knowledge, CAT involves its dealers in its product development and quality improvement programs—frequently and intensively.

For example, CAT engages its high volume dealers in a program called Partners in Quality. Under the program, each participating CAT plant selects dealers who have a high concentration of its products in their product-line mix and names them "high-C dealers" (C for concentration). Currently 40-plus in number (out of a total of 200), these dealers then engage in joint efforts to identify opportunities for improvement in product quality. These dealers are connected to CAT by a special dedicated toll-free phone number. If they encounter any problem in a CAT machine during machine preparation prior to delivery to end users, or later while the machine is in the field (usually during the first 1000 hours of its operations), they would call CAT immediately; a CAT quality engineer will then immediately investigate the problem and find a solution. CAT would subsequently implement that solution proactively on all other similar machines. "When any one of these dealers calls in a problem," explains Dale Roberts, CAT's commercial manager for TTT division, "CAT has a commitment to give a written response to that dealer within seven days."

These and other high volume dealers also serve as a "Dealer Advisory Group." The company brings them together about once a year to Peoria to jointly identify product problems and possible improvements. The company also uses them as sounding boards for new product ideas and prototypes. Beyond effecting improvement in product quality, this level of participation and involvement generates a sense of identification with the company and true partnership between dealers and CAT.

CAT also works through its dealers to obtain feedback from end users, surveying a purchaser of a CAT machine, for example, three times during the first two years, and then every time a part is replaced or some service is performed. The feedback helps both the company and the dealership by identifying improvements in the dealership organization and operations. "Our single focus," says Donald V. Fites, retired chairman and CEO, "will continue to be helping customers all over the world succeed in their businesses. When we do that—when we make them winners—then employees, dealers, and stockholders win as well."

CAT abolished its functional silos in 1990 and each region and division and product line became a profit center. Since this reorganization, everyone in the company, from the young design engineer to the vice president, makes it his or her business to be in frequent touch with dealers, and through them with large end users. Management holds annual regional conferences of dealers where they share company plans and help dealers with their goals and plans. There is substantial discussion of strategy and business issues; but there is also camaraderie and celebration and emotional bonding. CAT's sales and marketing managers, and senior executives as well, know dealers personally, as friends and as family.

Performance ValueSpace

CAT customers seek, first and foremost, equipment that performs—that is, they seek equipment that is reliable, durable, and does its job in the most efficient and effective way. CAT products offer superior performance, compared to its competitors. For example, consider the D11R Carrydozer, CAT's latest, most advanced track-type tractor for mining applications, introduced at the Mine Expo 1996. In comparison to the Komatsu 575-A2, its closest competitor, CAT claims superiority on a number of dimensions: most technologically advanced engine (3508 EUI) ever used in a track-type tractor with electronic injection (versus Komatsu's mechanical); average overhaul life of 12 to 16,000 hours; easier to access modular transmission; a more efficient torque converter (versus the lock-up converter of the 575 A-2); a stronger cast steel frame (versus Komatsu's fabricated plate frame); a monitoring system that keeps records of performance data (575 A-2 does not); and longer life of many parts such as cutting edges, end bits, roller frames, and blades.

Consider the experience of Charolais Coal, a coal mining operation in Madisonville, Kentucky. It leased a Komatsu D575A-2 "SD" tractor for 12 months. The tractor developed, within the first year, some engine problems, necessitating the installation of a replacement engine. Track bushings were worn 120 percent after only 2500 hours of operation. After two years of trial operation, Charolais returned the tractor to the local Komatsu dealer and replaced it with a CAT D11R! At the time of this writing (in 2000), Charolais is a very happy user of D11R.

One important source of performance value to the user is product-availability for use. CAT excels on this value in two ways. First, its machines are better built and are more reliable, so inherently, their uptime is higher. Second, the company offers well-designed maintenance contracts. Dealer service reps monitor its products in the field, and often maintain the machine for the customer who is freed from that burden. CAT dealers call their visits to customer sites "house calls"; their purpose is to monitor the health of CAT machines in the field.

CAT's Quality Obsession

CAT measures its product quality by defect rate. (*Defects* defined as any failure in machine operations.) It tracks these defects by the age of the machine in three brackets—VEHR—very early hour failure, registered within the first 21 hours of operation; DRF1—Dealer Repair Frequency One, registered during 22 to 200 hours of operations; and DRF2, registered during 201 to 1000 hours of operations. Such close tracking is part of its vigorous continuous quality improvement (CQI) programs.

CAT's CQI programs are comprehensively conceived. For example, while some might think of paint on a heavy machine as a mere cosmetic feature, CAT recognized that the quality of the paint job (good or poor) is the first thing a customer notices. And, indeed, customers noted and complained about such paint defects as poor coverage, runs and sags, embedded dirt, and uneven gloss and finish. So the paint line team in the TTT division set up a CQI project. The team identified and implemented improvements in equipment, processes, and worker tasks. The result? Within 20 months since the project started, the CQI team virtually eliminated all paint defects. And CAT counts, mind you, any slight unevenness in finish on any square inch of the tractor surface as a defect. And customer response? Customer complaints about paint on the machines had declined from 113 in 1990 to 7 in June 1995, and to zero since then!

CAT achieves such high product quality by high quality production processes—and by a rigorous certification process, for both its internal and external suppliers. The painstaking initial certification process takes one year, and then suppliers must be recertified every year! One of CAT's divisions, Solar Turbines Incorporated won the Malcolm Baldrige National Quality Award in the manufacturing category in 1998. Of course, the same high quality prevails in other CAT divisions.

Throughout CAT's history, its machines have had a significant quality edge over its competitors. With time, the competitors have been attempting to catch up, lessening the distance between themselves and CAT. The drive for maintaining and improving that quality leadership is an ambitious project called 16X. Begun in 1996, the 16X project aims to reduce the already low defect rate by 16 times by 2001. Achieving that rate meant that CAT worked to improve, in any given year, its quality by 100 percent, and then double it again the next year. The outcome of this intense quality effort was that by the end of 2000, the company had virtually eliminated all systemic defects, that is, defects that occurred repeatedly in a consistent pattern. Under attack now are the defects the company considers random; and these are being addressed under its Six Sigma CQI program. CAT executives believe that they now have processes in place that will drive continuous improvement to achieve breakthrough levels of quality. "When that happens," says CAT's Despain, "no competing machines will even come close!"

Performance Value through Innovation

Innovation is a CAT tradition. Its D10 tractor was the world's most technologically advanced track-type tractor at the time of its introduction in 1977. The D10's elevated drive design was a first, making the tractor easier to operate. Barely three years later (in 1980), CAT completely redesigned its tractors loaders. With its engine in the rear, these provided better operator visibility, machine balance, and serviceability, and they became the talk of the industry. Then in 1987, CAT introduced Challenger 65—an all-purpose farm tractor with a revolutionary Mobil-trac traction system. The tractor's rubber track allows speed and mobility and excellent floatation. *Business Week* magazine declared the tractor one of the best-designed products to hit the market in 1987! Over the last five years, Caterpillar has introduced 296 new or improved products, including gas turbine engines, backhoe loaders, hydraulic excavators, and so on. And it has won over 2000 U.S. patents since 1995.

A major thrust in CAT's innovation program is to harness electronics and hydraulics technology into its machines. Imagine, if you will, that you were a construction worker, removing earth on a specific terrain. Instead of completing the job in a random sequence of tractor movements, what if you could just program it for autopiloted optimum cutting path? Now you can! This is achieved by, as we mentioned in Chapter 1, the Computer Aided Earthmoving System (CAES) technology, introduced in CAT machines in 1996. The CAES displays the topography of the ground under the tractor in-action and relays it on a real-time basis, using the Global Positioning System (GPS) to a CAT office, where CAT technicians can calculate an optimal operating cycle and beam it back to the tractor operator. Likewise, CAES technology can also give the operator the capability to exactly duplicate a particular result or task. When a particular task is being performed, say leveling a particular piece of land, the computer chip inside the machine stores this information. If the operator wants to repeat that performance exactly, he or she simply hits a button, and the machine will perform that task repeatedly.

Another innovation is *Dozsim*, a PC-based software program that predicts dozer productivity in specific mining applications. Feed it tractor, operator, pit, and material parameters, and it will spew out on its monitor a visual of the selected mine profile and calculate tractor productivity and per-yard cost.

To drive its program of innovation, CAT has a technical services division, with a technical center in Mossville, Illinois. Here some 2000 engineers and scientists are at work, constantly innovating, constantly finding new sources of customer value. One of their charters is to develop operator-less tractors; vehicles that move without people. These tractor machines will be useful in such jobs as removal of hazardous waste, and operating in unsafe areas.

Customization

Nothing fits like a custom-made shoe. Can there be a customized 230,000-lb tractor? The answer is a "Yes"! A CAT salesperson (actually a CAT dealership salesperson, since CAT sells its machines through its dealership network) can sit down with a customer—a farmer, a miner, a construction contractor—and have the customer pick and choose the features and modification needed for a specific application. The tractor will then be delivered to the customer, with those customized features, exactly as the customer specified it. This of course would be but one of a myriad of configurations that would have been possible on that machine. "Many of our products have some custom modifications on them," says Randy Williams, TTT marketing manager (now retired). "A customized product could be anything from having a spotlight or a special heating attachment on it to a complete main-frame change."

What is more, such customization does not stop at the production stage. CAT engineers and marketing personnel roam in the field, observing their machines in operation. If they find a machine in a situation where its effectiveness or efficiency is compromised, they go to work to change it. For example, one of its oil excavator machines was operating in a highly corrosive environment, an oil field in northwestern Canada. The corrosive elements in the ground were attacking the metal in the undercarriage. CAT designed and manufactured corrosion resistant components and placed a modified guarding configuration on the machine. These custom-modifications would double the life of the undercarriage in that corrosive application!

Building Price ValueSpace

In the price ValueSpace, customers seek at least a fair price for tractors and if possible a value price. Most CAT customers are businesses and to them value price translates into economic benefits from using CAT machines. Caterpillar delivers economic value to customers in innovative ways. CAT wants to be the quality leader, not a low-price supplier. Commensurate with its superior product quality, CAT charges a premium price for its machines. However, what CAT strives to offer in terms of economic value is a lower total product cost—that is, the cost of owning and using the machine over its lifetime. CAT and its dealers are committed to making the customer's acquisition of a Caterpillar product the best value money can buy. CAT machines are more reliable and their uptime greater than competing machines, more than making up for its high initial price. CAT also believes that the resale value of its machines is significantly better than its competitors. CAT machines can be rebuilt because the frame lasts a lifetime. To help customers figure out the total product cost, CAT offers them software that permits factoring in acquisition price, operating costs, insurance costs, and resale value.

CAT also offers price value to customers by making buying CAT more affordable. CAT dealers offer its equipment for lease, for example. Some customers have limited, specific needs, and they would say, for example, "I have this much dirt to remove." The dealer would charge them a fixed price for using the equipment for that particular job. CAT dealers have also opened CAT rental stores in many locations worldwide, which rent out smaller machines and tools to a new set of customers whose needs were too small to even justify leasing the machine. CAT's rental capability is now worldwide.

Another avenue of economic value that CAT offers is a "forward repurchase program." Selling or getting rid of an old machine used to be a headache for customers; now CAT relieves them of this ordeal by agreeing, at the time of initial sale, to buy the old machine back after a certain number of years at a predetermined price. In fact, CAT has a dealer network to resell the used machine, so it doesn't even have to bring it back to the factory. And selling used machines is in itself a profitable business for its dealers, so it is a win-win strategy for all parties involved.

An even more intriguing avenue for making its machines affordable for the customer is CAT's innovative "barter" program—in lieu of cash, the company would accept a variety of merchandise as payment. The former Soviet Union, for example, was short on currency, so the company accepted men's suits and jackets as payment for its machines. The barter system works like this: Suppose one of CAT's customers, say a mining company, also makes steel; then CAT would sell its machines for steel. Then to get rid of steel, the company would find a sewing machine manufacturer and exchange steel for sewing machines. Next it would find a garment maker to whom it would sell the sewing machines in exchange for some suits. And then it would sell the suits to some mass merchandiser for cash. It has accepted in barter a wide range of products including TVs and generators. To manage all these barter operations, CAT has a subsidiary, called Caterpillar World Trade Organization. This subsidiary is also a profitable business unit in its own right!

More than enabling the sale, it is a goodwill opportunity for CAT. Says Dale Roberts, commercial manager of CAT (TTT division), "At the top of our vision pyramid we say, 'We make machines that raise the standard of living.' It does not say, 'We raise that standard only for developed nations or for well-off customers.' Many governments in underdeveloped nations never thought they could afford a CAT machine, but we make it possible for them. We are in the business of helping build infrastructures for developing nations. To be global is part of our charter."

Better Price Value through Cost Leadership

To remain able to offer great overall price value to customers, CAT is working on becoming a cost leader. It recognizes that as price pressures intensify in the marketplace, it must continuously improve its costs to maintain margins. Its program of cost management is as unique as they come—every component that CAT buys internally must compare favorably in price terms with any comparable external sources. And each component manufacturing unit is treated as an independent profit center, responsible for generating targeted profits. This forces every unit manager to act like an entrepreneur, striving to offer price value to its internal customer. Of course, the pressure to deliver superior price value is on CAT's external suppliers as well. They too must demonstrate that their offering is better than alternative suppliers'—dollar for dollar. In effect, CAT does not push its suppliers (whether internal or external) toward lowest possible prices; only toward superior products commensurate with the price demanded. Thus cost-management is pulled through its entire supply chain.

To drive its costs down through the supply chain, CAT will provide some of its parts suppliers with the raw materials needed to make their parts. For example, it would supply steel to forgers who would then supply forged parts to CAT. CAT buys that steel from steel mills, and because it buys so much of it, it gets a better price than its individual forgers could get.

Then there is the Virtual Prototyping System that aids target costing; it enables, via satellite, design engineers in the United States and Belgium to work together. Using virtual reality and cutting-edge software programs, CAT's design engineers are able to evaluate a machine before it is built. A process called Rapid Prototyping allows it to optimize the design before tooling.

Price Value though Lean Production

CAT also aims to run its manufacturing processes with the "best-in-class" efficiency. The company spent close to $2 billion to modernize its factories in the late 1980s and early 1990s. Its material handling system is now state-of-the-art. Its machining centers are computer controlled, enabling parts to be machined to tight tolerances, allowing even for tool wear. Its track links forge presses are fully automated. Track shoes are made in flexible manufacturing systems, which use materials delivered just-in-time. Components are machined in large flexible machining centers. The welding of various components is done by robots that are computer-controlled. Robotic welding delivers high quality, consistent welds. Major components are first assembled into modular subassemblies and individually tested, which reduces errors on the mainline assembly and enables customization at the final assembly stage. Its factories use high-speed lasers to cut and heat-treat the machine components. Produced with lasers, structures are now twice as strong. Tough steels (better materials) extend product life. And technology has been harnessed to reduce time from design to market.

Constantly, the TTT division is reengineering its production processes. The CQI project in the paint line (mentioned earlier) is a good case in point. One of the equipment modifications in that project was the installation of new pressure regulators to eliminate variations and decrease air pressure in the paint guns from 60 to 30 psi. This reduced paint and filter consumption and associated labor costs. Indeed, nearly all of the modifications instituted to improve paint quality (for example, increased oven temperatures, shifting the painting of the attachments from the tack paint stage to the finish paint stage, staggering the two finish painters to start half an hour later so that the last tractor coming out of the tack paint stage received the finish coat on the same day, etc.) also resulted in significant reductions in waste (indirect materials and expenses dropped from \$450 to \$282 thousand, annually), cycle time (from 25 to 21 minutes per tractor), and manpower (from 33 to 24 for the whole unit). The whole project resulted in cost savings of more than \$800 thousand per year. And this of course was just one of hundreds of projects implemented for leaner production and CQI since then.

Personalization ValueSpace

Beyond performance and price values, CAT also works diligently to build personalization ValueSpace, doing so through a number of activities it calls customer service. (Personalization is our term, not CAT's.) CAT builds this ValueSpace for its end users primarily through its dealer network. Recall that these dealers are the direct customers of CAT. CAT thus has two layers of customers, end users and dealers. In order that dealers may offer good value to end users, it is important that they themselves first receive good customer value from CAT. And CAT goes the distance to offer its dealers excellent customer value.

Excellent Dealer Network

CAT has perhaps the strongest dealer network in its industry. (CAT sells direct only to OEMs and governments.) To all other end users, it sells through its global dealership network of some 207 independent distributors (144 of whom are outside the United States). CAT views its dealership network as one of the most critical drivers of its marketplace success, as important as its engineering excellence and world-class, efficient manufacturing. Many of its dealers have been with the company for more than 50 years, even though the dealership agreement allows them to terminate without cause on a mere 90 days' notice. So much do they trust the company that twice a year they open their books to CAT for review and advice. Without reciprocating their trust and without offering solid value to them as customers, CAT could not expect to command such fierce loyalty from them. How does CAT offer this value to its dealers?

First, the performance value of CAT machines that end users experience is also a prime value for CAT dealers. As independent business establishments, they naturally seek good economic returns; however, what gives their business an identity distinct from those of other dealerships and other businesses is that they sell CAT machines. The quality and performance value of CAT machines is thus inextricably linked to their self-identity, their pride in what they do, and their enthusiasm to add further value in the value chain. The addition of an innovative feature on a CAT machine—such as the self-guided, operator-less tractor described earlier—is as much a source of excitement to them as to the intended end-user market.

Having said that, good economic returns remain a basic, universal value to all dealers, and CAT certainly makes sure its dealership operations are profitable. In fact, CAT adopts a paternalistic posture, nurturing their business capabilities in good times, and protecting their economic viability if times get rough. During much of the 1980s, for example, when the industry suffered a recession and CAT's edge in product quality and manufacturing costs were challenged, it absorbed about a million dollars a day in losses by accepting lower margins for itself so that its dealers could retain their business in the end-user markets. Likewise, in the early 1990s, when the market slumped again, CAT protected its dealers by supporting inventory financing. During normal times as well, if a particular end-use market experiences an aggressive competitor pressure, CAT will offer a case-by-case price support to the involved dealer. Generally, though, CAT is a price leader in the market, and its dealerships profit from the higher margins they earn on CAT products. That, and the fact that its end-user customers—delighted with the performance value of CAT machines, return for more business year after year.

Of course, the dealers need and look for more than just a good product and decent margins—specially, given that most dealers depend on CAT for 90 percent of their revenues, some indeed the entire 100 percent! They need training, merchandising help, and technical support. CAT provides its dealers with extensive training that covers not only product knowledge and technical information, but also various aspects of managing the business, such as planning, inventory management, logistics, and cost and financial management. CAT dealers are responsible also for the maintenance of CAT machines in the field, and they receive both training in equipment maintenance and on-line technical help. CAT supports them also by sharing market information, sales trend forecasts, customer satisfaction survey results, and company plans.

Easy Access, Rapid Response, and Relational Nurture

Dealers have easy access to the company. Product information is available online, as is technical assistance. When dealers need a part in a hurry for one of their customers, they need easy access and rapid response from CAT. And CAT's distribution network delivers. The distribution network links 23 CAT distribution centers and major parts depots located around the world. This network of distribution centers, enhanced by dealer storage locations in several countries, enables 94–96 percent parts availability on an immediate basis. When a customer needs a part, dealers first search their own stock, then the closest CAT distribution center, and if needed can expand their search to include the entire distribution network. This distribution network gives dealers easy, immediate access to all the available inventory and enables customers to receive the parts they need usually within 48 hours, if not sooner.

In fact, Caterpillar's capability for logistics and distribution is so good that in 1987 it started a new business called Caterpillar Logistics Services, Inc. (CAT Logistics). This wholly owned subsidiary today moves goods for such companies as Daimler-Chrysler and Ericsson!

CAT displays rapid response also in its day-to-day dealings. For example, when a dealer calls in a potential sales transaction, the CAT finance representative will type in the information, process the application promptly, and electronically download to the dealer's computer the paperwork to be signed by the buyer. The approval is as quick as is the subsequent funds transfer to the dealer for whom quick availability of cash is a significant value.

CAT considers its relationship with its dealers an unmatched resource. To be sure, there are the usual points of conflict—CAT has a tendency to push higher retail prices, and new model introductions sometimes overwhelm the dealers. However, while CAT is very demanding of its dealers, just as it is of itself, the company nurtures them with passion and acts to guard their interests. If a dealer were in crisis financially or otherwise, the company will do its utmost to be of help. Likewise, if CAT needed help from dealers, they (the dealers) put all their differences aside. "We have tremendous respect for each other," says Dale Roberts, commercial manager (TTT division) for dealer relations. CAT has invested heavily in building a trusting and personal relationship with its dealers. The regional sales organization is frequently in contact, and dealer/owners can call the CAT CEO anytime, direct.

The paternalistic attitude we spoke of earlier takes CAT deeply into its dealership operation. Dealers open their books and CAT's regional sales managers review and advise dealer/owners not only on how to improve sales and performance, but also their financial strength, organizational structure, and skills and capabilities of its sales and technical persons. CAT even worries about succession—hoping to keep the dealership in the family, the company frequently organizes business seminars for the families of owners. And to interest the young, they arrange for summer jobs and internships, and invite dealer's young sons and daughters (as young as 15) to Peoria for a plant tour and for a hands-on exposure to the pride of working for a CAT dealership. So important does the company consider the intergenerational continuity of dealerships that, should all efforts to rehabilitate a debilitating dealership fail, the CAT CEO must personally authorize any dealership termination.

The CAT culture of high service and relational attitude toward its dealers rubs off on those dealers, who then carry the same value to the end users. They are easy for the end user to access, they respond rapidly, and they display and nurture the same relational attitude toward the end users that they receive from CAT.

Consider rapid response for a minute. What can be more rapid than taking care of your problem even before you request it? CAT's high-tech vision is to achieve just that. Some CAT machines now have built-in sensors that monitor the machine performance continually and immediately alert a computer located regionally, say with a local dealer, about an impending breakdown in a specific machine. The dealer's technician immediately locates a part on the global inventory network (which links all of CAT's dealers and all of the distribution centers and factories), and determines the best source of the part. If a part is unavailable, it sends an order to the factory or to a CAT supplier. The part is delivered to the customer site on the appointed day for the technician to make the repair. Thus, the machine is repaired even before the customer would ever know of any potential breakdown.

ValueSpace Expanders

CAT has a roster of value-added services for both end users and dealers. Some offer value to both and some are offered to the end user via the dealer.

Financing and Insurance

Customers purchasing heavy equipment like CAT machines need two important services, financing and insurance; and CAT offers them both through its own subsidiaries, Caterpillar Financial Services Corporation and Caterpillar Insurance Services Corporation. This is a value-added service for end users not only because it enables one-stop shopping, but also because CAT offers merchandising programs that allow financing at below-market rates. One reason CAT can offer better-than-market rates is its unique insider knowledge of CAT customers, products, and markets (which means it assumes lower risk). Moreover it services its customers with a world-class service quality—a quality that in 1999 earned it Tennessee's (where the subsidiary is head-quartered) highest Quality Excellence Award with Global Excellence Commendation.

CAT financing is especially appealing to many government customers. Typically, many government budgets are annual appropriations rather than multiyear investments. Taking advantage of CAT Financial's government lease-purchase plans that offer low interest rates and flexible terms, a governmental buyer can appropriate ownership of say one-fifth of the machine during any given year, and acquire full ownership over five years. CAT Financial's corporate mission is to be a "significant reason customers select Caterpillar worldwide." And it is.

Likewise, CAT machine customer's need for product liability insurance is met by CAT's wholly owned subsidiary, Caterpillar Insurance Services Corporation (CAT Insurance). Formed in 1983, it provides a wide array of insurance products to CAT dealers and customers. With over $8 billion worth of CAT equipment under coverage, CAT Insurance ranks among the top 1 percent of all U.S. agencies. It is so intent on offering customers significant value that it self-defines its charter as follows: "We will be a significant reason customers select Caterpillar worldwide. We will deliver outstanding services, enhance the Caterpillar name, and grow on our strong foundation as a caring and learning organization." Its current vision is insuring "every piece of CAT equipment throughout the life of the machine."

End-User Product Support

Other ValueSpace expanders directed at end users are intended to enhance the life of CAT machines and their performance. One of these is the Certified Rebuild Program. CAT machines can be rebuilt after 10–12 thousand hours of operation, and again after a total of 20–25 thousand hours. The rebuilt machine even gets a new serial number and a new warranty, and it costs less. Another program is the CAT Lubricant program. Under this program, the company specifies and sources, and through its dealers distributes, the lubricants customers should use. It also offers an oil-sampling service—offering to sample and test the oil from its machine at scheduled intervals to assess machine performance. CAT is also prompt in responding to machine breakdowns. If a component breaks down, CAT will (again through its dealers) exchange it immediately with a remanufactured part. Its undercarriage inspection program evaluates the wear pattern. And, as previously mentioned, its technicians often repair machines even before they break down.

End-User Training

A third set of value expanders relates to enhancing the user/operator's skills. Operator training is available, and business seminars teach a small business customer how to manage the construction or agricultural business, for example. For high-volume end users, there are VIP days at the factory.

ValueSpace Expanders for Dealers

The financing and insurance of CAT equipment that is a considerable value to end users is also of value to the dealership. It helps sell the equipment and it yields selling commission for the dealer. The program is very effective—about seven out of every ten machines are sold with CAT financing. CAT dealers' participation in CAT Finance is totally voluntary. When CAT Finance started its operations, it told its dealers: "We don't want you to buy financing from us because you have to, but rather because you want to. We want to earn your business." And it does.

A number of other CAT programs are a source of value to CAT dealers. One set of these expands the scope of a dealer's business. Not only do dealers sell CAT tractors, they service them in the field, for example. They also rent equipment and buy and sell used equipment (some of it, after some value-added repair). They also make money by selling CAT lubricants, parts, and components. CAT dealers also sell maintenance and repair contracts (called Marc). CAT offers Marc support and life-cycle planning software that can help dealers predict the maintenance requirements of a specific machine. This becomes an important tool for estimating the profitability of maintenance and repair contracts, and indeed for structuring the maintenance contract. Maintenance contracts are administered by dealers and offer value both to dealers (via additional revenues) and end users (by enhancing machine uptime).

CAT also invests heavily in dealer training. At its Big Iron University, CAT brings together its big mining dealership salespersons for a program of information exchange, sales training, and peer group consultation.

Corporate Values as the Foundation for Building Customer ValueSpace

CAT's culture and the corporate values that define it are the fountain source of all of CAT's activities. It would be no exaggeration to say that CAT owes its success in continuous pursuit of quality and innovation to its values culture. These values (which CAT's TTT division calls Common Values) are embodied in the company's *Code of Worldwide Business Conduct*, which reads, in part:

> **The Company's most valuable asset is a reputation for integrity. If that becomes tarnished, customers, investors, suppliers, employees, and those who sell our products and services will seek affiliation with more attractive companies. We intend to hold to a single high standard of integrity everywhere. We will keep our word. We won't promise more than we can expect to reasonably deliver; nor will we make commitments we don't intend to keep.**

> **We seek long-lasting relationships—based on integrity—with all whose activities touch upon our own.**

CAT's TTT division's Common Values inform and guide all the foregoing customer ValueSpace building processes. Stories of empowerment of the rank and file and their innovations abound in the TTT division's roster of achievements. Here is one story. It pertains to the CQI project on the paint line for tractors, the project we described earlier. The project had begun with a customer complaining about paint that had chipped off a little. One of the workers took upon himself the responsibility to improve the painting process. He helped set up a CQI team and the team achieved near zero defect paint job. He then entered the process in a national contest sponsored by *USA Today* and the Rochester Institute of Technology. TTT division was one of the three finalists and was a runner-up for the award. At the award ceremony in Arlington, Virginia, CEOs and presidents of a number of other recipient companies received the award. When they called out for CAT, three

TTT representatives (Greg Liles, Sarge Schwartz, and Ernie Murray) walked up to the podium and each introduced himself: "My name is——, and I paint tractors!" "Today," declares CAT's Jim Despain, "there is no paint job better in the world!" And he means not just on tractors, but on any metal surface in the world, period.

Here is another story. Carmon Rose is staff manufacturing specialist in the TTT division. Most people fondly call him "Mr. Clean!" And it has nothing to do with a grooming fetish or the like; rather, a few years ago, he was the person responsible for devising a method that ensured that CAT tractors are shipped with a clean power train oil system. Today when customers visit TTT division, they will see assemblers filling machines with clean oil and using unique processes to guarantee cleanliness. A cleanliness roll off specification of ISO 18/15 is met by using a particle counter on all hydraulic and power-train oil before every tractor is shipped. Today, an active "Mr. Clean" and his SS Contamination Control Team are the forces that drive the SS clean oil system effort.

Finally, there is the story of an assembly-line worker who saw a customer walking with some dizzying movements. The worker left his station, walked up to the customer, inquired about him, and took him to the medical facility. "Without the Common Values," says Jim Despain, "such voluntary behavior may not have happened."

Two planks in the Common Values are *mutual respect* and *trust*. Walk around in the CAT compound for a few minutes. These values are everywhere—writ large on the faces and behaviors of all CAT employees—on the shop floor, and in the offices, manifested in CAT employees' everyday behavior toward each other and most certainly toward the visitor and customers. As a visitor to this world leader of the industrial age, you expect to see an impressive twenty-first-century industrial complex. You do see that, of course. But what will truly impress you is the realization that "how nice it must be to do business with CAT people." CAT customers—dealers and end users—already know it. And they cherish it as value unequaled anywhere else.

United Parcel Service: Big Brown's Package for Customer ValueSpace

"Rather than being pushed upon by the seller and the supplier, the customer will 'pull' the product or service of his/her choice through the supply chain. . . . The term 'customer loyalty' has been turned on its head. Today, we're the ones with no choice. We've got to be loyal to customers. The hunter has become the hunted."

Jim Kelly, *chairman and CEO, UPS*

For 17 YEARS IN A ROW, UPS has been named by *Fortune* magazine as the "America's Most Admired Company" in its industry. The same magazine, in 1998, 1999, and 2000, also ranked UPS as the World's Most Admired company in its industry, ahead of such global leaders as Nippon Express, and the Postal Services of the United States, Japan, Britain, Germany, and France.

Do customers also admire UPS? Ask Daimler-Chrysler, who for the last three years in a row has named UPS its "best in class" supplier and the winner of its most prestigious Platinum Pentastar award. This demanding customer evaluates about 8000 of its suppliers annually on such criteria as quality, service, performance, and cost savings. UPS saved it $1.5 million in its international operations in Mexico.

UPS revenues for 1999 were $27.05 billion, up 9.1 percent from the previous year. During the same year, its operating profits rose by 29.1 percent to $3.99 billion. Even its international operations turned profitable in 1998, earning it an operating income of $252 million. To run these operations, it owns and manages a fleet of some 160,000 vehicles, 500 planes, 2400 package sorting centers, and 330,000 employees—in sum a capability to handle 13 million packages a day globally, and to more addresses worldwide than any other company on earth!

This juggernaut was started in 1907 by James E. Casey, as a local message delivery service in Seattle, Washington. The now legendary Jim Casey was then only 19, when he saw an unfulfilled need in the market. At the turn of the twentieth century, few homes had a phone and the U.S. Postal Service would not begin the parcel post service for another decade. All messages and packages had to be delivered by hand, privately. With the help of a few friends, young Jim started the American Messenger Company. He contacted local retail stores and began delivering their packages in his car. Over the next two decades, his fledgling company grew rapidly, expanding its operations to all major West Coast cities and serving its markets by a large fleet of delivery vehicles. Since it now delivered more packages than messages, Jim and his partners changed the name to United Parcel Service. "United" reflected the fact that shipments were consolidated—then a pioneering concept that the merchandise from different shippers addressed to a certain neighborhood be loaded onto one delivery vehicle. And "Service" because, as one of Jim Casey's partners, Charlie Soderstrom, then noted, "Service is all we have to offer." Back then, Jim's slogan was "Best Service and Lowest Rates." Nearly a century later, UPS executives still invoke this slogan whenever they want to pep up the troops. And fulfilling customer needs remains, then as now, the engine of its global growth.

Being Customer Centered

The first requirement for creating customer ValueSpace, as our framework suggests, is for the company to become customer centered, and UPS certainly is focused on the customer. UPS invests heavily in researching its customers, in learning about them, and in helping them understand their own future needs. It conducts two large-scale surveys of its target customers. One of them is to measure its current customers' satisfaction. Called CSI (Customer Satisfaction Index), this survey questions some 14,000 customers every year, across all segments, sampling them throughout the year, and asking them a comprehensive set of more than a hundred questions. The CSI index is computed by segments, by regions, and by managers. The index is also computed for other carriers—most customers use multiple carriers, and they are asked to rate all carriers, without knowing that UPS is the survey sponsor.

How does UPS fare on its CSI? "In CSI, we are at the top, tied with FedEx; then other carriers are far below," says Joe Byrd, who is responsible for the survey analysis and its utilization. What does UPS do with these CSI scores? "The CSI varies by districts and industries, and we then try to tackle each district separately. We tell managers not only that their CSI is in need of improvement, but also what needs to be done; our model tells us that, and then we monitor whether those things were done and whether doing those things helped improve the CS. The important thing is that we relate CS to profitability measures," explains Byrd.

The other tool for understanding the customer is *Dialog*—a survey of all shippers, not just UPS customers. Done by a third party (so the survey respondents are blind as to the identity of the survey sponsor), about 40,000 shippers representing all segments are interviewed every year. Respondents are asked to rate their carrier and answer a few questions pertaining to all carriers. The findings of the survey are reviewed closely by senior management.

How important is customer research at UPS? Explains Frank Slaymaker, UPS's market research chief, "Our decisions at UPS have always been made based on information, but mostly it has been operations information. Now we are also incorporating customer information as basis for decisions. It is 50-50 right now; in the future, we would like it to be 70 (customer information) and 30 (operations information)." The value a company can offer its customers has to depend a lot on constantly measuring customer views of the service they are getting. UPS is measuring customer response to its service with the rigor of a mathematician, applying sophisticated statistical analytic techniques. This rigor and dedication was recently recognized by the American Productivity and Quality Center, who in 1999 named UPS as Best Practices Partners for Customer Value Measurement.

In addition to these two large-scale surveys, UPS is constantly doing more focused projects—focus groups and open-ended interviews. As Bruce Mack, UPS's new products group manager puts it:

> **We are always attempting to figure out customers' future needs. We are constantly asking them questions—playing out possible future scenarios. Like "What happens if we handle your packages this way or that way? Where are you going in the future: What would your growing business's shipping needs be? What kinds of information do you need about the package movement? How important is it to you that the package arrive in the morning rather than in the afternoon?" We are asking these questions in a consulting environment where we are counseling them on their future shipping needs.**

Creating Performance ValueSpace

How does UPS create performance ValueSpace for its customers? By investing considerable resources in making its package moving operations the "best in class." As Grady Hopper, vice president of corporate sales, puts it:

> **In on-time movement of packages, we are SECOND TO NONE. In tracking the package data, we are SECOND TO NONE. We offer quality of service that is first-rate in our industry. And we**

offer scope that is much broader than our competitors. We offer ground and air both, and we offer them in more locations around the globe than do our competitors. Finally, we offer them assurance that we are a long-standing company and that we will be there in the long haul.

Like other companies in our study, UPS too builds its performance ValueSpace through exceptional quality, innovation, and customization.

Quality Obsession

Quality is fundamental to what UPS does. To move a customer's package from point A to point B, by the guaranteed time, and to do so for about 13 million packages everyday, reliably and cost-effectively—that takes an extremely high level of quality operations. One clear indication of its quality in operations is its service guarantees. For many years, UPS has offered day and time definite delivery guarantees on all of its domestic air shipments. In 1998 UPS began to offer guarantees even on its international services to and from the United States. The same year, the company also launched a Guaranteed Ground service, which assures "day-definite" delivery of domestic ground packages shipped business-to-business. This is a first-of-its-kind guarantee.

And to make good on such guarantees, it applies all the quality tools it can. In 1996 all employees received quality strategy training. In 1997, to ensure system-wide precision schedule, it launched an initiative called On-Time Network Management. Under this initiative, every package was to leave a workstation and arrive at the next workstation on schedule. Necessary hub staffing and driver start and finish times were adjusted. Package mis-sorts were closely monitored to identify and prevent problems. One tool UPS uses to assure package delivery accuracy is the capture and use of what it calls "package level detail," basically by scanning the complete information on the package. And it pays great attention to the accuracy of that scan, a goal it terms and prizes as "data integrity." In fact, for all of its service offerings, the company has established higher reliability goals for the coming years.

In 1997 UPS received the *Distribution Magazine's* annual Best of the Best Quest for Quality award, among all carriers in the ground delivery service industry. The award is based on some 3500 subscribers' (mostly shipping managers) ratings of carriers on such criteria as on-time performance, value of service offering, equipment safety, shipment handling, and customer service. In July 1998 the *Air Travel Consumer Report* also ranked UPS Airlines (UPS owns its own fleet of airplanes) first for on-time arrivals within 15 minutes compared to the ten largest passenger airlines in the United States!

Many companies have quality projects. UPS has done it too. But UPS is well past quality projects now. Quality is no longer a project with UPS; rather it is an integral part of operations. It is built into all processes and into everyday operations. This is how Chris Mahoney, senior vice president of operations, explains it:

> **We have benchmarked every process, from vehicle maintenance to billing. We have learned it from the best in class; and we have honed on what we have learned. Now, quality is everyone's responsibility. We have standards, and we measure performance against those standards.**

Likewise, Raj Penkar, president of Professional Services, Inc. (PSI), a UPS subsidiary, says of quality:

> **We are absolutely obsessed with quality; you would find the evidence of it very clearly in our operating buildings, for example; you would not find a single package lying around after the sorting is done. Every package that comes in must be sorted. And we measure it. And we have targets. These targets are linked to performance review and salary reviews for all employees and for all managers.**

Innovation

For UPS, innovation means coming up with new services to meet customer needs. Over the years, UPS has introduced a number of new shipping services and has extended its product line beyond package movement. First, consider the new product introductions in its core business. In 1929 the company was a pioneer in launching the air cargo industry. In 1982 it inaugurated its Next Day Air Service. Over the years, it has added Next Day Air Saver (3 p.m. delivery next day at a lower cost than the morning delivery), UPS Early A.M. (delivery by 8 a.m.), UPS Sonic Air Service ("next-flight-out" service), among others. As already mentioned, its Guaranteed Ground Service, introduced in 1998, was an industry first.

The second component of a customer's package shipping need is his or her need for information about the package. And UPS has pursued major innovation in package tracking service, using state-of-the-art technology. In 1991 UPS was the first company to capture delivery and pickup information electronically. It scans the package every time the package changes hands en route, and these data are instantly transmitted over its highly advanced global satellite system. This package tracking information is available instantly to any UPS customer service agent. While other carriers gather recipient signatures on a paper form, UPS drivers carry a smart board, which captures customer's signatures as an electronic image. Consequently, alone in its industry, it is able to offer a facsimile proof of delivery instantly to customers either over the fax line or on the Internet.

UPS exploits technology to place new performance value in its customers' hands. A vivid example is its alliance with 3Com to harness the latter's Palm VII technology. What does UPS have to do with Palm VII? Palm VII has wireless communications capability for Internet access and other applications. What Palm VII also has is a UPS icon. Click on it, enter the tracking number for the package you shipped via UPS, and out comes information on the package status including the name of the person who received it.

Suppose you are traveling on the road and want to know the nearest UPS service location. Palm VII will tell you the location of the nearest drop-off box, customer counter, or an authorized shipping outlet, and you don't even have to tell it where you are—it actually *knows* where you are, or rather where *it* is. Of course, if you want to know the service centers somewhere else, you will need to type in the zip code.

But even more dramatic is its innovation in the movement of funds. Suppose you ship something COD, you would typically have to wait for your shipping company to send the package recipient's check in the mail, and then for that check to clear in your bank. In an innovative practice, UPS has short-circuited this long cycle—for a fee, the company will deposit funds in your bank account, directly and immediately.

Then there is a plethora of innovation that extends its business beyond the package movement, leveraging the resources and competencies it has acquired in its core business. One of them is its consultancy service, delivered under the aegis of its Professional Services, Inc. (PSI).

Consider the work PSI did for American Airlines. A few years ago, American Airlines was looking for a more cost-effective method for maintaining its ground support vehicles (for example, baggage carts, etc.). They came to UPS for help. UPS not only suggested a new maintenance program, but also provided on-site implementation training for managers and mechanics. The program resulted in reduced cost per vehicle and greater overall vehicle availability for American Airlines. How did UPS acquire the expertise in this area? By mastering its own fleet management program for its more than 150,000 ground vehicles. That experience is now stored in a knowledge bank that contains some 500-plus preventive maintenance and repair methods. It utilizes that knowledge bank as a foundation to design customized maintenance plans for other fleet managers.

Another innovative offspring of its core business is its logistics group, UPS Worldwide Logistics (WWL). WWL is really a company within a company and would warrant, in this book, a chapter of its own. Consider a typical WWL offering. In 1996, OfficeMax, a U.S.-based office supply retailer, expanded its operations to Mexico. UPS's WWL helped the company set up its operations, and took responsibility for running its distribution system. You will see trucks with OfficeMax emblems and you will see drivers wearing OfficeMax uniforms, delivering merchandise from its stores to corporate clients throughout Mexico City. What is not obvious is that those trucks actually belong to WWL and those drivers are actually WWL employees!

The Mexico operation still looks like a package movement operation (except that WWL manages it from start to finish). For a glimpse of its breakthrough innovation in new services, consider its parts management operation for some clients. A case in point is what it does for a wireless company. Here is how John Wilson, WWL's marketing vice president, explains it:

Typically, wireless is programmed not only by the manufacturer but also by the consumer, for example speed dialing. What we

can do for this wireless company is "manage" the outbound unprogrammed wireless set. We would be holding the set for the wireless carrier who is passing the order from its order-entry system to UPS/WWL; here, we can actually program the phone in our warehouse-cum-factory, and activate the service. Now when a customer places an order with the wireless company, we will deliver it within 48 hours, already preprogrammed with a specific set of services. Moreover, if that phone breaks down in the future or if that phone becomes capable of accepting some higher level of services with additional software (and if the user wants to retain the same phone), we have tracking capability in our Returns Management System where we can track that individual phone customer, bring the phone back into our Louisville warehouse, reprogram it, and return it to the same user.

These offspring of the core business are amazing innovations. But they still pertain to the physical movement of goods and documents. This latter business is rapidly transforming in the digital age. As we all know, people now have the capability to send these documents digitally via e-mail. This means we will now be sending fewer documents via carriers; which means reduced business for these carriers. Isn't this a threat to carrier businesses? Hardly. Rather than view it as a threat, UPS has converted it into new business opportunity. Explains Dale Hayes, formerly UPS vice president of marketing and e-commerce, and now its process manager for customer relationship management: "E-mail is a wonderful medium for speedy delivery of digital files. There is only one snag. No one knows who opens the file and when; that is, there is no security. This is where UPS's new Internet courier service comes in."

What this pioneering service (another UPS first) does is to let the user (that is, the shipper) download free software that enables the shipper to input the document. The carrier system then uses 40-bit encryption technology to scramble the document before sending it to the receiver's e-mail address. The recipient must use a password selected by the shipper to open the e-mail file. To customers using this service, the document security this new UPS service offers is a great performance value.

Customization

UPS offers customization in two ways. One avenue is simply to offer a large variety of service options to suit a range of customers' shipping needs. UPS's array of services is long: Its letter and package shipping services include:

- UPS Early A.M.—Delivery by 8 a.m. in major U.S. cities, and by 8:30 in most other domestic and major international cities.
- UPS Next Day Air and Next Day Air Saver—Delivery next day by 10 a.m. or 3 p.m., respectively.
- 2nd Day Air A.M. and 2nd Day Air—Delivery by second day noon or afternoon respectively.
- 3-Day Select—Guaranteed three-day delivery at a price between ground and air express.
- UPS Guaranteed Ground—Commercial ground shipment with a time-definite delivery (most commercial ground shipment services do not guarantee delivery time or delivery day).
- UPS Sonic Air—A 24-hour, 365-days service for same day or next flight out delivery.

Likewise, for international shippers, UPS offers five levels of service: Standard, Expedited, Express, Express-Plus, and Sonic Air. Analogous to domestic services, shippers have the option of choosing from same day or next flight out deliveries to three- to six-day time-definite deliveries.

A second avenue is custom-designing a shipping service specific to a client. Yes, indeed, the company has the capability to put in place a custom designed package movement operation either as a one-time or ongoing operation. Case in point: A few years ago, a music company was launching a new CD record featuring a Beatles' anthology of songs never published before. The company's plan was to introduce the CD on Sunday night network TV and have the CDs in the stores on Monday morning. Secrecy was their top concern—and for fear of a leak, it would not even deliver the product to UPS before that Friday. UPS agreed to take on this special task. The client delivered the packages on Friday evening in armored vehicles. From that point on, UPS assumed control, and "staged" the product movement to meet both security and on-time delivery requirements to music stores all over the country. The special network UPS put together for this music company is testimony to the company's customization capability.

Such capability comes in part from its scope—coverage of both ground and air for time-definite next-day or later delivery, and acquisition of a special air service, called Sonic Air, for same-day service. Consequently, UPS can configure different combinations of air and ground.

John Sutthoff is the president of UPS's Worldwide Logistics Group (WWL). His unit specializes in installing and operating customized logistics on behalf of clients. He knows first hand the importance of offering to customers performance value that is superior to the offerings of competitors and other vendors:

No one competitor can match us on all of our offerings. We offer very broad-based comprehensive logistics services. Some of our major competitors are primarily focused on those logistics services that feed their core network, namely express services. A lot of the services we bring to clients—such as the transportation and warehouse services management of non-package carriers—these are outside the realm of our competitors. Furthermore, we engineer up front; we go in a consulting environment, and design the service. And then, unlike other consultants, we are also at the back-end, implementing the solution we had designed. So this area of design and implementation is our differentiation in offering our customers superior performance value.

Building Price ValueSpace

Shipping is a very price-competitive business. Obviously, UPS offers competitive prices. However, beyond its competitive rate chart, UPS has found a unique way of offering better price value to its customers. This is how it works: Suppose you have to send a package from Boston to Seattle, and you ship it for 2nd-day delivery. UPS can suggest that the package be routed from Boston to Chicago by road and then from Chicago to Seattle by air. This would be less costly than sending the package all the way by air and it would still accommodate the delivery deadline. UPS's competitors—who generally specialize either in ground or air but not both—cannot offer this flexibility. Or competitors who operate both ground and air service (such as the United States Postal Service) have not integrated the two operations as fully as UPS has done. Indeed, such customization is now routinized and automated—the packages are automatically routed for optimal cost-effectiveness. This is what enables UPS to offer a *mass customized* service, from a price value standpoint. UPS's Raj Penkar explains how this offers customers price value:

> **What we have done (sometimes at a risk to our revenues) is that we have told some of our customers that rather than give you another 5 percent discount, let us show you how, by more wisely using ground/air combination for example, you can reduce your total costs. "See, all these packages to these locations you shipped by air, they should have gone by ground because they would have still made the next day delivery." We call it transportation and distribution analysis; and we have developed a software for it. It actually allows us to save our customers considerable money over other carriers who have either air or ground operations but not both.**

Lean Operations

In the shipping business, just to stay competitive, a courier must run its operations efficiently. UPS knows it has to offer a good price value to customers. So its eyes are focused on streamlining costs. Its industrial engineers are constantly analyzing and redesigning its network, processes, operations, vehicle and driver scheduling, and even vehicle design. For example, to design the most optimal cars, UPS brings vehicle manufacturers to its facilities, has them ride with its drivers, and helps them see how UPS drivers would see the road. UPS engineers have also developed vehicle maintenance guidelines that are now available online to technicians and maintenance staff everywhere within UPS. By using a more effective maintenance schedule, the company has improved its average time between breakdowns to 319 car days, from 200 car days five years ago. The total vehicle costs have also declined due to other factors such as better vehicle design, better routing, and a more efficient purchasing program.

In the same vein, process streamlining and process redesign are important avenues of cost reduction at UPS. As Mike Eskew, executive vice president, explains:

Every company begins with simple operations limited in scope. Then when the scope of business expands, new activities are added on to the current ones. UPS was no exception. When new services such as 8 a.m. delivery were launched, the required processes were simply tacked on to the existing processes and schedules. Recently, however, UPS engineers took a fresh look at these processes, asking questions like "suppose we could redesign the entire operation from scratch? Or suppose, in launching the 8 a.m. service, we didn't have to be bothered with the existing UPS infrastructure?" So we reengineered the process for this service. Such reengineering is resulting in great operating efficiencies.

Automation of operations is yet another avenue of making operations lean. The package checking and sorting is now fully automated. When you ship a package, for example, your address label is automatically checked for address accuracy—soon it will use the Zip+4 system for even higher accuracy. The package is then automatically sorted out as to the best routing and is automatically loaded onto the appropriate trucks. That is, the system decides, based on destination and desired delivery time, what route and transportation mode it should be assigned to. At the destination, the system knows automatically which car to load it on and also in what sequence to load it on the car. That way the early delivery packages would get delivered first. All this automation reduces errors as well as costs.

Then there is the automation of the customer operations—that is, getting customers to service their own package shipping and tracking needs. The company has given its customers software for installation on their PCs or mainframes. Customers who do not have a PC or mainframe computer are offered an enhanced telephone. Currently, about 50 percent of its customers (by shipping volume) use this automated shipping option. Customers can also track packages in self-service environments either through an automated menu on the phone or on the company's Web site. According to Ken Lacy, the company's chief information officer, the estimated savings would be more than $50 million a year if all of its customers were to make its tracking requests electronically. The company is already realizing a substantial part of such savings.

"Of course, customer automation lowers UPS's costs," explains Dudley Land, the vice president of customer automation, "but what is noteworthy is that it also lowers customers' own costs of shipping. Using the automated shipping equipment, customers can print shipping labels, they can track package information, and they can print the proof of delivery, which then helps them collect on accounts receivable."

Yet another innovative means UPS has adopted for cost minimization is effective *asset utilization*. As you can imagine, UPS does not have to fly as many planes over the weekend. So what it does is to convert those planes into passenger planes and lease them over to a charter service. Chris Mahoney, senior vice president of operations, explains, "Every Thursday, on some of our planes, the cargo bins come out and the passenger seats go in. The planes are reconfigured and equipped with all the amenities. And the passengers love it, because our planes (when reconfigured) are more roomy, more comfortable, and more pleasing than the passenger-carrying airplanes of commercial airlines." Moreover, this asset utilization is not limited to planes. Airport equipment is rented to passenger carriers not only over the weekends, but even over the weekdays, for part of the day—after all UPS does not need them until after the early hours of the night, by which time the passenger airlines have loaded and unloaded their last flights!

Building Personalization ValueSpace

Most of the shipping customers have to interface with UPS couriers frequently, some almost daily. The quality of this interface constitutes the customer's personalization ValueSpace. To excel in this ValueSpace, UPS uses all three processes of our framework—easy access, rapid response, and relational nurture.

Customers can access its services by phone or the Internet, or by visiting one of its service locations. It has a widespread network of some 1000 customer service counters located across the country where it can accept all ground, air, and international shipments. Also, for air packages exclusively, it runs about 50 air service centers, located in high traffic areas such as airports, shopping centers, and office complexes. Then there are 48,000 dropboxes and 91,000 independently owned shipping service centers such as Mail Boxes, Etc. In addition, UPS routinely picks up packages and documents every day at every business location that does business with UPS on a regular basis. Finally, it picks up packages "on-demand." And the number you call is easy to remember—it is 1-800-Pick-UPS! Lastly, of course, a customer can reach its customer service by phone 24 hours a day, 7 days a week.

As already mentioned, customers can ship and track packages using their PCs (with a software from UPS) or the smart telephone. Customers can also do business with UPS using the Internet. It has a very extensive home page on the World Wide Web. By logging on to it, customers can obtain information about UPS services and its service center locations, calculate shipping costs, order supplies, and track packages. Today, UPS Web site tracking is available in 16 foreign languages!

Rapid Response and Relational Nurture

UPS also is cognizant of the value of rapid problem resolution and of building a positive relationship with customers. When a customer makes a claim (say, for a late delivery or a damaged package), the UPS service representative has authority to credit the customer account right away, with the final settlement contingent upon the outcome of the investigation. On a day-to-day basis, the builders of the relationship with the customer are its drivers. UPS is finicky about driver appearance and behavior, with detailed corporate guidelines. UPS drivers are pleasant and courteous, and they take the time to greet the customer and exchange pleasantries. Since the same driver visits the business customer and meets the same person repeatedly (either the mail room staff or the front office staff), there develops between them a friendship of sorts. Besides, all business accounts are assigned an account executive who maintains regular contact with customers.

While UPS provides good personalization value across the board, its superior personalization value really comes full steam for a select class of customers it calls *preferred customers*. Designated on the basis of account profitability, about 10 percent of its customers qualify. In addition to the account executive, a preferred customer associate (PCA) is assigned to each account. The relationship begins with a letter that informs the customer of his or her newly acquired preferred status and its benefits. Then a PCA makes an introductory call and, later, a personal visit. The PCA is accessible by phone and voice mail anytime, and is equipped to answer all customer questions about UPS services. He or she also assists the customer with filing and processing claims, resolving billing inquiries, making adjustments on the spot, and handling unusual tracking requests.

UPS realizes that regular communication is necessary to nurture a relationship. So the company sends its preferred customers a quarterly newsletter. Called *Preferred Report*—it keeps these customers informed about new products and services. From time-to-time, preferred customers receive special promotions, sometimes even fun prizes—a recent promotion featured a prize drawing for a trip to the Superbowl. Other activities of the "feel good" variety include occasional gifts—one recent item: a 1-oz. bar of luxury chocolate, custom packaged, delivered two days before Valentine's Day! Needless to say, preferred customers not only get superior performance value, they also find UPS "nice to do business with."

UPS is now taking its relationship with customers to new heights—it is partnering with them for mutual advantage. This is how Grady Hopper explains "partnering with customers":

> We are a very dynamic business. We now have a vast portfolio of products and services. And one of the things we are moving toward is consultative selling, that is partnership—they [the customers] have to open up their books as much to us as we to them. So that we may begin to develop solutions for their future needs.

> A good example of partnering is how UPS has established a reciprocal relationship with Kodak. Kodak has entrusted to UPS all of its transportation and distribution function. UPS offers to Kodak its expertise and core competencies in the shipping business. We are no longer a commodity for them; but a value-added resource. In turn, UPS has sought to benefit from Kodak's expertise in imaging solutions—the company is moving toward being able to capture shipping data in digital image, and it needs Kodak's help on that front.

ValueSpace Expanders

ValueSpace expanders, in our framework, push the boundaries of the three major customer ValueSpaces—performance, price, and personalization. UPS offers its customers a number of value-added services. For example, under its authorized return service (ARS), package recipients can return merchandise to the original shipper without any paperwork. Likewise, under its delivery confirmation service (DCS), customers are sent a proof of delivery (POD) with the recipient's signature (reproduced with electronic imaging technology) along with the weekly bill; or they can retrieve it via electronic data interchange (EDI). One money-saving, value-added service is UPS Hundredweight, wherein customers who ship multiple packages on the same day to the same address can receive up to 50 percent cost savings. Yet another value-added service is consignee billing (CB); with this service, customers who receive large volumes of packages from multiple senders with inbound shipping costs charged to themselves receive a weekly consolidated billing statement, customized to allow the customer to gain greater control over total costs.

Even more value-added services are available to preferred customers. For example, preferred customers can get a complimentary proof of delivery (POD) on their PCs or via fax. They can also receive a phone confirmation of the UPS Early A.M. Delivery. Damage or loss claims are settled quickly (usually within 24 hours) and funds are transferred electronically. Preferred customers also receive a number of discounts, such as an automatic 20 percent discount on Sonic Air and discounted (up to 50 percent) or free seminars of interest to shippers and management. One of the most important benefits is its management reports, which summarize by categories all the shipping activity during the preceding quarter or year. These reports are available free of charge and are useful to customers in forecasting and streamlining future shipping activity.

Perhaps the most innovative ValueSpace expander is its funds flow process innovation. As previously explained, tied to the movement of packages is the movement of funds. UPS's shipping customers receive money for the goods sold from their customers after the goods have been received. By promptly providing its shipping customers with proofs of delivery (POD), it enables those customers to collect its accounts receivable that much sooner.

"Do It My Way"

Beyond the eight ValueSpace components of our framework, and above all else, what is needed for creating customer ValueSpace is top management commitment to the customer. Are the senior managers at UPS committed to delivering customer value? None other than the company's CEO is a champion of customer value. In a speech delivered to the Economic Club of Detroit on January 19, 1999, Jim Kelly, chairman and CEO of UPS, titled his speech "You'll Do It My Way: The Consumer As Old Blue Eyes." That title reflects Kelly's—and UPS's—conviction that the Internet revolution gives customers the power to find the supplier who will offer customers what they want, whenever and wherever. Kelly believes that customers sitting at keyboards at their homes are already turning the conventional retailing model upside down. Rather than being pushed upon by the seller and the supplier, customers are "pulling" the products or services they want through the supply chain. Kelly puts it bluntly: "The term 'customer loyalty' has been turned on its head. Today, we're the ones with no choice. We've got to be loyal to customers. The hunter has become the hunted!"

Fossil: Crafting Customer ValueSpace in Niche Markets

IF YOU ARE 17 TO 24 YEARS YOUNG (or better still, if you are young at heart), you no doubt are familiar with the brand name FOSSIL. Fossil is a brand name as well as the name of the company behind that brand. With headquarters in Richardson, Texas, it makes, you guessed right, a line of watches sold in better department stores. Or does it?

The fact is that Fossil does not view itself as a watch company at all. Rather it views itself as a design company and a marketing company and a distribution company whose principal product at the time happens to be watches, but it could just as well make any related products that would benefit from its design resources. In fact, currently, it already applies its design resources to make and market other accessories, including sunglasses, small leather goods, belts, and handbags. Its latest line extension—Fossil brand of casual apparel!

Just what are its design resources? The answer to that question is at the heart of how this brilliantly innovative company creates ValueSpace for its customers. Here is how Fossil does it.[1]

Performance ValueSpace

Watches tell time. But we wear them for more than that—especially the "typical young at heart" types who buy and wear FOSSIL. We wear them as fashion accessories, and as shapers of our moods and reflections of our lifestyle. Performance ValueSpace for such a product then consists of more than its functional performance, that is, its ability to keep time; it includes also the product's symbolic meanings—the psychological benefits the customer seeks in the consumption and use of a brand. Fossil is cognizant of this and indeed creates a unique Performance ValueSpace both on the functional and symbolic factors. And it does so using the same three components of our framework: quality, innovation, and customization.

Quality

Its customers—the "young at heart" types—love its watches.

They are solid performance watches—well-constructed, reliable, good looking. Although their principal distinction and appeal lie elsewhere (described later), Fossil makes sure their quality is flawless—both on the inside and out. As to the inside, it obtains its components from certified and high quality suppliers. Rather than manufacture its own movement—the core mechanism that keeps the watch running—Fossil procures it from outside, and it procures the same precision movement that goes into Citizen and Seiko watches—watches many times more expensive than Fossil. These components are assembled in its Hong Kong factory in a high-quality production environment. How sure is it of its quality? Most watch manufacturers give a 5-year warranty; some give 10 years. Fossils come with an 11-year warranty. Now 11 years is not considerably longer than 10 years, but Fossil goes for 11 just to make a point!

How good is its performance record against this warranty? Its repair shop, located at its headquarters in Richardson, has a meager staff of about 50; and it sells 10 million watches a year! Some rough calculation would show that it spends less than a quarter a watch on repairs or on honoring its warranty.

Design Distinction

The 11-year warranty on materials and craftsmanship that go inside the watch is a nice edge over other comparable watches, but Fossil's real distinction comes from its edge on the *outside*—the aesthetics and the brand personality. In aesthetics, Fossil seeks to be neither pure classic nor ultra trendy, but in the comfortable middle. That is how it differentiates itself from its direct competitors—the trendy Swatch and Guess—the two brands that most directly target the same young consumer. This middle *positioning* is also what extends the brand's appeal beyond the 17- to 24-year-old core market. While the ultra-trendy (and occasionally faddish) Swatch and Guess designs appeal mainly to youth, Fossil draws considerable audience from the age brackets that flank (on both ends) the core group, and this is just what Fossil wants.

Innovation: Rampant Creativity

Imagine you are in a mall. Let us walk up to a storefront. The one we have in mind has an intriguing display in one of its windows. There are beakers of different sizes (the kind you would find in a chemistry lab), half-filled with liquids of various colors. Amidst them are a few mock models of a particular body part. Perhaps this is a medical supplies store. It could well have been, judging from the paraphernalia. In actuality, however, it is a section of Fossil watches display for one of its recent innovative watches—called Fossil *Brain* (yes, the mock body part is a cutout section of a human brain)! The "brain" comes equipped with dual time, chrono/stopwatch, a six-setting timer, 7 alarms, 5 schedule memos with a 30-message capacity, and a digital display. This is but one innovation among many.

Within the moderate spot (between the classic and the trendy), the consumer has a choice of a wide assortment of watch faces—the Fossil *Arkitekt* (with stainless steel cases and bracelets), *Titanium* (which is stronger and lighter than steel), *Chronograph* (with three dials and stopwatch movement), and the *Blue*—the underwater sports watch.

Its innovative design team spews new styles like forest fire. Visit its design studio—its "skunkworks"—a crisscross of cubicles and meeting rooms generously *littered* with multimedia artifacts that serve as office decor as well as design-concept props. There, maverick artists in diverse ensembles ranging from cargo pants and platform shoes to more sedate officewear mingle freely (the company has a liberal dress code that prohibits only shorts and T-shirts—everything else is fair game). Some are in deep contemplation over the fresh pencil sketches they drew only minutes ago; others are focused on recontouring the lines of the digital image of a watch casing on their new neon-blue iMacs; still others are playing with a collection of antiques, trying to receive divine vision for some new design. There is abundant vibrant energy, even some chaos perhaps. But all chaos and all maverick energy is directed toward one single goal—design innovation that its consumers will love.

Five times a year the company introduces new styles. At any given time, about half of its styles were introduced within the preceding one year. Of course, some of the watches are "evergreen" (for example, its FOSSIL BLUE line of watches), forever popular; but even here, there will be some rejuvenation from time to time. And don't expect the company to shirk opportunities for *small* innovations five times a year; it also introduces new print designs on *the tins* as well. Ah, "the tin"—that is a product paraphernalia with a charm of its own. But more about it a bit later.

To keep their creative juices flowing, two or three times a year its army of designers descends on Europe. There, in small groups, they visit the malls, the stores, the art galleries; they scan through hundreds of magazines, take thousands of pictures, buy tons of sample objects, and head back home. Back at the Richardson headquarters, in the design "war rooms," they lay these images and objects on the central conference table, and start brainstorming—and putting ideas to physical shapes. Some will prepare a collage depicting a particular theme. In one such war room that we visited, there were three collages hanging on the wall, inspiring three new designs in the works. "How do these multimedia collages help you design the watch?" we asked the head of one of the design groups and our guide through the studio. His explanation: "Well, we would try to capture these looks in our watches. From these dresses (pointing to a photo from a fashion magazine), for example, we might want to capture the pastel colors. And from these objects here, we might replicate the contours in the casing."

Emotional Bonding: Raising Performance ValueSpace to a Higher Plane

While Fossil produces watches of solid quality, the watch in and of itself is *not* the principal source of value to its core customers. Sure enough, were the watch of inferior quality, it would be hard to find a customer. But what really draws the consumer to Fossil is the brand's unique personality—it is an identity that is reminiscent of the Fifties. To cultivate this personality, the company has taken the images, visuals, and artifacts from that era and surrounded the brand with them. These images are everywhere—in the architectural style of its headquarters building, in the artwork that decorates its offices, on the in-store displays, in point-of-sale materials, on company stationery. The company executives scout antique shops, flea markets, garage sales, old magazines, and the like for ideas and for actual objects.

Perhaps the most offbeat incarnation of this image is in its packaging. Fondly and simply called "the tin," it is a tin box with imprints of the images of the 1950s—about a hundred designs at any time. The customer chooses a watch and then he or she chooses a tin (which is given free of charge). The company executives believe that choosing the tin after one has bought the watch adds immensely to the buying experience. Once home, it sits on the consumer's desk, dresser, bookshelf, or whatever, reminding the user of the brand's unique identity.

Just what is Fossil's brand identity? To capture and describe this identity, Fossil uses a set of words: Authentic, Classic, 1950s Americana, Innovative, Aspirational, Emotional, Sense of Humor, Surprise, Quality/Value, and Casual. On a product-positioning map, it places itself right in the middle of the classic and the trendy; in reality, its success owes to making the classic trendy. What the company has done is taken 1950s images and made them trendy and fashionable.

As to the other adjectives in its brand-associations, spend a short time in its office and you would find them alive everywhere and in most people. Everyone, including senior executives, dresses casual; they have a very unassuming attitude about them. "Surprise" and "a sense of humor"—yes, you will find these too. The day one of us visited the company, Fossil's vice president of marketing was making a PowerPoint presentation to a group of merchandise buyers from Bon Marche. About halfway through, suddenly a slide of a cat pops up on the screen. "This is Shadow, my cat," he says nonchalantly. At the end of the presentation, just when he is finished, he asks, "Now who can tell me the name of my cat?" Later he would confide in us and say, "We don't mind acting a little goofy around here!"

Of course this element of surprise, this sense of humor is also stamped on some of the merchandise itself. One of the watch styles is called *Big Tic*. *Big Tic* features a digital display of seconds—the two digits are big enough to cover the whole dial face, and are crooked and curved—sort of a little goofy, but also fun. And its line of *BLUE* watches come not only in blue but also in green and gunmetal and gold and silver and champagne! A little goofy yes, but nice goofy!

Let us return to a key phrase we used to capture its brand identity— "images reminiscent of the 1950s." "Reminiscent" is actually a wrong word. Its core audience (17 to 24 years old) was not around in the 1950s; therefore, it doesn't remind them of anything. What then do these images mean to them? "What appeals to the 17 to 24 youth," explain Fossil executives:

> is that the images are unique and so different. They look like they are from—not just a different era—but a different planet; the art-work looks surreal—depicting people that are happy, people with a little goofy smile. There is a certain casual attitude about life in these characters and in these artifacts. And it has just caught on the fascination of young people. It has become an aspirational brand. The target consumer thinks that if they buy this watch they belong to a certain group of people; that they are part of some surreal culture; that they are living a certain experience.

Now that adds a whole new layer of performance ValueSpace for the consumer. And Fossil has created that ValueSpace partly by serendipity, partly by rampant creativity.

Customization

Although Fossil does not customize individual watches, its customization takes the form of leveraging its design and production resources to new and diversified lines of merchandise. To begin with, under its flagship brand name, Fossil, it brings out a range of design variations. But it also has designed the watches under the Eddie Bauer, Disney, and Emporio Armani labels. The last one is a high fashion, upscale brand. That Emporio Armani would choose Fossil to manage its namesake (Fossil manages the entire operation from design to production to sales and distribution) is a tribute to Fossil's design creativity as well as to its quality production capability. Lately it has even extended its design talent to other fashion accessories, such as ladies' purses and apparel. Although this sort of customization offers value to a different group of customers, the ability to customize to such vastly different brand concepts as Eddie Bauer and Emporio Armani speaks highly of the company's knack for creating new performance ValueSpace.

While the end users are the final customers, in a sense, companies like Eddie Bauer and Disney are also Fossil customers. What customer ValueSpace does Fossil build for them? Fossil put its design creativity to work and captured the Disney spirit in the watch. Or as Fossil would like to put it, "it took the Disney images and put Fossil spirit in them." Fossil spirit in Disney images—now that is a powerful testimony both for the design resources and customization skills of Fossil. The Disney watch line would appeal to someone who, like the customer of Fossil's own watches, likes the somewhat offbeat, goofy style *and* is, at the same time, a fan of Disney's other merchandise. That is a rare value combination, a rare ValueSpace, that Fossil brings to this group of consumers.

Price ValueSpace

After reading the above tale of its quality, innovation, and distinct brand identity, one would think the watch would be priced to exploit its unique appeal to the consumer. Here too, Fossil embodies a paradox— it really avoids lofty prices! Its prices are low not only because it wants to make the watch very affordable for its core customers (17 to 24 years old), but also because its business model (discussed later) demands that its pricing objective be to gain high volume rather than high margin. The trick to its profitability is to find the "sweet spot" price that gives it the volume it needs for high efficiency and which, at the same time, its customers would love. Here is how it does it.

Target Costing

At Fossil, all design work on new styles begins with a certain product concept broadly specified. One unmistakable element in that concept specification is *price point*. That price point guides both the style design and manufacturing. Product leaders would approve or disapprove design elements within the price point parameters. Then in sourcing components, price points would play a prominent role. "We do not, however, talk price until later in our discussions with our suppliers," says Fossil's production planning manager. "We first discuss the design and performance and quality that our design assumes, and then jointly explore how the targeted price points can be achieved." The company has partnership relationships with its major suppliers of components, sharing each other's cost information, so the value-exploration, in terms of the "desired performance within the targeted price points" becomes a genuine, joint pursuit of value.

Lean Operations

The other leg of its price value capability is lean operations. We have already spoken of its extremely efficient inventory management using analytical models. But cost efficiencies are pursued in all operations across the organization. It owns three watch assembly plants, where it makes all of its mainstream watch lines, which account for most of the production, and all three of these are in Hong Kong, where labor costs are low. The rest are styles in experimental market trials, and it subcontracts these to other assembly shops, which can do such small runs more efficiently. It manages its entire world inventory from a warehouse in Dallas, Texas, near its headquarters, where it holds merchandise in duty-free zones, packed at the factories in packages easy to unbundle and ready to ship in small lot sizes to retailers worldwide.

Fossil's business model deliberately eschews charging "lofty prices." One of its distinctive competencies (other than design) is its skill in efficient management of inventory throughout the distribution channel. The company has built analytical models to predict inventory movement levels, and it has become so good at managing inventory that it makes good profit only on those lines that are large enough and that sell fast enough to allow its inventory models to play themselves out. Therefore it wants to price the watches where the product will move consistently fast. It tries to find a "sweet spot" in the middle. The "sweet spot" price helps inventory management. The sweet spot price gives enough volume to exploit the company's expertise at inventory management; efficient inventory management reduces costs, and that, in turn facilitates or enables the lower sweet spot price.

The company pursues lean operations in other places, in fact, in every activity. The artistic design work is done in Richardson, and manufacturing engineering is done in Hong Kong, closer to the three assembly factories it owns. The design and engineering drawings are exchanged between the two offices digitally over the Web, making for instant, even interactive, and cost-free coordination. All designs are archived on CD-ROMs and are available to all designers throughout the company, enabling them to leverage old designs toward new improvisations or line extensions. Images on paper or real objects are now photographed using advanced digital cameras, saving on photo development costs as well as time. Advertising and POP materials are designed in-house; executives scour for artifacts in flea markets, finding potential treasures for pennies. There are high tech computers and the latest in printing equipment, but the working spaces, conference rooms, and executive offices are spartan and functional. All executives travel coach class and stay in middle-priced hotels. "We take pride here in being 'cheap'—meaning, frugal," says one senior management executive.

Price Value for Retailers

Fossil sells through retail stores—both department stores and some trendy Generation-Y stores like Gadzooks. These stores are its direct customers. The company makes sure it offers good value to these direct customers—so they may in turn offer good personalization value to consumers.

The value retailers seek most is good profit margins on a product with good performance. Fossil's scientific inventory management at the retail level is a source of higher margin for retailers because their inventory costs are significantly reduced. Fossil acts almost like a partner in managing a retailer's inventory. The average watch inventory turnover in department stores is 4 percent—that is, 4 percent of the inventory moves every week; Fossil make its inventory move 5 percent—that is, the retailer has to carry only 20 weeks' inventory (instead of the usual 25 weeks). And the company aims to make 65 percent of the watch lines move at this speed. The other 35 percent are newer styles, not yet established. Recall that five times a year, the company introduces new styles. Fossil claims, that by its initial margin and by enabling lower inventory costs, its watches are one of the most profitable product lines for its department store merchants.

Personalization ValueSpace

Fossil has attended to the need for personalization for both sets of its customers—retailers and distributors who buy its watches to resell, and consumers. Let us first consider retailers and distributors, Fossil's direct customers. Fossil builds personalization ValueSpace for its retail customers, that is department stores, using all three components in our framework: easy access, rapid response, and relational nurture.

Easy Access

For starters, all of its retail customers are linked to the company by an electronic data interchange (EDI) system, and of course, retailers can call customer service anytime, toll-free. And Fossil's account executives are stationed in regions and visit retailers regularly and they provide in-store merchandising help to improve point-of-sale presentation.

Rapid Response

Rapid response is Fossil's forte, based on its inventory management skills. Fossil has 65 percent of its SKUs that turn 5 percent every week on what it calls a quick response (QR) system. How quick is QR? "Our account executives will go into the store, will set up the models for QR items, and specify minimum and maximum models," explains a senior manager. "Then, on Saturday night, say, the EDI system will kick-in the order into our system; on Sunday we would get the order; and on Monday and Tuesday, we will ship the order."

Relational Nurture

Finally, Fossil nurtures its relationship with its distributors by close partnerships. Five times a year, the company meets its buyers in New York. The buyers coming to these "markets" (for example, Merchandise Mart) are always excited about Fossil—knowing that they will get to see new styles—and that Fossil will always have something to chuckle about. To one such trade show, Fossil brought "Fossilized" teddy bears as souvenirs. In 1996 it had created a character, Fred Fossil, who was running in the presidential campaign! Buyers coming to these shows have fun, not only because they have new styles to look at, and new merchandising props to chuckle about, but also because Fossil simply treats them with personal, individualized attention.

Beyond the five-times-a-year reunion with central buyers, the company establishes partnering relationships at the store level. Indeed this relationship is one of coaching and mentoring the stores' in-house merchandisers. Most of the Fossil managers who deal with stores come with a retailing background. With such background comes true empathy— the ability to put oneself in the retailers' shoes, a quality much appreciated by retailers. "We get deeply into our customers' business," says the marketing vice president:

> We design fixtures for them, we do packaging, we set up their showcases and we furnish them with our unique point-of-sale display merchandise, we do warranty work for them, we do planning for them, we set up the economic order quantity inventory models and we set up EDI systems. We use our expertise on selling watches, we give their salespersons a point-of-view about our watches and about how to present them to the customer, and we sometimes even hire our own salesclerks and place them in the stores. In effect, we offer them a "wraparound" service. We really wrap ourselves around retailers' operations!

Personalization ValueSpace for Consumers

Similarly, the company builds personalization ValueSpace for its end-user consumers via all three components: easy access, rapid response, and relational nurture.

Easy Access

Consumers can find Fossil watches in all major department stores. And fashionable malls in major cities have Fossil's own dedicated company-owned store. Consumers can also access its Web site, where they can browse product information, locate a store, build a self-profile to store an address and other information in the company's database, and of course order merchandise online. They can also read instructions on how to operate the watch—simply click on the icon of the specific watch and up pops a screen with directions on setting various watch features, for example.

Rapid Response

When you visit a company-owned store, the store employees approach you and greet you as soon as they are available—which is "right away" on a normal day, but maybe 10 to 15 minutes later on a typical weekend. However, if they are attending to some other customers, they will send you a smile as soon as your glance meets theirs. And no one really minds waiting, for there is so much to browse in the store. Once when they get to you, they will attend to you 100 percent for as long as you need them.

You can return a watch for instant refund or exchange, and if a watch needs warranty work, you can simply return the watch to any retailer, who will instantly replace the watch and send the original watch to the company for repairs.

Relational Nurture

For a consumer product, the relationship is mostly psychological—how consumers feel toward the company and toward the brand. The watch on your wrist and the fondness you feel toward it keep you in that psychological relationship with the brand. And remember the tin? That adds further salience to your feelings. Consumers who are fans of the brand also enjoy visiting the company-owned stores and browsing the point-of-purchase materials and the new watch styles, vicariously consuming the imagery. And the store employees embody the lifestyles of its buyers, young and casually trendy (and occasionally, even funky). Fossil's youthful consumers like chatting with them, and viewing themselves as being part of the Fossil culture.

Finally, the company is building a Web-based affinity group—fans of the Fossil brand who want to become connected to the company communications and with each other in chat groups, information exchanges, and so on. This is relational nurture as best as it can get!

Customer Focus

Our hope was to be able to report for Fossil that the company monitors the consumer pulse closely and frequently; that it does a lot of consumer research—by consumer focus groups and surveys, for example. But that would be out of character for this rampantly innovative company. Oh, it is focused on the customer all right; only, the way it keeps an eye on the customer is, true to its character, also unique.

Recall that its first layer of customers is actually the retailers and central buyers. It meets those buyers five times a year at the accessories market in New York. To these markets, it takes everything—new watch styles, new package designs, proposed point-of-purchase materials, half-baked prototypes, sketches, materials, and so on. And it observes buyer reactions. And back at the drawing board, it tries to benefit from ideas its customers have shared. Occasionally, it invites major retail customers, such as Gadzooks, to its headquarters to react to projects under development.

As to its end users (consumers), it tries to understand their tastes through surrogate consumers and surrogate indicators. As we mentioned earlier, its designers—many of the same attitude if not the same age group as its target customers—scout the trends and cultures around the globe three times a year. They read everything that is going on in the broader culture. And they have an eye for what they think might appeal to its consumers. Furthermore, the company doesn't have to *follow* its target customers' unarticulated tastes; sometimes it might *lead* the consumer into new trends. Leading rather than following is itself, conceivably, a source of value to its target consumers, many of whom aspire "to belong."

The ultimate consumer pulse is of course when the products are actually placed in the market. The company has a keen eye for detecting, very quickly, which new items are moving at the desired, conventional, Fossil levels, and which ones are not. And it is able, then, to quickly rearrange its production cycles and schedules to keep only the fast moving items. That is, the product styles that the consumer liked and bought. And who can argue with that?

ValueSpace Building Processes

How can businesses create customer value? What actions would you as a business organization need to undertake to propel your journey into the customer ValueSpace? What resources would you need to command each of the three ValueSpaces—the 3P's of customer ValueSpace? What business processes must you put in place to accomplish each of the eight ValueSpace components? How would you, in other words, implement ValueSpace? We address this question in this chapter.

First, there are certain overarching processes that constitute the essential foundation for all customer values and for all ValueSpace components. One of them is already part of our framework—*customer centeredness*. To this, we add two more: top management commitment and sound strategic vision.

Foundational Processes for Customer ValueSpace

If you want to create superior ValueSpace for the customer, if you want to rule that space, then you must adopt *that* as your organization's principal mission. You should make that as the organization's be all, end all; its raison d'etre. Making money will follow. Shareholder value will follow. But building customer ValueSpace must be first and foremost as the organization's purpose.

Table 11.1   Foundational processes for customer ValueSpace.

a. Customer centeredness as a way of organizational life
b. Top management commitment to ValueSpace building
c. Sound strategic vision that aligns resources with target markets

This cannot happen without top management commitment. And the senior management must be committed not only to the customer and to the mission of creating customer ValueSpace, but also to the eight ValueSpace components discussed in this book. They must also have a widely shared understanding of the specific organizational processes required to implement the eight value drivers. They must believe, in other words, in the *instrumentality* of the implementation processes we outline in this chapter.

Our ValueSpace framework also requires the existence of a sound strategic vision. It assumes that the organization has successfully addressed various strategic questions: Who is our customer? What markets will the company serve? What technologies will it embrace? What alliances will it build? What will be the geographical scope of its operations? Our framework is not a substitute for an organization's need to "seeing the future first," as management scholars Gary Hammel and C. K. Prahalad put it.[1] Rather, our framework presupposes that the choice of markets and target customers has been aligned with the company's resources and competencies. In assessing that alignment, our ValueSpace framework can play a pivotal role—the alignment is right only if the company has the competencies and resources to deliver the best combination of performance, price, and personalization Value-Spaces to its target customers.

Once these overarching prerequisites are in place, each component of our ValueSpace requires a set of specific organizational processes, which we will describe.

Building Performance ValueSpace

Performance ValueSpace comprises three components: quality, innovation, and customization. Each in turn requires certain implementation processes, as described in Table 11.2.

Table 11.2 Building performance ValueSpace.

Driving Quality

a. Defining quality in customer terms

b. Establishing process and outcome standards

c. Measuring everything

d. Deploying technology for quality

e. Implementing "Continuous Process Improvement"

f. Investing in human resources

g. Rewarding and compensating desired behaviors

Driving Innovation

a. Innovation culture

b. Encouraging and rewarding *intrepreneuring*

c. Research and application fusion

d. A strong futuristic orientation

Driving Customization

a. Deep customer knowledge

b. Mass customization production processes

c. Broad skills base and cross-training of staff

d. Infinite variety

Driving Quality

Quality in products and services is implemented by these processes: defining quality in customer terms; establishing standards for business processes and outcomes; measuring everything; deploying technology for quality improvement; implementing continuous process improvement; investing in human resources; and rewarding and compensating desired behaviors.

An organization's quality obsession must be guided by how customers define quality. If keeping delivery vehicles spic and span (rather than merely adequately clean) does not add to the perceptions of quality by customers, as UPS realized, then it need not burn money on it. When Caterpillar wanted to reduce paint defects on its tractors, it asked customers what was paint quality to them; based on their responses, CAT identified three areas of the tractor surface—high visibility, low visibility, and "ground engagement"—that needed different degrees of paint perfection.

Once quality is defined in customer terms, detailed performance standards must be established. In the tractor paint quality improvement project cited above, CAT defined the standards in the high visibility areas as "100 percent coverage, 2 mils dry film thickness, no runs/sags, no dirt, no dry spray, and uniform gloss." Hilton Hotels Corporation has extensive brand standards, which it monitors rigorously through a mystery guest program. Companies focused on quality must closely monitor compliance with brand standards, and measure every performance component. American Express's merchant customer service center in Phoenix, Arizona, measures every call detail—response time, call duration, calls dropped, customer problem resolution, customer satisfaction with the call, and so on. An external behavior measurement agency measures, sampling at random, even the mannerism of its telephone representatives and provides instant feedback!

Quality is built into products and services by deploying the most current production technology and wherever possible by deploying technology to substitute for the more error-prone manual processes. UPS has implemented, for example, technically sophisticated label designs that eliminate address misreads and an automated zip code sorting procedure so that a wrong package will simply not get loaded on the wrong delivery truck. PPG ensures high quality in its phosgene derivatives by adopting good manufacturing practices. And Caterpillar has accomplished a near-zero-systematic-defects level under its 16X initiative by an all-fronts attack comprising design, procurement, and manufacturing operations. It is also improving product quality in use by building in automatic diagnosis and performance-signaling technology. Furthermore, quality obsessed companies don't sit on their laurels once a specific high level of quality is achieved. Rather, for them it is a continuous journey. At Xerox Business Services, on-site associates are charged with improving operational processes every day.

Deployment of technology, continuous process improvement, constant measurement, and so on, are very important for quality; the single most important element, however, is the quality of human resources. Our sample companies all invest heavily in their employees. They hire through a rigorous screening process, and then subject the new hires to extensive training programs. At XBS, for example, all of its 22,000 employees have received TQM training. Hilton has invested heavily to bring cutting-edge technology to its training—a CD-ROM based module is designed to allow individual property managers to customize its contents by dovetailing its individual elements into the universal core supplied by the corporate headquarters. And Rosenbluth International's training program is so exceptional that the company is on constant lookout for competitors who may be pirating it.

Finally, competent and well-trained employees need a reward structure to feed their contribution to quality. At American Express, everyone's compensation is tied to customer satisfaction ratings; and every time its call center supervisor (who is monitoring individual call quality on a real-time basis) spots an exceptionally good execution of a customer call, a red wagon *immediately* pulls up at the desk of the customer service rep and delivers a gift and cheers from coworkers!

Driving Innovation

What does it take for an organization to innovate performance value in its products and services? You can find more than a dozen books on the subject of innovation in organizations. Our list is short and simple. We believe it takes at least four elements: innovation culture; encouraging and rewarding *intrepreneuring;* research and application fusion; and a strong futuristic orientation.

Organizations that spew a constant bevy of innovative products and services have a culture of innovation where employee creativity is nurtured and encouraged by empowerment and by commitment of resources. At 3M, known to be a leader in product innovation, for example, employees are allowed freedom to deploy some of their time and allocated resources to unspecified projects of personal whim! At XBS, on-site associates are free to do whatever it takes to become a customer "amazer." And individual innovators—that is, *intrepreneurs*—are recognized and rewarded for their creativity. At CAT, the three workers who came up with innovations in painting the tractor were nominated to *represent the corporation* in a national award where other award recipient companies were represented by their presidents and CEOs! Such are the rewards—ego building recognition rather than just material giveaways—on which intrepreneurs thrive.

Bringing innovation from the lab to the market requires an infrastructure for rapid commercialization. This takes two elements: First, more and more of the R&D work is done close to the market, with research scientists working in close contact with customers. Much of the developmental work is actually done with specific customer applications in mind. This is the prevailing 3M mode, of which the bonding system's work to replace rivets in bus bodies with VHB tape, as described in Chapter 4, is an example. Second, there are production and technical resources to support prototype and commercial model development. 3M has process innovation technology centers that help researchers scale up an idea from the lab bench to production. Engineering systems technical centers help technicians develop and scale up key manufacturing process technologies (for example, coating and inspection processes) for a specific innovation, to ensure successful transition to commercial manufacturing. Such is the sort of research and application fusion that is required for innovation as a source of customer ValueSpace.

Finally, innovation-centered companies have a strong futuristic orientation—they have a keen eye for emerging trends in technology as well as customer tastes. XBS, for example, saw the coming revolution in digital documentation, and redefined its business from mere management of outsourced corporate printing centers to helping companies manage their knowledge in the digital world. Rosenbluth International views its business as not merely facilitating corporate travel but indeed as *business interaction management.* It is exploring, consequently, technology that might enable interaction between two businesspersons without necessarily traveling!

Driving Customization

Finally, how can businesses implement customization as a component of performance value? We believe it takes four things: deep customer knowledge; mass customization production processes; broad skills base and cross-training of staff; and infinite variety.

First and foremost, to be able to customize products to customers' needs, companies need a deep knowledge of its diverse customers. 3M develops customer-specific bonding applications by closely collaborating with customers. UPS's World Wide Logistics group spends considerable time studying customer operations before bidding on a job that entails customized logistics. Rosenbluth International interviews employees as well as corporate travel managers in a prospective client organization to understand end users' needs; this knowledge then becomes the principal basis for it to custom-configure a travel service operation for the client. American Express has, uniquely in its industry, a merchant transaction database that it utilizes to develop marketing support customized to each merchant. XBS has organized itself around major industry segments such as health, finance and banking, publishing, manufacturing, education, and public agencies. Such organization allows a cluster of employees to develop intimate knowledge of specific industries and develop capabilities to serve that industry in a more customized way.

Customization also requires mass customization production processes. Scholars such as Joseph Pine have described various methods of mass customization. We group them into four: modular production, flexible manufacturing, assembly at the point of purchase, and digitized customer database. Modular production entails design innovation so that various components, produced independently, can be configured to custom-fit specific customer requirements. Dell is a prime example, drawing on separate modules to configure a computer only after a customer order is received. Similarly, Rosenbluth International custom configures various travel service sites according to clients' needs, drawing upon its different modules of service delivery—centralized call centers, on-site office, dedicated reservation centers, or a combination of these. And Caterpillar's engine assembly, drive train, undercarriage, and special attachments are produced as separate modules and then assembled per distributor or end-user demand.

Flexible manufacturing entails production systems that can be switched on and off efficiently from one setup to another, corresponding to multiple product requirements. 3M's focused factories exemplify this; depending on varying customer demand across product lines, individual focused factories can be switched on or off. Pushing final production closer to the customer order either in time, or in the channel is another method. For example, window blind factories will manufacture standard size blinds in a central factory for inventory and then cut them to custom-size upon receiving customer orders; or the retailer would install special equipment to cut them to custom size. In the computer industry, value-added retailers (VARs) combine modular production and postponed assembly methods. UPS's World Wide Logistics group helps its clients customize their products by completing the last step of production upon receiving the order (for example, it stores wireless phones at its various warehouses, ready to ship, but it does not preprogram them until customer requirements are known).

Flexible manufacturing enables mass customization of physical products. For services, the corresponding resource is digitized customer-database and cross-trained employees. In order to serve a customer in an individualized manner, what a service company needs most is a customer database that stores customer preferences and retrieves them at the time of service. John Peppers and Martha Rogers' *One-to-One Future* is essentially a relationship marketing approach based on computerized customer databases.[2] Customization based on digitized data has the inherent efficiency of mass-customization; it costs virtually nothing to pull data specific to a customer. A hotel, for example, could unobtrusively observe and record its guest's preferences during the guest's stay; on subsequent guest visits, it could retrieve that information and arrange service to meet those preferences. Among our companies, Hilton Hotel is setting up such a database to automatically arrange for its frequent guests such amenities as a hypoallergenic pillow if the guest had requested it during an earlier visit.

At American Express, customization is based on data-based marketing using customer data from individual merchant's trade areas. 3M's new Web site is mass-customizing its information—making it specific to particular customer categories, such as carpenters or office workers.

In order to customize effectively, service companies need broadly skilled employees. Thus, cross-training of employees can be a good customization strategy. A hair salon can customize a person's hair styling to his or her taste if the stylist is trained and skilled in a broad range of styles. Chefs skilled in diverse cuisine can customize their offerings to special dietary needs of individual guests. XBS trains every associate in every operation, for example, and this improves its ability to move associates from one site to another to match individual client's specific task needs.

Finally, producing near infinite variety is another means of customization. Although it doesn't actually customize a product to individual customers, it does enable a better match by offering a much broader product range. Lee jeans has utilized this approach in offering jeans in 27 sizes, for example! Among our sampled companies, UPS approaches customization by offering a long slate of services, from Early A.M. Delivery to 4-Day Ground. And Fossil offers a wide range of watches—all of which still share a common brand personality. But for Fossil what really adds great customer value is the customization-enabling variety in its large collection of tins—the combination allows each customer to identify his or her personality in the Fossil product *and* its packaging.

Building Price ValueSpace

Price ValueSpace has two components, fair price and value price. Corresponding to these are two organizational processes, namely, target costing (which primarily addresses fair pricing) and lean production (which primarily addresses value pricing). While there is some overlap between the two, each in turn has a set of individual implementation processes.

Table 11.3   Building price ValueSpace.

Driving Fair Price
a. Designing for target costs
b. Better sourcing and "outsourcing"
c. Supplier partnering

Driving Value Price
a. Low-cost production sites
b. Asset utilization management
c. Just-in-time manufacturing
d. Process reengineering
e. Automation and technology deployment
f. Mass customization

Driving Fair Price

Target costing to achieve a fair price can be implemented through the following processes: designing for target costs; better sourcing (including outsourced production); and supplier partnering.

Once a firm has determined what target cost will enable it to offer the product or service at a fair price, it has to produce it within that cost. To do this, it must design it so that the parts and components and production and assembly processes required to produce it are within target costs. Design for target costing will entail a judicious use of available materials, technology, and product engineering. In addition, better sourcing of required parts and components could keep costs within targets. Furthermore, portions of the production job could be outsourced to low-cost contract manufacturers, including off-shore locations. Partnering with suppliers can also aid achieving target costs: suppliers can help at the design stage by suggesting cost-saving components and applications such as 3M is trying with its customers; they can also pursue long term cost-improvement goals since the longevity of the customer patronage is assured.

Among our sample companies, Caterpillar employs all three enabling processes for target costing: It designs new components and machinery within certain price targets, sources materials wisely in partnership arrangements with many suppliers, and outsources production of cast iron castings to other foundries. For some foundries, it even sources raw iron and steel, using its buying power to get price advantages. XBS, Rosenbluth, and World Wide Logistics Division of UPS target-cost their services by designing service configurations for individual client's cost goals. On behalf of clients, Rosenbluth also negotiates favorable rates with airlines and hotels (that is, suppliers). Hilton Hotels, in launching its new product line, Garden Inns, worked within the target costs that would deliver a fair price identified through extensive customer research.

Driving Value Price

Moving beyond merely fair price to value price requires a set of processes we collectively call *lean operations*. (Recall that under "operations" we subsume both factory and office/managerial processes.) Lean operations are achieved by a number of avenues, the principal ones being: low-cost production sites; asset utilization management; just-in-time manufacturing; process reengineering; automation and deployment of technology; and mass customization.

Locating production facilities in low-cost locations (that is, where costs of real estate, labor, utilities, and taxes are low) or shifting production to low-cost sites is the first step in lean production. Fossil achieves low cost by assembling its watches in Hong Kong—since watches are a low volume item, shipping costs are not a major barrier. And locating its call centers in low-cost sites in North Dakota is a major enabler of value price for Rosenbluth International.

Another avenue is asset utilization management. It includes both preventive maintenance of equipment and leasing spare capacity. UPS does both: By better maintenance, it has increased the uptime for its delivery vans (now a car breaks down, on an average, every 319 days instead of every 200 days a few years ago). And it leases its airplanes over the weekend to commercial charter services.

Lean operations also result from just-in-time manufacturing and, related to it, efficient inventory management. The cornerstone of cost containment for Fossil is its expertise in managing its inventory turnover both in its assembly plants and in retail stores.

Process reengineering is another tool to streamline factory and office processes. American Express has reduced more than $1 billion over the past decade by streamlining all processes. UPS has reengineered its process of handling C.O.D. payments; instead of sending the actual check (received from the C.O.D. package recipient) to the shipper, it now directly deposits it in the shipper's account, which not only saves UPS check-mailing costs, but UPS even earns a fee for offering this service. Moreover, the C.O.D. shipper also receives his or her money sooner, thus improving his or her cash flow. And at SYSCO, modifying the ways that workers record their activities helps warehouse employees to allocate their time wisely, thus improving their productivity.

Automation and technology deployment is perhaps the most potent and lately most utilized tool for achieving lean production. XBS is using automation tools for its salesforce to reduce its selling costs. It is also reorganizing its selling organization for better cost efficiency; for example, its call centers will identify prospects and prequalify leads to improve the productivity of its salesforce. For AutoNation, integration of its brick-and-mortar stores with e-commerce gives it a much needed shot in the arm in the otherwise thin margin industry of new car dealerships. And SYSCO streamlines its warehouse and delivery operations through such simple technologies as a shrink-wrapping machine for its pallets and software (*Roadnet*) that charts optimal routes for each delivery truck.

Indeed, technology and automation even serves process reengineering. For example, enterprise resource planning (ERP) systems link all departments for sharing process information, thus reducing or eliminating manual transfer of information across transactions handled in different departments. At SYSCO, for example, when sales receives an order, separate paper copies need not go to production, shipping, and accounting where they will have to be manually keyed in. The information is simultaneously available to everyone, and job progress can be tracked on any connected PC. UPS's C.O.D. innovation actually uses this sort of technology. UPS also offers self-shipping software to customers. Likewise, Rosenbluth's suite of self-booking tools, and its computer network that enables every reservations agent to access a customer record are examples of automation. American Express has achieved significant economies in its operations by making transaction information available to merchants online. The remarkable thing about such deployment of technology is that while it saves on the cost of operations, it also enhances performance and personalization ValueSpaces for customers.

Finally, mass customization, which we described earlier as an enabler of better performance value through customization, also is a means of leaner production. That is the case, for example, with 3M's focused factories—small one-product, one-process dedicated factories can be switched on and off on demand, avoiding the costs of between-run clean up and set up of the more generic factory.

Building Personalization ValueSpace

Personalization ValueSpace has three components: easy access, rapid response, and relational nurture. Here is how to build each.

Table 11.4   Building personalization ValueSpace.

Driving Easy Access

a. Locational ubiquity

b. 24-7 hours of operation

c. Multiple channel access

d. Near zero-wait access

Driving Rapid Response

a. Frontline information systems

b. Well-trained and empowered customer contact
    personnel

c. CS measurement with teeth

d. Flexible resources

Driving Relational Nurture

a. Customer retention as business model

b. Digitized customer database capability

c. An ethic of nonopportunistic behavior

d. Social bonding

Driving Easy Access

Easy access entails locational ubiquity; 24-7 hours of operation; multiple channel access—mail, phone, voice, fax, e-mail, and automated and self-service channels (ATMs, Web sites); near zero-wait access. Most of our Most Admired companies have adopted these diverse enablers of easy access. You can access Rosenbluth, Hilton, SYSCO, American Express, or XBS anytime, via phone, e-mail, or Web sites. And their phone lines are not busy, their voicemail menu not annoying (most offer the option to "press zero to speak to a customer service rep immediately"), and their Web sites are state-of-the-art, award winners for customer friendliness. PPG customers can call its plant directly without going through customer service to order or check on product availability. UPS enables its customers to access package tracking information via phone, e-mail, or Web site. And at American Express Establishment

Services Division and at Rosenbluth, among others, when customers call, they are answered within three rings.

Driving Rapid Response

Rapid Response requires frontline information systems; well-trained and empowered customer contact personnel; CS measurement with teeth; and flexible resources. Frontline information systems allow customer service personnel to quickly access information about customers and about service capacity and resources necessary to construct a proper and prompt response to customer problems. When an American Express merchant calls, for example, the customer record is already on the computer screen of the service representative. At Rosenbluth, all service associates can access all customer data from any office in the world. At AutoNation, its in-house software (COMPAS) automatically delivers to its salespersons a pager alert whenever there is an e-mail referral or a direct inquiry from its own Web site from a prospective customer.

Information systems merely provide the necessary data; to act on them and to construct a rapid and effective response based on that information requires employees who are both well-trained and empowered. XBS exemplifies both. Its site associates were recently trained in document machine repair so they can now fix machine failures almost immediately. Likewise, there can be no better illustration of empowerment than the fact that XBS site associates can do—are charged with doing—whatever they need to, in order to be a customer "amazer." At SYSCO, its salesforce has full authority—and we mean *full* authority—to decide the sale price (save that their total earnings are intimately linked to the profits they make for the company). At AutoNation, the company has determined that the single dominant driver of inquiry-to-close-ratio for its e-commerce is the speed of its response; so it took its most seasoned salespersons, made them internet sales specialists (dedicated to Web-based customers), and then gave them further intensive training.

All of our sampled companies employ extensive customer satisfaction (CS) measurements. And these measures have teeth—at these companies, employee as well as executive compensation significantly depends on CS ratings. At American Express, for example, as much as 25 percent of the bonus for everyone, president down to the service rep is tied to CS ratings! At Hilton, guest surveys are used to plot the customer-perceived quality of hotel attributes; and individual property managers are required to improve on attributes that customers rated poorly and which they also rated as being important to them. At Rosenbluth International, quality experts from corporate headquarters visit operations sites to coach associates on deficiencies identified in CS surveys.

Another helpful capability for rapid response is flexible resources that can be deployed or moved around from one application to another or from one client site to another. Examples of flexible capability include access to a temporary pool of employees, cross-trained employees, and production lines that can be quickly switched from one application to another without undue set-up and retooling costs. In cases of emergencies, XBS on-site teams can call upon their fellow XBS associates from neighboring sites. For more systemic problems that require major restructuring of operations to respond to client concerns, XBS has what it in fact calls "rapid response teams"—teams of process design experts at headquarters who will fly to a customer site and analyze and redesign the entire process to solve a problem. For CAT customers (dealers and end users), rapid response means availability of parts and a repair technician, and CAT has linked all of its parts warehouses and dealer inventories on its intranet. About 96 percent of all parts are shipped within 48 hours. And repair technicians show up, based on built-in remote diagnosis technology, even before the customer notices the problem. PPG customers can call the factory direct (that is, rather than wait for customer service to be open) for a crunch order in the middle of the night, and the plant will ship the order ASAP without even first notifying sales or customer service. At 3M's roofing granules division, if a customer believes he got a wrong or flawed shipment, a lab technician will fly out by the next flight. And at SYSCO, marketing associates will personally pick up and deliver a foodservice customer's emergency order—or the order the customer forgot to place at the time of scheduled delivery!

Driving Relational Nurture

The last component in the personalization ValueSpace is relational nurture, and it requires customer retention as business model; digitized customer database capability; an ethic of nonopportunistic behavior; and social bonding.

First, companies should explicitly recognize the benefits of long term customer loyalty and make customer retention the goal of their strategy. XBS does it most explicitly. In fact, its business model is "retain and grow": Retain current customers, and grow revenues from them by satisfying them so well that they expand the scope and volume of what they buy from you. Hilton is also focused on retaining its frequent guests by offering them a frequent guest reward program (called HHonors) unparalleled in the industry—only with HHonors can you exchange rewards between the airlines and the hotel. UPS has a preferred customer program wherein it offers a slate of special and exclusive services of great value to these customers. At AutoNation, they don't make much money selling a new car; their hope is to earn their corporate "living" from keeping you as a customer over the entire ownership of the car. And then the next car.

The second requirement of relational nurture is a digitized customer database. If you visit your car mechanic and if he writes the service request anew every time, including the type of car and your address—obviously he does not maintain the history of the car. How can he then provide a relational service? On the other hand, Lexus cars have a built-in chip to record the car's performance history so that any mechanic anywhere across the United States can read that chip and provide a relational service—service based on "knowing the car as an individual car." Likewise, information about customer preferences stored in a digital medium helps businesses maintain a relational interface with customers. At the very least it allows customer service reps to offer customized service. More importantly, it allows analysis of individual customers' evolving needs and preferences, and meets them with some continuity, such as a financial services planning consultant monitoring his or her individual clients' changing needs. Among our Most Admired companies, most have such a database, but more importantly companies like American Express and UPS use them to analyze and understand what products and services would be of value to their customers in the future. And SYSCO marketing associates can pull up on their laptops a customer's purchase history for the last four weeks, which helps the customer understand his or her restaurant's consumption pattern.

The third requirement of relational nurture is that businesses not be opportunistic, taking advantage of circumstances that disfavor the customer. For example, in times of shortage, to raise the price or to drop specific customers in favor of others or to divert scheduled delivery of products to higher paying customers or to otherwise take advantage of customers' ignorance or inattention would amount to opportunistic behavior. In the growing academic body of knowledge on relationship marketing and relational selling, trust between the customer and the supplier has been found to be the most important factor, and a key determinant of trust is the absence of opportunistic behavior. When a company discards opportunistic behavior as a means of growing its profits, it begins to search for opportunities of mutual gain. PPG's specialty chemicals division holds periodic business planning meetings with customers to project and plan for future needs as well as to identify opportunities for joint cost-savings. UPS does the same—it will analyze, for specific clients, last years' shipping practices to identify and advise on better shipping practices that would save the client money without sacrificing delivery deadlines.

Finally, what is needed for relational nurture is social bonding. As any savvy salesperson knows (and any person who deals with a client is a salesperson, from a CEO down to an account assistant), all other things being equal, interpersonal relationships matter. They will not substitute for poor performance in products, or unfair price, or lack of rapid response, but once these value-components are in place, customers like to deal with those they find pleasant, respectful, and friendly. University of Nebraska marketing professors Linda Price and Eric Arnould have studied commercial relations in consumer service markets and have found that many consumers tell personal stories to their hair stylists, behavioral therapists, personal physicians, interior design advisors, and stockbrokers—stories that they may not even tell their close friends. These service providers have earned the trust of their customers; consequently, they have earned lifelong patronage of their customers. What companies need to do to establish social bonding are two things: first, frequent contacts and frequent communications by a designated account rep as well other senior executives; and second, a personable attitude and personal warmth on the part of this person and indeed on the part of everyone who comes in contact with the customer.

UPS has dedicated account managers for its preferred clients. American Express does the same for its large merchants. 3M is reorganizing its salesforce so that there is now a single point of contact—while sales reps from different divisions with product specific expertise would still continue to visit customers, they would be coordinated by that single point of contact. PPG and Caterpillar have account reps who keep close contact with customers. SYSCO's marketing associates visit each customer at least once every week; and SYSCO executives ride with sales reps or delivery drivers and call on individual customers at least once a year, and they know them one-to-one. Rosenbluth has a general manager for each site in addition to account associates who meet with clients regularly. And XBS takes this concept to a new height: A senior executive, called a Focus Executive, builds a link with his or her counterpart in the client organization.

As to personable attitude and personal warmth, customer-centered companies make it their second nature. Executives at our sampled companies speak of their personal relations with clients wistfully. XBS's "customer amazer" associates and Focus Executives boast of this attitude. CAT dealers cherish it as do 3M's roofing granule customers. American Express customer service reps are always personable—call and find out. Finally experience the "be nice" credo by the travel service associates (TSA's) at Rosenbluth. Their goal is nothing short of bringing happiness to the caller. When you deal with these companies, all of them in our sample, what you will find is that to do business with them is indeed a *pleasure*.

Such social bonding, to borrow a tag-line from MasterCard, *is priceless!* For the customer and the supplier alike!

12

Customer Value, Value Discipline, and the Pursuit of Excellence

Our book is a blueprint for becoming a market leader. But it is not alone. Indeed, some insightful business bestsellers have all provided admirable blueprints. Six are particularly noteworthy: *In Search of Excellence* (Thomas J. Peters and Robert H. Waterman, Harper & Row, 1982), *Built to Last* (James C. Collins and Jerry I. Porras, Harper Business, 1994), *The Discipline of the Market Leaders* (Michael Treacy and Fred Wiersema, Addison-Wesley, 1995), *Competitive Strategy* (Michael Porter, Free Press, 1982), *Competing for the Future* (Gary Hammel and C. K. Prahalad, Harvard Business School Press, 1994), and *The Innovator's Dilemma* (Clayton M. Christensen, Harvard Business School Press, 1998). Our book invites a close comparison with these, especially the first three.

In Search of Excellence (Peters and Waterman) and *Built to Last* (Collins and Porras) identify traits of excellent and visionary companies. Both are now classics and a sheer joy to read, to say nothing of the insight and practical lessons for managers that each offers. A number of organizational attributes suggested by these authors are absolutely essential to building the ValueSpace we describe in the present book; some of these attributes are included in our discussion of ValueSpace implementation (Chapter 11).

One of the attributes Peters and Waterman suggest is "being close to the customer." We call this "customer centeredness" and deem it the foundation for ValueSpace. Three more attributes suggested by them are being "value driven," possessing "autonomy and entrepreneurship," and achieving "productivity through people." These too ought to be, in our view, a prerequisite and foundation for all excellent and visionary companies, certainly for those striving to excel in building customer ValueSpace. These attributes are value-driver processes rather than value-components—which is the focus of our book. Consider "being value-driven." Excellent companies harbor and promote a number of core values (for example, "respect for the individual," "honesty," "open communication," etc.) and use them to guide their everyday behavior. Among our sample companies, we saw the strongest and most articulated example of being value-driven at Caterpillar. "Autonomy and entrepreneurship" is recognized in our framework as a driver process for innovation, a ValueSpace component. And "productivity" (through people as well as through machines and technology) in our framework is the driver for lean operations, which is a driver for the value price component of ValueSpace.

Two other attributes Peters and Waterman suggest are to "stick close to the knitting," and to have "a bias for action." We consider these too as desirable qualities for a company striving to create customer ValueSpace. "Sticking to one's knitting" is a matter of strategic choice, and we view a strategic vision (that is, what marketspace to compete in) as a prerequisite to adopting our ValueSpace framework. And by "a bias for action," Peters and Waterman really refer to a rapid implementation of ideas, frequent experimentation, always trying out new things, and always searching for better methods, better products, better everything. We agree, of course, that companies should have a predisposition to act; however, that action should not be haphazard; it should not be action for action's sake; it should not be action void of thought. Our ValueSpace framework can serve to channel that bias for action: *Every action must add to customer ValueSpace.*

Collins and Porras actually express a reservation concerning "being close to the customer." They argue that organizations should not succumb to giving what customers want if that does not sit well with its core values (for example, Hewlett Packard not giving customers cheap IBM-compatible computers). A stronger reservation is actually made by Christensen who in *The Innovator's Dilemma* shows convincingly that being too close to the customer will keep companies from exploring really innovative products that might be of little perceived value by current customer's current perspectives. Our take here is that it is certainly true that exploiting breakthrough technologies might require a research and development cell (or "skunkworks," if you will) driven by a far-reaching vision of the technology rather than current customers' current needs; however, once the technology and its applications are developed, to successfully deliver them to customers in a form customers would find of value would certainly require close customer orientation.

Collins and Porras researched a set of truly exceptional companies vis-a-vis their lesser-performing leading competitors, and through years of meticulous analysis, identified "the timeless management principles" that set the two groups of companies apart. They report their findings in their 1994 book, *Built to Last*, in which they describe "nine successful habits of visionary companies." Of these, three are, we believe, overarching enduring values of universal application for any organization: "clock building, not time telling" (that is, investing in the organization), "more than profits" (having some higher mission than just making money), and "cultlike culture" (where there is an obsession with certain style, certain organizational mission, and certain core processes). The attribute of "more than profits" might include such lofty a mission as "developing a cure for human suffering," for example; however "customer ValueSpace" can serve, in our opinion, as a nexus around which any cultlike zeal should be nursed.

Another insight from Collins and Porras is that visionary companies have "big hairy audacious goals" (BHAG). Such goals excite and propel the organization fast forward. However, what kinds of goals? How do we know if those goals are the correct ones to follow? Our answer: Ask the question, "Do they enhance one or more of the customer ValueSpaces of our framework?" Thus our customer Value-Space framework can give BHAGs their desired *anchors*. Two other attributes—"try a lot of stuff and keep what works" and "good enough is never enough"—are a call for "continuous improvement." Who can deny the utility of continuous improvement? Indeed, our framework calls for continuous pushing of the boundaries to invent new frontiers of customer ValueSpace.

In sum then, both these works admirably highlight the attributes of excellent companies. To these, we would add one more: Excellent companies have a clear perspective on what constitutes customer ValueSpace and they are constantly driven by that goal. The attributes these authors credit excellent and visionary companies with—those attributes are the bedrock on which any viable organization should be built. Such an organization can, based on this solid foundation, pursue other processes of customer ValueSpace building, as outlined in this book.

The Discipline of Market Leaders (Treacy and Wiersema) comes closest to resembling our framework. That resemblance is superficial, however. In reality, *The Discipline* addresses a question different from ours. In *The Discipline*, Treacy and Wiersema argue that a company must adopt one of the three business strategies: operational excellence, product leadership, or customer intimacy. Operationally excellent companies offer customers lowest total costs, which they make possible by running their operations with utmost efficiency. Product leadership companies offer their customers the most innovative products, usually at premium prices. Finally, customer intimate companies engage in close personal relationships with customers, devising for them a customized total solution. On the face of it, the three strategies would correspond respectively with offering customers great price value (lowest total cost/operational excellence), performance value (product leadership), and personalization value (customer intimacy). Treacy and Wiersema argue, convincingly, that a company cannot be everything to everybody; that it must choose among these three value disciplines. We, on the other hand, advance a case for a simultaneous pursuit of all three ValueSpaces: performance, price, and personalization. How come?

Very simply, Treacy and Wiersema's operational excellence implies nothing about performance and personalization values. That is, a company could do well on operational excellence, but it could still be poor on performance value or poor on personalization value. Similarly, a product leadership company could be delivering poor personalization and price values. And finally, customer intimacy does not mean predominant focus on personalization value, nor does it mean absence of performance or price values. Indeed, the primary goal of pursuing a strategy of customer intimacy would be performance value (by generating customized solutions) rather than personalization value. We argue that there is no one-to-one correspondence between the three disciplines and our 3P's of ValueSpace, and that no matter which one of Treacy and Wiersema's three strategies a firm uses, it can and must attend to all three customer values of our framework.

Consider operational excellence first. What operational excellence really means is that the customer is offered a standardized product or service of high quality, produced with a standardized and highly efficient process on a large scale. Mastery of operations is the key competence of operationally excellent companies; however, such competence would have no market value unless it is applied to a product or service of attractive performance value and it is built around a delivery mode that entails good personalization for customers. Treacy and Wiersema cite McDonald's and AT&T Universal Card Services as exemplary "operationally excellent" companies. We argue that they both offer all 3P's of our ValueSpace. McDonald's offers a quality menu in clean, comfortable restaurants delivered with courteous service. It researches and expands new menu items constantly (performance ValueSpace in our framework); it adds new locations to make it more convenient for customers (easy access in our framework). It has brand standards that are rigorously maintained (quality component of performance ValueSpace in our framework). Every detail of the production process, every step in the delivery process is standardized and scripted—even the sequence in which the order will be arranged on the tray, and the exact words that cashiers will use to greet customers. In effect then, McDonald's offers customers good performance value (quality menu items), good personalization value (convenient locations and courteous employees), and good price value (reasonable prices and a value menu). But don't expect daily or weekly menu innovations there (product leadership) or individualized or customized menu (customer intimacy). You will find McDonald's offering a high quality fast food, at good prices, delivered with a good service, and you will find this every time you go there, with remarkable consistency.

Treacy and Wiersema's showcase example of operational excellence companies is AT&T Universal Card Services. And operationally excellent it is. But no one could deny the performance value the company offers. In fact, the very premise of the start-up company was a product innovation—a credit card and a calling card combined into one! And it was a pioneer in adding such features as purchase protection and rental car coverage. And its customer service? That is legendary. The company has courteous, well-trained, and empowered service reps who resolve most problems on the spot (that is, rapid response in our framework). And of course it offers great price value—it was a pioneer in "no annual fee" pricing. So this operationally excellent company offers excellent performance value, excellent personalization value, and excellent price value, all at once.

Both McDonald's and AT&T Universal Card Services are exemplary executioners of organizational and production processes that produce a combination of particular product, price, and personalization levels delivered with near-zero variance. This near-zero variance is the core of operational excellence. That core is powerful, however, only when it is deployed with a certain configuration of performance, price, and personalization values attractive to the market. Operational excellence then is these companies' operating model, not their ValueSpace position.

Now consider product leadership as a value discipline; Treacy and Wiersema use Intel as their showcase. Intel is a leader in technology innovation—it invests heavily in R&D, and when it brings out a new chip, its engineers are already working on the next chip that will soon make the current chip obsolete! But that is work being done inside the R&D labs. Outside of the labs, those units of the company that would be responsible for commercializing the next generation chip are already working on figuring out what would be a good price value to the customer for the new chip and how that price can be enabled during the design and manufacturing process. And the company has built an organization that interfaces with its customers in a high personalization mode—responding to customer needs during application development and making it easy for customers to do business with it.

Finally, consider customer intimacy and Airborne—the company Treacy and Wiersema use to showcase their third value discipline. Airborne custom configures specific logistics solutions for individual clients. By definition, those solutions are not off-the-shelf, and their custom configuration entails knowing the customer real close. But the kind of solution the customer wants is the one that not only meets the customer's special task needs (for example, deliveries by 8 a.m. or accept pickup as late as 9 p.m.), but that it also has to be economically sound and that it also has to be hassle-free for the customer to work with. The customized solution must in fact combine, therefore, all 3P's of the ValueSpace in our framework. Once the customized solution is designed and put in place, it is then run with the same clockwork efficiency that marks the operationally excellent companies. Airborne thus is a combination of customer intimate and operationally excellent companies. This becomes possible for Airborne because the scale of operations for a single client for whom it custom configures a total solution is large enough to run the operation in a standardized, efficient way. Of course, Airborne does it for its large business clients. It could not afford to follow the customer intimacy discipline for its consumer markets, where it therefore runs the operational excellence model. And to both groups of customers—consumers and large business clients, it offers, or at least strives to offer, all 3P's of ValueSpace—performance, price, and personalization. So does the rival UPS, a company we showcase. They have to, they all do, if they want to survive, sustain, and grow in their competitive marketplace.

The crux of Treacy and Wiersema's blueprint, then, is not a trade-off between performance, price, or personalization ValueSpaces; rather it is in the choice of a marketspace. Large size current markets seeking established products require companies with operational excellence; significant potential markets seeking innovative products demand "product leadership" companies; and individual, high volume customers seeking customized total solutions require firms practicing the "customer intimacy" operating model. A similar triad (low cost, focus, and differentiation) is suggested by Michael Porter in his historic *Competitive Strategy*. This is a strategic choice companies must make; but by itself such a choice is not telling enough. In each of these three cases, each company, whether it be an operationally excellent company, or a product leadership company, or a customer intimate company, it must build all three ValueSpaces of our framework.

Thus, our work overarches the three strategies. No matter which of the three marketspaces (and the corresponding business models) one chooses, the next task is to plan for and build ValueSpace for the customer. Our framework is a blueprint for planning and for process implementation. It is a guide to a comprehensive reckoning of the values customers are seeking. It reminds managers that there are three values customers seek, and that organizations must consider creating and delivering in this *entire* ValueSpace.

13

A Roadmap for Action

I F YOU ARE THE CEO of a moderately successful company, and if you have read this far, you could be saying to yourself: "But we are already doing it all!" Either this, or its exact opposite: "Nobody can do it all!" However, these thoughts most likely were early reactions, if they occurred to you at all. What you really intend to say is, "Okay, tell me how my organization can proceed?"

Two Myths

We will take up that challenge momentarily. But first to those early thoughts. We need to exorcise them; we need to put them to rest, once and for all. True market leaders recognize that both thoughts are misplaced. Both are self-serving myths. Consider the second myth first.

"Nobody Can Do It All"

For years, a familiar refrain among many market followers in business has been that no business can offer customers all three values; that customers have to sacrifice quality or service to get a lower price; or sacrifice price value for performance and/or service. This management perspective is ill informed. Or at least ill phrased.

When ill informed, it leads managers to give up quality or service and embrace a "we will not be undersold" low-price strategy. Or the reverse: "We don't compete on price." Our research shows that in fact, everyone does!

This myth surfaces in other forms: "We compete on quality." Or that "we want to be known for excellent customer service." We hear these claims of strategy in everyday comments from many a manager. To our pleasant surprise, then, no one in our sample companies—not one manager, not one CEO—professed these views. To the contrary, their guiding precept was that they had to do the very best they could on each of the 3P's of customer ValueSpace. Any assumed trade-off among the three value components is a false choice. It is a nonstarter.

In part, the misguided precepts arise because, as managers, we sometimes tend to make comparisons among offerings across different market segments; comparisons that are more or less misguided. We get misguided by the fact that there is Chevrolet, and then there is Cadillac. And the two make a trade-off, between price and quality and service. There is Kmart and there is Macy's and then there is Nordstrom. Surely, we might say, Kmart competes on price; Macy's on merchandise; Nordstrom on personalization. No one can compete on all three; no one can offer all three values. Or so we could argue. But what we forget is that Kmart isn't competing with Macy's and Macy's isn't competing with Nordstrom. Kmart is competing with the likes of Wal-Mart and Target. And Macy's is competing with the likes of Dillard's and Rich's. And Nordstrom with the likes of Neiman Marcus. In cars, Chevrolet is competing with a Camry and Cadillac with Lexus. For some consumers, a Camry beats a Chevy hands down in all three ValueSpaces: performance, price, and personalization. For others, a Chevy beats a Camry. Whether they buy a Chevy or a Camry, and likewise whether they buy a Lexus or a Cadillac, they buy the car they buy because they all believe that they are getting the best overall value combination from these cars.

If we went to Kmart and found a very limited selection of merchandise or we found that it carried brands of shoddy performance, we would not buy from there no matter how favorable the price was. And if we had difficulty finding in-store help or the lines were too long, we would leave in frustration. And if we found out, over time, that its prices are often higher than competitors, we will, just as likely, take our patronage elsewhere.

Now what happens if we were shopping at Nordstrom. The amazing thing is that we would, again, be appraising the performance, price, and personalization value we are getting there. All three of them. Only one or two of them would not do. We would be applying the same calculus at Nordstrom!

The fact is that the value criteria remain the same; as customers, we continue to use the same three values for assessment. What changes is the reference point for assessing the three values. The trade-off is not between performance, price, and personalization value. The trade-off is between one combination of performance, price, and personalization and another combination within a narrow range of ValueSpace. It is between the performance, price, and personalization value combinations offered by Nordstrom and Neiman Marcus; or by Kmart and Target. Within the same market segment, in other words. The race is among near equals. And "near equals" compete on all 3P's of ValueSpace. If as a business, we differ sharply on price, or performance, or personalization, we are running a different race. Is there any fan, any spectator for that race? And we should start benchmarking our competitors in *that* race, not in any other race, and from the vantage point of that spectator, that fan who has come to watch *our* particular race.

There should be no mistaking that as a business we must and can offer all three values. Our Most Admired companies do it. Take Rosenbluth International. If it made one wrong ticket, if the reservation it made violated a single client corporate policy, if it did not select the best flight schedule possible, if it forgot a single minor customization request from a traveler, then it would lapse on its performance value; and it will not do that—not even to save on the price of the ticket. But at the same time, it must absolutely ensure the lowest possible annual travel spending for the client for the specific amount of travel. And it must display its usual interpersonal charm in its dealings with travelers and corporate travel managers alike. Its act in each of the three ValueSpaces must be first class. Absolutely.

Likewise, at the PPG's fine chemicals division. The desired purity level in the phosgene derivative must absolutely be ensured. And there is constant price pressure it must respond to, so it is constantly exploring avenues of total cost reduction to the client, in product application, and in inventory and supply chain management. Given these performance and price values, does it then relax its personalization? Far from it. Whether a client needs help in the process qualifying stage or an urgent shipment, it will respond with both enthusiasm and diligence.

Now to the other myth.

"We Are Already Doing It All"

The fact is that none of the companies we feature are doing it all. And they would be the first to admit that. By "doing it all" we don't mean "doing all three." On that, there is no choice. We mean rather that they are not doing all they can on any of the value components. They are constantly striving, but the effort is far from being concluded. On all three value dimensions (the 3P's), they are good, very good. But they could be better. Especially when considering the eight individual ValueSpace components, progress is usually uneven. Caterpillar is making strides in achieving unparalleled quality, and its innovations with hydraulics and electronics in tractors are remarkable, but extensive tractor customization has the status of a "vision for the future," rather than a current value reality. Its dealer relationships are exemplary, but an end-user-level comprehensive database—a prerequisite for proactive relational nurture at the end-user level—or a centralized end-user support system must await management focus. And at 3M, customer access to the company—whether via its salesforce or via the Web site is still being reconfigured from its historic company-centered (organized by separate product divisions) to customer-centered (organized by customer application) organization.

Ready for Action? A Roadmap

All right, so you are convinced you are ready to embrace the comprehensive customer ValueSpace framework. How do you proceed? Our roadmap is comprised of three steps: value audit, bridging the gap, and leading the customer.

Value Audit

The first step is an audit of where you currently are. It is an assessment of where you stand on the nine ValueSpace components (the eight components of the 3P's and, as the ninth component, the ring of ValueSpace expanders). To help you in this assessment, we have developed an audit form (see Figure 13-1). We list "indicators" you can use to judge each ValueSpace component, such as the existence of and compliance with brand standards as an indicator of quality. The maximum possible score is 300. Three Foundational Prerequisites are allocated 30 points. Individual ValueSpace components receive weights proportionate to their relative significance: performance: 100 points; price: 60 points; personalization: 90 points; and ValueSpace expanders: 20 points. We have tried to maintain the same logic within each of the 3P's: within performance ValueSpace (total max score, 100), quality gets 30 points, innovation: 40 points, and customization: 30 points. And so on.

After you have done this audit, you need to get underneath these nine components—what builder processes drive these ValueSpace components? We described these processes in Chapter 11, and summarize these in Figure 13-2, in a form ready for use in audit. Rate these too.

A starting point would be to get all senior managers to rate the company using these two audit forms. And then rate, using the same audit form, each of your direct competitors. Various managers would obviously differ in their ratings. The ones who rate more stringently are the ones of special value. Ask them to explain the gaps. Their explanations can become training ground for other executives.

The next logical step would be to get a similar audit from customers. This would be similar to the customer satisfaction surveys you are perhaps already doing. A customer audit form would differ from satisfaction surveys in two important aspects: First, competitor's customers and prospective future customers would be surveyed as well as your current customers; and second, it would assess elements of the ValueSpace. Subsequent data analysis of both the satisfaction and the ValueSpace surveys would serve the important purpose of identifying specific satisfaction attributes that are linked to specific ValueSpace elements. This in turn would make current satisfaction surveys more meaningful. The ValueSpace audit forms for customers would be modified from those given in Figures 13-1 and 13-2 (much of the information sought on these two forms is privy only to managers). When such customer audit data become available, an analysis of the gap between executive audit and customer audit would be an eye-opening reality check. For now, let us work only with the executive audits.

Figure 13.1   Executive self-audit: ValueSpace components.

ValueSpace Component
(Rate each on a 0–10 scale—10 is best; rate indicators
first and then write total for ValueSpace Component)

Foundational Prerequisites

- Customer centeredness as a way of organization's life
- Top management commitment to ValueSpace building
- Sound strategic vision that aligns resources with target markets

---

Performance Valuespace

1. Quality of Products or Service
   - Brand standards and compliance (demanding rather than modest)
   - External recognition of quality
   - Customer returns/complaints near-zero

2. Innovation
   - Percent of revenue from products <3 yrs. old (0 to 40%)
   - An active program of R&D
     A stream of truly breakthrough products introduced; Products are of latest generation; Products are "distinct" in design vs. "me too"
   - Considered an innovation leader in the industry
   - Tales of "customer wow" (with "product") abound vs. absent

3. Customization
   - Customer-specific applications aplenty
   - Long a la carte menu/deep product line
   - Build to order rather than sell from stock

Price ValueSpace

4. Fair Price/Target Costing
   - Pricing policies shun opportunism, are equitable across customers, and are open and honest
   - Product development driven by cost targets; able to meet customers' budget constraints

5. Value Price/Lean Operations
   - Documented performance/price ratio superiority exists; performance/price ratio has an up-trend
   - Cost reduction programs in place; all productivity measures have up-trend
   - Customer-participation in identifying reductions in cost of doing business
   - Productivity gains shared with customers

My Company
Rating   Gap (indicate what is lacking)

_____ (Grand Total, Max 300)

_____ (Total, Max 30)

_____   _____

_____   _____

_____   _____

_____ (Total, Max 100)

_____   _____

_____   _____

_____   _____

_____   _____

_____   _____

_____   _____

_____   _____

_____   _____

_____   _____

_____ (Total, Max 60)

_____   _____

_____   _____

_____   _____

_____   _____

_____   _____

_____   _____

Continued

Personalization ValueSpace

6. Easy Access
   - Customers have ability to reach us anytime, from anywhere
   - Customers can reach us through hassle-free processes

7. Rapid Response
   - Rapid response standards are high and closely monitored
   - Customer requests for information, assistance, and problem resolution fully met; industry-leading "recovery" procedures exist
   - High flexibility built into customer service operations

8. Relational Nurture
   - Customer retention adopted as a primary business model
   - Ethics of nonopportunistic behavior valued; high level of mutual trust exists
   - Collaboration with the customer in planning common future
   - Customers rave about our relationships

ValueSpace Expanders

9. Value-Added Offerings
   - Patronage reward programs—none to modest to substantial
   - "Surprise" offerings not normally associated with core product or service (e.g., training, annual spend analysis, e-mail helpful alerts, etc.); ad hoc assistance to customers (e.g., product use support, coaching in business, resource loan)—none to many or rarely to often

Bridging the Gap

Take note of certain gaps, but note especially the gap between the scores you and your competitors received. And look at the gap between your actual scores and the perfect scores. At a minimum, you will need to bridge the first gap. Once that is achieved, you can act to move your scores toward their maximums.

That is easier said than done. This requires detailed planning; and a more detailed analysis of ValueSpace builder processes (summarized in Figure 13-2). This is where your next layer of management would need to be involved—those who are process owners. With their help, senior management must check their assumptions about the ValueSpace drivers: Do we have a relational database on customers? Do we have multi-

_____ (Total, Max 90)

_____
_____

_____
_____

_____

_____
_____

_____
_____

_____ (Total, Max 20)

_____

_____

ple channels of access? Are our employees sufficiently empowered? How deep is our customer knowledge? Does our customer satisfaction measurement have sufficient teeth? Do we have resources for rapid response to customer personalization needs? Are employees and managers rewarded for customer retention? And so on.

The next phase is planning. The central planning question is, How can we deploy the resources to garner these capabilities? At this stage, the next layer of managers get involved—the operations managers and subject-matter specialists. These would include IT managers; logistics design people; production process engineers; HR specialists; financial analysts; and so on. All options are explored; and a plan of action is prepared and implemented with the usual Plan-Do-Check-Act cycle.

Figure 13.2   Executive self-audit: ValueSpace builder processes.

ValueSpace Component
(Rate each on a 0–10 scale—10 is best; rate indicators
first and then write total for ValueSpace Component)

Drivers of Customer Centeredness

    a. High investment in customer research
       (Total immersion into understanding the customer's ValueSpace)

    b. Organizational processes built around the customer
       (validating with customer feedback all organizational actions)

    c. Top management displays true customer commitment
       (doing well by the customer is everyone's second nature)

Drivers of Performance ValueSpace

Quality

    a. Defining quality in customer terms

    b. Establishing process and outcome standards

    c. Measuring everything

    d. Deployment of technology for quality

    e. Implementing "Continuous Process Improvement"

    f. Investing in human resources

    g. Rewarding and compensating desired behaviors

Innovation

    a. Innovation culture

    b. Encouraging and rewarding intrepreneuring

    c. Research and application fusion

    d. A strong futuristic orientation

Customization

    a. Deep customer knowledge

    b. Mass customization production processes

    c. Broad skill base and cross-training of staff

    d. Infinite variety

Drivers of Price ValueSpace

Fair Price: Target Costing

    a. Design for target costing

    b. Better sourcing or outsourcing

    c. Supplier partnering

My Company
Rating   Gap (indicate what is lacking)

_____ (Grand Total, Max 400)

_____ (Total, Max 30)

_____   _____

_____   _____

_____   _____

_____ (Total, Max 150)

_____   _____
_____   _____
_____   _____
_____   _____
_____   _____
_____   _____
_____   _____

_____   _____
_____   _____
_____   _____
_____   _____

_____   _____
_____   _____
_____   _____
_____   _____

_____ (Total, Max 90)

_____   _____
_____   _____
_____   _____

Continued

Value Price: Lean Operations
   a. Low cost production sites
   b. Asset utilization management
   c. Just-in-time manufacturing
   d. Process reengineering
   e. Automation and technology deployment
   f. Mass customization

Drivers of Personalization ValueSpace

Easy Access
   a. Locational ubiquity
   b. 24-7 hours of operation
   c. Multiple channel access
   d. Near-zero-wait access

Rapid Response
   a. Frontline information system
   b. Well-trained and empowered customer contact personnel
   c. CS measurement with teeth
   d. Flexible resources

Relational Nurture
   a. More resources per customer spent on customer retention
      than on customer acquisition
   b. Digitized customer database capability
   c. Linkages exist with customers at multiple levels with frequent face-to-
      face contacts
   d. Joint planning with customers is in place
   e. All customer contact employees and executives maintain integrity and
      empathy and enjoy interfacing with customers

Leading the Customer

It is good to start your value improvement project with a customer audit; and to base all your actions on their reactions. But once you have made significant progress in bridging the value gap based on customer audits, the next frontier in value creation will come, not from customers, but from within you. You will have to innovate value that customers don't yet see. In essence, you are going beyond what anyone else offers customers; beyond what currently exists. You are going to be

_____   _____
_____   _____
_____   _____
_____   _____
_____   _____
_____   _____

_____ (Total, Max 130)

_____   _____
_____   _____
_____   _____
_____   _____

_____   _____
_____   _____
_____   _____
_____   _____

_____   _____

_____   _____
_____   _____

_____   _____
_____   _____

inventing new customer ValueSpace. Only you know the capabilities of your technology, of your processes, of your human resources. So you must deploy them; contemplate them in relation to each of the value components in our framework.

Several of our Most Admired companies are doing just that. Caterpillar's innovation in remote piloted tractors is an example. This is a tremendous value for hazardous site operations, but no customer could have guided CAT into it. CAT had to think of it alone. American Express's merchant customers could not have led it to customized merchant-specific promotions; or toward Web-based transmittal of transaction summaries. No customer told UPS to place shipping functionality on every Palm wireless device. And not one customer could have told Hilton they needed a Sleep Tight$^{(SM)}$ room!

Nor are such "lead the customer" value innovations limited to performance value. Price and personalization ValueSpaces also present opportunities for such innovations. UPS invented a process where it assumes the responsibility to determine the transport mode combination for a customer's package so as to save the customer money (a price value invention). XBS came up with the invention of Focus Executives without any hint from clients (a personalization value invention). And 3M's roofing granules division invented economic forecast seminars, without any roofing manufacturer asking for it (a ValueSpace expander invention).

Companies that invent new values such as these possess certain traits. They observe customers real close. They dig customer need to its essential core. And they keep their eyes on a singular target: creating far-reaching new ValueSpace for the customer. These traits indeed lead a business to mold its own self-concept in the customer's image. Rosenbluth redefines the very nature of its business as "business interaction management." 3M comes to view itself, instead of being a maker of masking tapes, abrasive papers, and adhesives, as a provider of bonding, protection, and masking solutions. And XBS employees never fail to remind themselves who they are—*customer amazers!*

This reinvention of oneself as a corporate being, this customer-centered adoption of a new self-identity, the constant contemplation of the customer desires—this is what it takes to invent unparalleled ValueSpace for the customer. This is what it takes to become, ultimately, a "customer admired" company. And this is what it takes to win the battle for market leadership.

Epilogue: The Science and the Art

SO NOW YOU KNOW!
The secret to building the customer ValueSpace.
And the realization of the following truisms.

- Customer value creation is the only path to long-term sustainability of organizational growth. Shareholder value flows from it and will not accrue without it.

- Customers seek three market values—performance, price, and personalization. These value names in our framework are common names. But their meaning is specific. Know what they mean, specifically. And there are eight value components. Know them too.

- Customers seek all three values, not one or two. They seek these three, in all their marketplace exchanges. Always.

- You cannot compete on price, or performance, or personalization alone. And the claim that you do not compete on price is nonsense. Everyone does!

- Customers do not choose between performance, price, and personalization; they choose between one performance, price, and personalization package and another within the same marketspace. A marketspace is a set of closely matching performance, price, personalization combination offerings. A business has to create the best performance, price, and personalization values in its marketspace.

- No, you are not doing it all already! Your current market offerings are not the best combination of performance, price, and personalization values. You can enhance your total customer ValueSpace significantly. By diligently pursuing each of the eight value components. And then by augmenting it further with value expanders.

- These components together have 40 drivers—organizational processes (see Figure 13-2 in Chapter 13). These processes produce, individually and collectively, targeted customer ValueSpace. You already have many of them in place. Direct them with a better understanding of their instrumentality—knowing which process produces which ValueSpace component.

- Our framework will guide you in your ValueSpace building excursion. Our stories of the World's Most Admired companies will inspire you on that journey.

- However, it will inspire your competitors too—some of them, anyway. They know what you know. What then will differentiate you from them? How will you outpace them? The answer: by the quality of your implementation. How exactly will you create performance ValueSpace, for example? By quality upgrade? By innovation? By customization? And what exactly will you innovate? And how will you progress from fair price to value price? What processes can be made leaner without sacrifice of performance or personalization values? How will you multiply your channels of customer access? How will you acquire a "fix it yesterday" capability? And will you acquire and demonstrate an attitude of relational nurture?

- You will outpace your competition, in other words, by how well you flesh out the customer ValueSpace framework; by your commitment to it; by a singular focus on customer ValueSpace creation as the organization's only goal. Its only true purpose.

- Learning the customer ValueSpace framework in this book is the science. How well you flesh it out is the art! Go ahead, practice your art. And experience where this blend of the science and the art of customer ValueSpace creation takes you.

Customer ValueSpace: Contemplate it. Build it. Live it.
Customer ValueSpace: If you build it, they will come!

Notes

Chapter 1

In our sample, three companies were ranked #1 on the 1999 list of the Global Most Admired Companies (GMAC) as well as on the America's Most Admired Companies (AMAC)—American Express, UPS, and Caterpillar. One (Xerox) was ranked #2 in the Imaging and Office Equipment category (#1 in 1998) on GMAC. The Global list placed 3M in Imaging and Office Equipment rank #4, but AMAC placed it in the Scientific, Photo, and Control Equipment category at rank #1. PPG Industries was ranked #5 on the Global list and #3 on AMAC in the Chemical Industry. AutoNation was placed #12 on the GMAC list, but it shared that list with a very heterogeneous group of retailers ranging from Wal-Mart to Home Depot to Mark and Spencer; the American list was more homogeneous, confined to Automotive Retailing and Services, and on that list AutoNation was placed #1 in 1999 (up from #9 in 1998, before AutoNation restructured to divest its used car superstores and car rental businesses). Hilton was #5 on the American list of the Hotels, Casinos, and Resorts Industry. Rosenbluth and Fossil were chosen from outside these lists.

Chapter 2

For further reading on topics covered in this chapter see:

Jadish N. Sheth, Banwari Mittal, and Bruce I. Newman, *Customer Behavior: Consumer Behavior and Beyond*, Fort Worth, TX: Dryden Press, 1999.

William A. Band, *Creating Value for Customers: Designing and Implementing a Total Corporate Strategy*, New York: Coopers & Lybrand, 1991.

Margaret Campbell, *Perceptions of Price Unfairness: Antecedents and Consequences, Journal of Marketing Research*, 36 (May 1999): 187–199.

Donald C. Fisher, *Measuring Up to the Baldrige: A Quick & Easy Self-Assessment Guide for Organizations of All Sizes*, New York: AMACOM, 1994.

Bradley T. Gale with Robert Chapman Wood, *Managing Customer Value: Creating Quality and Service That Customers Can See*, New York: Free Press, 1994.

Douglas B. Grisaffe and Anand Kumar, *Antecedents and Consequences of Customer Value: Testing an Expanded Framework*, Cambridge, MA: Marketing Science Institute, Report No. 98-107, May 1998.

Michael Hammer, *Beyond Reengineering: How the Process-Centered Organization Is Changing Our Work and Our Lives*, New York: Harper Business, 1997.

Noreen Klein and Janet Oglethorpe, *Cognitive Reference Points in Consumer Decision Making, Advances in Consumer Research*, Vol. 14, Melanie Wallendorf and Paul Anderson, eds., Association for Consumer Research, Provo, UT (1987): 183–187.

Yasuhiro Monden, *Cost Reduction Systems: Target Costing and Kaizen Costing*, Portland, OR: Productivity Press, 1995.

B. Joseph Pine II, *Mass Customization: The New Frontier in Business Competition*, Boston, MA: Harvard Business School Press, 1999.

Barry Sheehy, Hyler Bracey, and Rick Frazier, *Winning the Race for Value: Strategies to Create Competitive Advantage in the Emerging "Age of Abundance,"* New York: AMACOM, 1996.

Robert B. Tucker, *Win the Value Revolution: How to Give Your Customers a Quality Product, Excellent Service, and Still Make Money*, Franklin Lakes, NJ: Career Press, 1995.

Richard C. Whiteley, *The Customer-Driven Company: Moving from Talk to Action*, Reading, MA: Addison-Wesley, 1991.

Richard Whiteley and Diane Hessan, *Customer-Centered Growth: Five Proven Strategies for Building Competitive Advantage*, Reading, MA: Addison-Wesley, 1996.

Fred Wiersema, *Customer Intimacy: Pick Your Partners, Shape Your Culture, Win Together*, Santa Monica, CA: Knowledge Exchange, 1996.

Russell S. Winer, *A Reference Price Model of Brand Choice for Frequently Purchased Products*, Journal of Consumer Research, 13 (Sept. 1986), 250–256.

Robert B. Woodruff and Sarah F. Gardial, *Know Your Customer: New Approaches to Understanding Customer Value and Satisfaction*, Cambridge, MA: Blackwell Publishers, 1996.

Chapter 3

The authors wish to thank the following American Express (Establishment Services Division) executives who participated in discussions with one of the authors (BM): Dave House (group president), Robert Adams (director, Marketing Research), Charles Aubrey (vice president, Quality Operations), Ritu Clementi (manager, Value Story Library Group), Paul M. Dottle (vice president, Electronic Merchant Services), Jennifer Gold (vice president, Customer Services Strategy), Sharon Smith (vice president, Operations), Susan Sobbott (VP/GM, New Industry Development), Lisa I. Vehrenkamp (director, executive assistant to president), and Steve Zacks (vice president, Marketing & Communications). For further reading on many topics covered in this chapter, see:

George S. Day, *Market Driven Strategy: Processes for Creating Value*, New York: Free Press, 1990.

Frank Feather, *The Future Consumer*, Los Angeles: Warwick Publishing, 1994.

Edward F. McQuarrie, *Customer Visits: Building a Better Market Focus*, Newbury Park, CA: Sage Publications, 1993.

Banwari Mittal, *Determinants of Vendor-Patronage in Business Service Markets: An Integrated Model, Journal of Business-to-Business Marketing*, Vol. 6, No. 4: (1–32), 1999.

Robert B. Woodruff and Sarah F. Gardial, *Know Your Customer: New Approaches to Understanding Customer Value and Satisfaction*, Cambridge, MA: Blackwell Publishers, 1996.

Chapter 8

The authors wish to thank the following CAT (TTT division) executives who participated in round table discussions with one of the authors (BM): James E. Despain (vice president), Marylean Abney (business research manager), R. L. (Ron) Catton (supply chain manager), Mark S. Hanback (product manager, undercarriage products), David Newman (purchasing manager), Dale B. Roberts (former commercial manger), Thea Robinson (formerly, manager, human resources), and Randy Williams (former marketing manager).

Chapter 10

All names of company executives we interviewed are withheld at the company's request. Further exhibiting its character of being unique in almost everything, Fossil management believes that the company and the statements about it are important, not the executives who make them. Our interviewees included the president and several senior executives.

Chapter 11

1.   Gary Hamel and C. K. Prahalad, *Competing for the Future: Breakthrough Strategies for Seizing Control of Your Industry and Creating the Markets of Tomorrow*, Cambridge, MA: Harvard Business School Press, 1994.

2.   Don Peppers and Martha Rogers, *The One-to-One Future: Building Relationships One Customer at a Time*, New York: Currency Doubleday, 1993.

For further reading on many topics covered in this chapter, see:

William A. Band, *Creating Value for Customers: Designing and Implementing a Total Corporate Strategy*, New York: Coopers & Lybrand, 1991.

Leonard L. Berry, *Discovering the Soul of Service: The Nine Drivers of Sustainable Business Success*, New York: Free Press, 1999.

George S. Day, *Market-Driven Strategy: Processes for Creating Value*, New York: Free Press, 1990.

Michael Dell, *Direct from Dell*, New York: Harper Business, 1999.

Michael Hammer and James Champy, *Reengineering the Corporation: A Manifesto for Business Revolution*, New York: Harper Business, 1993.

Michael Hammer, *Beyond Reengineering: How the Process-Centered Organization Is Changing Our Work and Our Lives*, New York: Harper Business, 1997.

Index

Page references to tables or figures appear in **bold**.

About the Authors

Banwari (Ban) Mittal holds a Ph.D. in marketing from the University of Pittsburgh, and is a professor of marketing and management of Northern Kentucky University. He has previously held faculty positions at State University of New York at Buffalo and the University of Miami. His areas of expertise for research, teaching, and consulting are marketing strategy, services management, customer satisfaction and loyalty, brand equity, and customer value processes. Ban has made presentations to numerous audiences, is the coauthor of *Customer Behavior* (1999), and has published articles in *Journal of Marketing*, *Journal of Market-Focused Management*, and other prestigious professional journals. His current passion is contemplating what constitutes customer ValueSpace™ and how companies can build it.

(Dr. Mittal can be reached at BanMittal@MyValueSpace.com.)

Jagdish (Jag) N. Sheth, Ph.D., is the Charles H. Kellstadt Professor of Marketing at Gouizeta Business School, Emory University, where he is also the founder and director of the Center for Relationship Marketing. His areas of expertise are market strategy, global competition, and customer relationship management. Jag—a frequent consultant to Fortune 500 companies—has held chairs at USC and the University of Illinois, and served on the faculty of Columbia and MIT. Listed in *Who's Who in America* since 1985, he is the author of more than 200 articles and books, including *Clients for Life* (2000), *The Customer Is Key* (1987), and the classic *The Theory of Buyer Behavior* (1969).

(Dr. Sheth can be reached at Jag@JagSheth.com.)

L